THE GAA
V
DOUGLAS HYDE

The Removal of Ireland's First President as GAA Patron

CORMAC MOORE has a Master's degree in history from UCD where he completed his thesis on Douglas Hyde's removal as GAA patron. He is currently pursuing a PhD on a history of soccer in Ireland.

cormac.moore@gmail.com

In memory of my father, Paddy Moore.

CORMAC MOORE

THE GAA
v
DOUGLAS HYDE

The Removal of Ireland's First President as GAA Patron

The Collins Press

FIRST PUBLISHED IN 2012 BY
The Collins Press
West Link Park
Doughcloyne
Wilton
Cork

British Library Cataloguing in Publication Data

Moore, Cormac.
The GAA v Douglas Hyde : the removal of Ireland's first President as GAA patron.
1. Hyde, Douglas, 1860–1949.
2. Gaelic Athletic Association—Rules and practice.
3. Presidents—Ireland—Discipline.
4. Gaelic games—Political aspects—Ireland—History—20th century.
5. Ireland—Politics and Government—1922–1949.
I. Title
796'.09415'09043–dc23

Paperback ISBN-13: 9781848891524
EPUB eBook ISBN: 9781848899742
mobi eBook ISBN: 9781848899759

Typesetting by Carrigboy Typesetting Services
Typeset in Bembo 11pt/14pt
Printed in Denmark by Nørhaven

Contents

Acknowledgements

The genesis of this book came from meetings with Professor Diarmaid Ferriter and Dr Paul Rouse of University College Dublin who persuaded me to delve deeper into the incident of Dr Douglas Hyde's removal as patron of the GAA. Seeing the rich material available on the subject, I decided to complete my Master's thesis on the topic. Both Diarmaid and Paul helped me greatly with this. Their knowledge of Irish and sporting history and their willingness to help me at every turn was of huge assistance.

I would like to thank Mark Reynolds of the GAA Archive in Croke Park, Dónal McAnallen of the Cardinal Tomás Ó Fiaich Memorial Library and Archive in Armagh, and the staff of the Leinster and Connacht GAA Councils. I am also indebted to Deirdre O'Gara of the Dr Douglas Hyde Interpretative Centre in Portahard, Frenchpark, County Roscommon. The staff of the National Archives of Ireland, the National Library of Ireland and the UCD Archives deserve a special mention for the excellent service they provided throughout this project.

I wish to thank Kieran Hoare from NUI Galway, Eamon de Valera from the *Irish Press*, Arlene Crampsie from the GAA Oral History Project, Peter Deighan from *Gaelic Art* and Paul Carson from the *Belfast Telegraph* who were very helpful with the sourcing of images for this publication.

A huge debt of gratitude is owed to The Collins Press who have been a pleasure to deal with throughout the publishing process.

I would like to pay special thanks to Brian Murphy, who kindly read the first draft and suggested many, much needed, changes. He also provided additional material from his own research, which I feel add greatly to the finished book. A big thank you is owed to Gráinne Daly, Margaret Ayres, Kaye Duffy, Frank Mulcahy, Justin Sinnott, Hilary Delahunty, Deirdre Keane, Claire Egan and Simon Deignan for the time they took to read the original manuscript, for their support and for the advice that has helped make this a better book. I would also like to thank Aoife Ní Lochlainn, who kindly provided me with material from her studies on the Ailtirí na hAiséirghe movement.

To all my family, friends and work colleagues who provided me with encouragement and advice throughout the process, I am very grateful for your support. Finally, this book is dedicated to my late father, Paddy Moore, who instilled in me a great passion for history and sport and a thirst for knowledge that I will always have.

Cormac Moore
September 2012

Introduction

Our games were in a most grievous condition until the brave and patriotic men who started the Gaelic Athletic Association took in hand their revival. I confess that the instantaneous and extraordinary success which attended their efforts when working upon national lines has filled me with more hope for the future of Ireland than everything else put together.

I consider the work of the association in reviving our ancient national game of *comáin*, or hurling, and Gaelic football, has done more for Ireland than all the speeches of politicians for the last five years.

And it is not alone that that splendid association revived for a time with vigour our national sports, but it revived also our national recollections, and the names of the various clubs throughout the country have perpetuated the memory of the great and good men and martyrs of Ireland ...

... Wherever the warm striped green jersey of the Gaelic Athletic Association was seen, there Irish manhood and Irish memories were rapidly reviving ...[1]

Dr Douglas Hyde
November 1892

Dr Douglas Hyde, founding member and first president of the Gaelic League, became the first President of Ireland in 1938 under the new Constitution of 1937, Bunreacht na hÉireann. He was an early member and advocate of the Gaelic Athletic Association (GAA) and was friends with Michael Cusack, the man most associated with the founding of the GAA.

Hyde claimed that the GAA paved the way for the Gaelic League, an organisation he, more than anyone else, initiated and grew to levels unthinkable at its outset. It was for his work with the Gaelic League that he was made a patron of the GAA in 1902, an honour bestowed on only a few men even to this day. It was an honour greatly appreciated by Hyde.

This honour was taken from him in December 1938.

On 17 December of that year, the Central Council of the GAA met. Members in attendance included the then president, Ulsterman Pádraig McNamee who was chairing the meeting, Pádraig Ó Caoimh, general secretary, former president Bob O'Keeffe (1935–1938), and members representing the four provincial councils and different county boards. One item on the agenda involved a brief discussion relating to Hyde. It would lead to his removal as a patron of the GAA.

Hyde had attended an international soccer match between Ireland and Poland on 13 November 1938 in his capacity as Head of State. This was considered to be in direct violation of Rule 27 of the GAA, the ban on 'foreign games'. The 'foreign games' ban stipulated that members of the GAA could not play or attend any event organised by the sports of Association football (soccer), rugby, cricket or hockey.

At the meeting a resolution of the Galway County Board was discussed:

> That the Central Council at its next meeting be requested to consider the position of a patron whose official duties may bring him into conflict with the fundamental rules of the Association. The chairman said that his ruling was that such a person ceased to be a patron of the association. Some people thought that a patron should be above the rules, but that was not his view. It was no pleasure to rule as he was doing, but he saw no other course. Mr O'Farrell, Roscommon, dissenting from the ruling said Dr Hyde had done some good work for them in Roscommon. Chairman – He did good work in many places and in many ways. There was no further discussion.[2]

The meeting ended when a 'circular from the National Association of the old IRA was read, in which it was asked that the Central Council would send two representatives to a conference in connection with Partition. The Council decided not to appoint delegates as it may lead the Association into political connections'.[3] The GAA may have desired to remain uninvolved in politics but its decision to remove the President of Ireland as patron of the Association would ensure that the opposite would happen over the coming weeks and months.

The decision to remove Hyde was seen as an extraordinary one and garnered much interest both nationally and internationally. Not only was the decision made against the Head of the State but it was against a man seen by most as the embodiment of the Irish-Ireland movement, a movement that had the GAA at its forefront.

How did it come to pass that such a decision could be made? In pondering this question, this book will look at Hyde's career, one spanning over fifty years dedicated to the Irish-Ireland cause that culminated with him being elected unanimously as first President of Ireland. This book also explores the backgrounds of the two people in the GAA who were most associated with Hyde's removal, Pádraig McNamee, the president at the time, and, Pádraig Ó Caoimh, the general secretary. Both men contributed hugely to the Irish-Ireland movement in their own rights and it can be believed that the removal of a man they both respected greatly was a very difficult decision for them to make.

The GAA ban on 'foreign games' had experienced a colourful history before the Hyde incident was added to its catalogue of episodes. Installed shortly after the founding of the GAA in 1884 to stave off the growth of the Irish Amateur Athletic Association (IAAA), the Ban went through periods of being removed, then being reinstated to reach the point, by the late 1930s, of being a steadfast rule accepted by the majority of the membership of the GAA.

Hyde's removal coincided with club, county and provincial conventions within the GAA and this ensured the topic remained in the news until the GAA Annual Congress of April 1939. The media, with a few exceptions, were vehemently opposed to the GAA's stance. There was also a big divide within the Association itself.

This decision led to a great straining of relations between the GAA and the government that would be exacerbated by a number of incidents in the following years that tested their rapport to its limits. A resolution was finally reached in 1945 when Éamon de Valera, the Taoiseach at the time, met with members of the GAA and an agreement was made to ensure such an incident would never happen again.

The maintenance of the Ban was seriously questioned by many quarters after Hyde was removed as a patron in 1938. The Ban would remain in place as a fundamental principle for many years, only being removed over thirty years later in 1971. The credibility of the Ban was undermined significantly by the removal of Hyde as a patron; over the following decades his removal would be the main weapon used by opponents of the Ban to demonstrate its flawed nature as an antiquated rule that had no place in an Ireland looking to embrace the modern world.

1

'I Dream in Irish'

Douglas Hyde was born on 17 January 1860 in Castlerea, County Roscommon. A member of a family steeped in the Protestant religion, he was the third son of Arthur Hyde, a Church of Ireland rector, and his wife, Elizabeth, whose father was John Orson Oldfield, Archdeacon of Elphin. His two brothers were Arthur and Oldfield and he had one younger sister, Annette.[1] Hyde's ancestors had moved from Castle Hyde, Cork, where they had lived since they were planted there from England during the reign of Queen Elizabeth I in the sixteenth century.[2] Although his family was not wealthy, they 'moved in circles occupied by a relatively leisured, educated, privileged class'.[3] When Hyde was a young boy his father was made rector at Frenchpark, County Roscommon, and the family moved there to live. According to author, poet and translator, Seán Ó Lúing, 'The environment of Douglas Hyde's boyhood, embracing central and northern Connacht, played an important part in the development of his consciousness, superlatively rich as it was in bardic culture, legend and folklore'.[4]

Hyde was not formally educated except for a brief, unhappy stint in a school in Kingstown (modern day Dún Laoghaire) in 1873.[5] His move back to Roscommon turned out to be fortuitous for Hyde and for the Irish language movement in the long term. He was educated at home mainly by his father

Castle Hyde in County Cork. Douglas Hyde's ancestors were planted there from England in the sixteenth century during the reign of Queen Elizabeth I. *(Courtesy of the National Library of Ireland)*

who, with an eye on Hyde following him into clerical life, taught him Greek and Latin, the primary languages he would need for that profession.[6] Hyde developed an extraordinary talent for languages and, in addition to Greek, Latin and English, he was able to communicate in German, French and Hebrew.[7] The language that he had most affection for was the one he learned from his father's servants, from local farmers and peasants, the native tongue of the land, Irish.[8] While studying at Trinity College Dublin, Hyde claimed it was the language he knew best, saying, 'I dream in Irish.'[9]

According to Doiminic Ó Dálaigh, in his book, *The Young Douglas Hyde*, Hyde picked up the language within a remarkably short period of time, which was astonishing considering he had no 'formal' teacher.[10] His first Irish teacher was a local Fenian, Seamus Hart, who instilled in Hyde a love for the language as well as a love for the idioms and lore of Irish folk tales handed down orally to generations of locals in the area. Hart's death in 1875, when Hyde was just fifteen, was a huge blow to the young boy. He wrote in his diary, 'Seamus died yesterday. A man so kindly, so truthful, so neighbourly I never saw. He was ill about a week, and then he died. Poor Seamus, I learned my Irish from you. There will never be another with Irish so perfect. I can see no one from now on with whom I can enjoy friendship such as I enjoyed with you.'[11] Other locals who took up the baton of teaching Hyde Irish included Mrs William Connolly and John Lavin.[12] Hyde was a meticulous and dedicated student, spending between five and six hours a day on average studying,[13] primarily concentrating on languages. His diaries document his first halting steps writing in Irish in 1874 and demonstrate his rapid progression with the language. Soon it would be the language he would use, primarily, for writing.[14]

Not a particularly robust youth, Hyde was, however, a keen enthusiast of the outdoors and there are many references to him participating in activities and sports such as fowling (hunting), tennis, cricket[15] and croquet as well as a ball game he played with his future brother-in-law Cam O'Kane.[16] Had he grown up a number of years later, he would not have been free to participate in some of those sports as a member of the GAA.

On many of these outdoor excursions he was to discover from locals a treasure chest of sources he would use as stories and folktales in later years. Hyde realised that there was no documentation of these wonderful tales, tales covering ghosts and fairies and many other mythical characters,[17] tales that had all been handed down orally to different generations. He was determined to record everything he heard, creating a new genre and power in literature along the way, according to his contemporary William Butler Yeats.[18]

Hyde did not learn just the language and stories from local people. He also developed a taste for their politics. Considering that he would be forever remembered as a non-political man, reading some of his youthful pro-nationalist and anti-British sentiments makes for surprising reading. His verses are covered with themes on the oppression of the local people as well as a need to remove the British Empire by physical force. In one poem, one could be forgiven for thinking that the author was a Thomas Clarke or a Pádraig Pearse, not a man who became widely known as a pacifist:

> And it (is) their power to free their country
> By rising and drawing their blades like men,
> To show to the Saxon that each man is ready
> To break the yoke with which he is bound.
>
> To frighten that most hateful country;
> Believe, oh believe that she will not withstand force,
> But she will grant easily, meekly, to arms
> What she will never grant to truth or to right.
> I hate your law, I hate your rule,
> I hate your people and your weak queen,
> I hate your merchants who have riches and property,
> Great is their arrogance – little their worth.
>
> I hate your Parliament, half of them are boors
> Wrangling together without manners or grace –
> The men who govern the kingdom, false, insincere,
> Skilled only in trickery and deceit.
> Smoke rises over no city more accursed
> Than London, for all its greatness, its wonder, its fame;
> It deserves the greatest chastisement from God,
> Like ancient Rome or great Babylon.[19]

He was an admirer of Fenians like O'Donovan Rossa and John O'Mahony who he eulogised in the poetry he wrote.[20] His political beliefs would change significantly over the years but his passion and enthusiasm for the Irish language would remain with him forever.

He enrolled in Trinity College Dublin in 1880; he started to attend lectures in 1882 and moved to Dublin to live a year later.[21] Due to pressure from his father, he took a course in Divinity studies, graduating with great distinction. A deep rift would develop between Hyde and his father, as Hyde, like his older brothers, had no interest in pursuing a life in the Church. Instead of returning to Roscommon to live with his father, he decided to remain in Trinity to study Law in 1886 and qualified with an LL.D. degree in 1888.[22] Hyde had a glittering academic career, winning many prizes and medals. It was his extracurricular activities at university that would be of most interest to him. He immersed himself in movements such as the Contemporary Club where he discussed topics of the day with minds such as Yeats, Maud Gonne, John O'Leary and Michael Davitt,[23] as well as the newly formed literary group the Pan-Celtic Society.[24]

Hyde did not find too many fellow students in Trinity College who shared his passion for the Irish language. His main outlet to interact with like-minded language enthusiasts was the Gaelic Union, an offshoot of the Society for the Preservation of the Irish Language. Hyde had been contributing to that society since he was a teenager, subscribing £1 to its cause in 1877.[25] Hyde immersed himself wholeheartedly in the nascent language movement and chaired many of the Gaelic Union meetings.[26] One of the people he befriended at this time was fellow language activist, Michael Cusack. Cusack, a Clare native, was, at that time, in the process of setting up another Irish-Ireland movement, one specifically catering for the native games, the Gaelic Athletic Association.

2

'Sweeping the Country Like a Prairie Fire'

Michael Cusack was born in 1847 in Carron, which is located in a remote part of the Burren in County Clare. As a child he was keenly interested in hurling, a game that would stay with him throughout his life. Cusack trained as a teacher and had teaching positions in all four provinces at various times.[1] He settled in Dublin in 1874. He taught in Blackrock College as well as in Clongowes Wood in County Kildare before setting up his own academy to prepare students for the British Civil Services examinations, an academy which would become quite lucrative for Cusack for a number of years before his extracurricular activities would take up more and more of his time. Like Hyde, Cusack was a keen Irish language enthusiast and he was an active member of the Gaelic Union. He played a leading role in the establishment of a bilingual magazine sponsored by the Gaelic Union entitled *The Gaelic Journal*,[2] seen by many as the spark for the language revival movement.[3] Douglas Hyde referred to *The Gaelic Journal* 'as the start of the resurrection of modern Irish'.[4] He would also become an early member and actively involve himself with the Gaelic League when it was established in 1893.[5] It was, however, for his interest in the national pastimes

Michael Cusack (*front row, second from left*) in a team photograph for a rugby match. Cusack, an accomplished athlete in many codes of sport, was the key driver in the founding of the GAA in 1884. *(Courtesy of the James Hardiman Library, NUI Galway)*

of Ireland that Cusack's name has been remembered. An accomplished athlete, Cusack played hurling, football, handball, cricket, rugby and athletic field events, and was particularly accomplished at weight-throwing events. As well as competing at athletic events, Cusack became involved in the administration side of sports. He soon became disillusioned with how sports were being organised in Ireland: he was against sports being run on a professional basis. There was a tendency to ignore sports such as weights and jumping events in which Irish people had a track record of excelling, and he believed the sports bodies in Ireland were too elitist and class-based as well as too subservient to Britain. Although there had been a revival in athletics throughout Ireland at this time, it 'remained the preserve of the well-to-do and of the small class of white-collar workers. Both groups were predominantly Unionist in outlook'.[6] Commenting years later on the elitism and exclusionist policies of sporting bodies towards many Irish

Maurice Davin, the first president of the GAA, was an internationally renowned athlete, whose public support for the GAA helped the nascent body gain a strong foothold. *(Courtesy of the GAA Museum, Croke Park)*

people, Cusack declared, 'From out this latter crocodile condition of things came an idea no bigger than my head'.[7]

Inspired by people like the renowned athlete P. W. 'the Champion of the West' Nally (an advanced nationalist from Mayo who would have a stand named after him in Croke Park in 1953), Cusack started a campaign for pure athletes, advocating amateurism, the inclusion of weights and jumping events, the lifting of class barriers, and unity in Irish athletics. Following

Archbishop Thomas Croke, founding patron of the GAA. His letter accepting the position as patron of the GAA, using pro-Irish and anti-British rhetoric became in many ways the *de-facto* manifesto of the GAA. *(Courtesy of the GAA Museum, Croke Park)*

Nally's lead of organising sports events for Irish people in Mayo,[8] Cusack followed suit in Dublin and started to organise sports meets there. In 1882 he established the Dublin Hurling Club, which would later become the Metropolitan Hurling Club. The momentum he created gathered pace in the summer of 1884 when he wrote a series of articles in William O'Brien's *United Ireland* and Richard Pigott's *Irishman* (Pigott would achieve infamy a few short years later as the man responsible for forging letters purporting to be from Charles Stewart Parnell), calling for a national athletic body to be founded.[9] On 11 October 1884, an article, almost certainly from the pen of Cusack, appeared in *United Ireland*, asking 'the Irish people to take the management of their games into their own hands, to encourage and promote in every way every form of athletics which is peculiarly Irish and to remove with one sweep everything foreign and iniquitous in the present system'.[10] Internationally renowned athlete Maurice Davin from Tipperary publicly offered his support to such a body and the wheels were set in motion for the Gaelic Athletic

Association to be formed. This happened in Mrs Hayes' Commercial Hotel on 1 November 1884 where at least seven men met, including Cusack and Davin. Davin was invited to become the first president and Cusack one of three secretaries. The main agreement reached at the first meeting was the names of the people they would invite to be patrons of this new association: Archbishop Thomas Croke of Cashel, Charles Stewart Parnell and Michael Davitt. The three men represented different strands of the nationalist cause in Ireland at the time.

Archbishop Croke was the clergyman most associated with the Irish-Ireland cause. He was an active supporter of the land agitation and the Home Rule movements of the time and was a patron of the language society, the Gaelic Union.[11] He led calls for the Gaelic Union and the parent group that it had split from, the Society for the Preservation of the Irish Language, to amalgamate with each other again,[12] a precursor to what happened when the Gaelic League was formed in 1893. He was very vocal in calling for a revival of the national pastimes whilst being a virulent opponent of foreign sports. He called existing sports such as cricket and polo 'effeminate follies' played by 'degenerate dandies', saying that 'if we continue condemning the sports that were practised by our fore-fathers, effacing our national features as though we were ashamed of them ... we had better, and at once, abjure our nationality and place England's bloody red exaltingly [sic] above the green'.[13] With his exemplary religious credentials and his support for all things nationalist, he was seen as the perfect choice to be the GAA's primary patron. His letter accepting the position, using pro-Irish and anti-British rhetoric became, in many ways, the *de-facto* manifesto of the GAA.[14]

Charles Stewart Parnell had shown no interest in or knowledge of native pastimes or sports prior to the founding of the GAA. As a youth he was more than likely to be found on a cricket field. There is still a cricket ground at his estate in Avondale, County Wicklow to this day.[15] He too, though, was

Michael Davitt, one of the founding patrons of the GAA. Douglas Hyde was not the only GAA patron to attend a soccer match, as Davitt was also a patron of Glasgow Celtic Football Club in Scotland. He placed the first sod at Celtic's new ground, Parkhead, in 1892. *(Courtesy of the National Library of Ireland)*

a perfect choice as patron. The most pre-eminent politician of his era, Parnell was at the height of his powers in 1884, known by many as the 'Uncrowned King of Ireland'. It may have been somewhat of a coup for the GAA, founded on such incon- spicuous terms, to receive the support of such a powerful figure who had previously not demonstrated an interest in Irish pastimes. However, Parnell saw the mood in Ireland moving towards a revival of all things Irish and was determined that his Irish Parliamentary Party would not let the Irish

Republican Brotherhood (IRB) take complete control of what could potentially become a very useful organisation. In accepting the invitation from Cusack he stated, 'It gives me great pleasure to learn that a "Gaelic Athletic Association" has been established for the preservation of national pastimes, with the objects of which I entirely concur. I feel very much honoured by the resolution adopted at the Thurles meeting; and I accept with appreciation the position of patron of the association which has been offered to me'.[16.]

Michael Davitt was another inspired choice as a founding patron. An advanced nationalist, Davitt had served time in prison for Fenian activities. He was the driving force behind the founding of the Land League in 1879 and was devoted to Irish-Ireland causes such as the Irish language[17] and native pastimes. Douglas Hyde was not the only GAA patron to attend a soccer match, as Davitt was also a patron of Glasgow Celtic Football Club in Scotland. In fact, he placed the first sod at Celtic's new ground, Parkhead in 1892;[18] the sod came from Donegal and was apparently stolen soon after.[19] He would subsequently become a regular visitor to Parkhead, occasionally accompanied by his son.[20]

The choice of patrons demonstrated the GAA's nationalist credentials, thus helping, as Cusack was to claim a number of years later, the association to sweep 'the country like a prairie fire'[21] in its first few years. It is estimated that there were over 50,000 individual members of the GAA after eighteen months and over 400 affiliated clubs after two years. In comparison, the soccer body, the Irish Football Association (IFA), which had been founded in 1880, had just 124 affiliated clubs ten years later, and the initial Irish rugby union of thirteen clubs on its foundation in 1874 had grown to merely 100 clubs six years later.[22] It is hard to pinpoint the exact reasons for the huge success the GAA experienced in such a short space of time, but there were a number of factors that helped to make it the most popular sporting organisation in the country. Neal Garnham in his paper, 'Accounting for the Early Success of the Gaelic Athletic Association', claims the primary reasons were the GAA's affiliation with the nationalist cause and the support it received from the Catholic Church. Its nationalist credentials were demonstrated through its choice of patrons, its connections with the IRB and the naming of GAA clubs after nationalist heroes and martyrs.[23] Nationalists were now afforded the first opportunity to participate in sports in Ireland; previous sporting bodies had kept their doors firmly shut to people of a nationalist outlook. The GAA also opened its doors to all classes and members included those from the ranks of teachers, clerks, small tradesmen and artisans. For example, the first All-Ireland Gaelic football winners of 1887, the Limerick Commercials, were all shop workers.[24] GAA events were also held on Sundays, the main day of rest for most people in Ireland, making it easier for people to participate in the new organisation. The rugby, soccer and cricket bodies in Ireland discouraged Sunday play.[25] The GAA had the full day of Sunday to itself, whereas the other major sports were competing against each other to attract members and attendances at their events. GAA affiliation fees and entrance fees to games were also cheaper. The GAA provided better additional forms of entertainment like dances and poetry recitations at its events.[26] The exclusion of fitter, more disciplined policemen and soldiers from participation at GAA events made it easier – and more attractive – for civilians to compete and win GAA competitions.[27] The bans the GAA introduced, although the reason for much controversy over the years, also helped to increase the GAA membership numbers and stifle the growth of its opponents. This was particularly the case when the GAA was looking to gain a foothold during its embryonic years.

The GAA today is primarily known for its field sports of hurling and Gaelic football and, to a lesser extent, handball. This was not the case when it was founded in 1884. It was mainly concerned with athletic events and its first ban, known as the Boycott Ban, was introduced to curb the growth of the IAAA, which was founded to combat the GAA in 1885. The word boycott had only recently made its way into the English language after Mayo based landlord Captain Charles Boycott had been ostracised by the local community in Mayo in 1880, following a battle to improve tenants' rights on his estate.[28]

At the third meeting of the GAA, held on 17 January 1885, the following resolution was passed: 'any athletes competing at meetings held under other laws than those of the GAA shall be ineligible for competing at any meetings held under the auspices of the Gaelic Athletic Association'.[29] This came into effect on St Patrick's Day 1885. The IAAA introduced its own ban disallowing its members to compete at GAA events and a battle for supremacy raged between the two bodies for most of 1885. The first big test between the two occurred in Kerry on Sunday 17 June 1885. The IAAA advertised an event under its code to be held on that date. Cusack, along with other members of the GAA, decided to hold their own event at the same place on the same day, calling for Irishmen to choose between Irish and foreign laws. Special trains with extra carriages were organised to bring people to its event. Between ten and fifteen thousand turned up for the GAA event where they watched over 450 athletes compete. A paltry few hundred attended the IAAA event.[30] This trend was to continue throughout the summer of 1885 and the GAA's supremacy over the IAAA was all but assured by October 1885. The *Freeman's Journal* intervened to have the Ban removed, calling the boycotts between the two bodies 'childish and ridiculous'.[31] Archbishop Croke agreed with the *Freeman's Journal* and after a letter he had written expressing those sentiments was read out at the GAA Annual Convention held on 31 October 1885,[32] the Association decided to remove the Boycott Ban in 1886.[33] The GAA decided to remove it, not out of a position of weakness but from a position of strength. The Ban had played its part in decimating the support of the IAAA.

The embryo of the ban on 'foreign games' came about almost immediately after the original ban was removed. 'With the organisation turning increasingly towards the cultivation and standardisation of hurling and Gaelic football, it would not be long before a similar ban would be required to counter-act the threat posed by "foreign games" and, in particular, that posed by rugby'.[34] At the first Annual Convention held in 1885, Maurice Davin loosely proposed that any athlete playing non-Gaelic football would forfeit his club's membership of the GAA. This became compulsory at the second Annual Convention held in 1886 appearing as Rule 12, which stated, 'Any member of a club in Ireland playing hurling, handball or football under other rules than those of the GAA cannot be a member of the Association and neither can members of any other athletic club in Ireland be members of the G.A.A.'.[35] According to GAA scholar Marcus de Búrca, 'each rule, especially that on foreign games, represented a positive application in amateur sport of the boycott idea, which had proved so effective in the agrarian campaign of the Land League'.[36] The bans, in their initial guises, were introduced for administration and organisational pur-poses primarily. However, within a few short years, a political element to the bans would be brought to bear, reflecting the changes in the leadership of the GAA.

The bulk of the credit must go to Michael Cusack for founding the GAA. He was, though, a very difficult man to get on with. James Joyce, in his novel *Ulysses*, modelled his character the Citizen on Cusack. Although a work of fiction, there were characteristics the Citizen shared with Cusack in real life. Joyce, it would appear, was fascinated with Cusack. Cusack also appears in *Stephen Hero, Portrait of the Artist as a Young Man*, and twice in *Finnegans Wake*.[37] Cusack was prone to making extreme statements that had an alienating affect on other people, such as his comment in 1886 that the IAAA was nothing but a 'ranting, impotent, West British abortion'.[38] In March 1886, he admonished Archbishop Croke and the *Freeman's Journal* for alleged 'vile' attacks on him. Archbishop Croke retaliated by dis-agreeing with Cusack's assertions and threatening to discontinue as patron if Cusack was going to be allowed to remain as 'dictator' of the GAA.[39] Cusack was condemned by leading GAA figures such as John McKay and Dan Fraher who called on Cusack to apologise for his 'disgraceful and wholly unjustifiable attack upon our most illustrious patron, the great Archbishop Croke'.[40] Cusack was also attacked for his incompetence as a secretary and organiser and when a special meeting was organised for Sunday 4 July 1886, a decision was made to remove Cusack from his position by a vote of forty-seven to thirteen. Cusack would remain a member of the GAA until his death in 1906 but he never again served in an official capacity. Interestingly, the meeting organised to expel Cusack had a notable absentee, the president Maurice Davin. He was also absent when another decision was made to ban members of the Royal Irish Constabulary (RIC) from the organisation in 1887,[41] a move that demonstrated the increased control the IRB was enjoying within the GAA. There was no ban on the army and navy, just the RIC who were viewed with disdain by most quarters in Ireland at the time.[42] Davin resigned as president primarily due to the increased control of the GAA by the IRB. He was persuaded, at the behest of Croke and Davitt, to come out of retirement in 1888. His second term as president was for a brief stint as the IRB maintained their control over the organisation and his precarious financial situation would not allow him to continue in his role with the GAA.[43]

The IRB had been steadily increasing its power base within the GAA from the moment the GAA was founded in 1884. Five of the ten people elected on to the GAA executive in 1885 were members of the IRB[44] and once Cusack was removed and Davin sidelined before his resignation, they were in complete control. A manifestation of this control was the choice of person selected to become the fourth patron of the Association, Fenian John O'Leary. O'Leary was invited to become patron in 1886, an invitation he duly accepted. The original three patrons – Croke, Parnell and even Davitt – represented the orthodox, more mainstream, strain of Irish nationalism. O'Leary, by contrast, was an active Fenian, known by some as 'the noblest of the Fenians', and was the then president of the Supreme

Council of the IRB.[45] He was immortalised as representing 'Romantic Ireland' in W. B. Yeats' poem 'September 1913'. His selection as patron was the first clear sign that the IRB fully controlled the GAA. On the same day O'Leary was proposed as patron a decision was made to have a monument erected in Tipperary in honour of his predecessor as president of the IRB Supreme Council, Charles Kickham.

There has always been a close link between politics and the GAA despite some of the GAA's claims to the contrary; this was amplified when the IRB had full control. It was now clearly more of a political organisation than a sporting one.[46] Many GAA members were not happy with this new turn of events and the clergy in particular provided strong opposition to the IRB. The conflict came to a head at the Annual Convention in 1887, held in Thurles, when a Tipperary priest, Father Scanlan, unhappy with proceedings at the convention, stormed out with over 200 of the 800 or so delegates, threatening to set up a new athletic association under the control of Croke, Parnell and the National League, and William O'Brien.[47] This was the closest the GAA has ever come to a split; were it not for the interventions of Croke and Davitt in early 1888 to get Davin approved as a president again as a compromise, the GAA as we know it would not exist.

At the re-convened convention in 1888, William O'Brien was proposed as the fifth patron of the GAA, which he accepted in May of that year.[48] O'Brien was a leading politician of Parnell's Home Rule party, serving as Member of Parliament almost without a break up to 1918. He was also a committed land agitator and editor of *United Ireland*, the paper that had done so much to promote the GAA in its early years. He was, at the time, serving a jail sentence in Tullamore for his participation in the 'Plan of Campaign', a strategy in the Land War that had engulfed the country for over a decade.

Although there was a temporary peace after the 1888 re-convention, the clergy and IRB-led GAA would be at loggerheads again over their respective treatment of one of the

The funeral cortège of Charles Stewart Parnell passes over O'Connell Bridge on its way to Glasnevin Cemetery in October 1891. The GAA provided a hurley-carrying escort for the cortège. The GAA's support for Parnell during the Parnell Split severely damaged the association, almost leading to its disbandment. *(Courtesy of the National Library of Ireland)*

founding patrons of the Association, Charles Stewart Parnell. The Home Rule Party and indeed all of Ireland became deeply divided after Captain William O'Shea issued divorce proceedings against his wife, Katherine, on 24 December 1889, naming Parnell as co-respondent. In Victorian Britain, of which Ireland possessed many traits and idioms, it was a huge scandal. Once William Gladstone, the leader of the Liberal party in Britain, withdrew his support for Parnell, Parnell lost his grip on the Home Rule Party and was ousted as leader. The clergy in Ireland was firmly against Parnell, whilst the GAA prominently supported him. The strain of the split and the bitter campaign to ascertain his authority took its toll on Parnell. He died on 6 October 1891. There still is a great deal of uncertainty surrounding the cause of his death; the most commonly ascertained diagnosis given is coronary heart disease.[49] There was a huge outpouring of grief at his funeral, where the GAA provided a hurley-carrying escort for the cortège as it made its way towards Glasnevin Cemetery.[50] The GAA's prominent role at one of the biggest funerals ever seen in Ireland presented a striking image, the 'G.A.A. bodyguard which received the remains of the fallen leader at Westland Row and, in their thousands – marching six abreast with hurleys draped in black – they led the huge funeral procession to Glasnevin'.[51]

The GAA suffered significantly for supporting Parnell; the clergy was decisive in convincing people to stay away from GAA events. When people were faced with choosing between the Catholic Church and the GAA, the Church won convincingly. The numbers participating at GAA events and meetings had been declining for a number of years: there were only seven counties represented at the 1890 Annual Convention. Things deteriorated further still after the 'Parnell Split'. At the 1892 Annual Convention, held in 1893, there were delegates from only three counties in attendance – Dublin, Cork and Kerry. There were 118 affiliated clubs as opposed to over 1,000 four years previously.[52] It was decided at this meeting to remove the ban on the RIC: the political climate was considerably calmer and there was also less revulsion towards the RIC at the time. The RIC ban's removal was also a direct result of the IRB losing their vice-like grip over the GAA. People like Richard Blake, Patrick Tobin and Frank Dineen were about to come to the fore and they recognised, as Dineen pointed out, that politics had been 'of considerable injury to our association'.[53]

The GAA received a further boost in 1893, albeit not recognised at the time, by the founding of a body that would be its sister organisation for many years, a body that would be as powerful a force in the quest for an Irish-Ireland as the GAA, the Gaelic League.

3

The De-Anglicising of Ireland

The Gaelic League was founded in 1893 after the Gaelic scholar and future nationalist politician Eoin MacNeill invited Douglas Hyde and a number of other interested people to a meeting with the objective of setting up an organisation to restore Irish as a *spoken* language. There had been a rapid decline in the Irish speaking population, dwindling from 900,000 to 700,000 in the period 1881 to 1891.[1] Although this meeting was initiated by MacNeill, the driving force and inspiration behind the organisation was undoubtedly Hyde. It was for this reason he was made its first president.

Whilst at Trinity College Dublin and through his involvement with the Gaelic Union, Hyde was the main advocate for restoring Irish as a spoken language. The Society for the Preservation of the Irish Language and the Gaelic Union were primarily focused on the written aspect of the language. Hyde believed that, in order for the language to survive, it needed to be spoken by the people of Ireland. He saw how Irish was spoken in his native Connacht, how it was declining there as well as elsewhere, and he called for a move away from the anglicising of the Irish people and back to the level where the Irish were proud of their native traditions and their language. He was not calling for Irish people to restore their language simply for the sake of keeping the language alive. He felt

This photograph of Douglas Hyde was taken around the time of the founding of the Gaelic League. Hyde was the chief inspiration and first president of the Gaelic League during its golden era from 1893 to 1915. *(Courtesy of the National Library of Ireland)*

Ireland as a nation, a people, had lost its dignity and self respect and the language was the optimal way to restore that lost pride. Hyde believed Irish people should focus on their positives as opposed to concentrating on the negatives of the British.[2] There is ample evidence of Hyde making these points in the years leading up to the first meeting of the Gaelic League.

Whilst a member of the Gaelic Union, he commented on the need to keep Irish as a spoken language, saying that if we allow the language to die out, 'We lay aside a language – which for all ordinary purposes of everyday life is more pointed and forcible than any with which I am acquainted, and we replace it by another which we learn badly and speak with an atrocious accent, interlarding it with barbarisms and vulgarity'.[3]

Contributing an essay in 1886 to the *Dublin University Review* entitled 'A Plea for the Irish Language', Hyde accepted the need for people to speak English for social and commercial reasons but called on people to speak Irish too, in order to restore national honour.[4]

This call to action was reiterated in 1889 when he published his book, *Leabhar Sgeulaigheach*, saying it would 'be an everlasting disgrace and a blighting stigma upon our nationality'[5] if Irish was allowed to die out without a struggle.

His voice was even heard on the other side of the Atlantic, calling for the restoration of Irish. Hyde moved to Canada for one year in 1890 to become Chair of Modern Languages at the University of New Brunswick. He made a trip to New York whilst living in North America and delivered a speech on how keeping the Irish language as a spoken language would be the glue that would 'weld together the Irish nation'.[6] The *Freeman's Journal* commented in 1893 that this speech was the opening shot in a quest to have a 'popular crusade' to revive the Irish language.[7]

All of these comments and speeches were a build up to the speech that was seen as the main catalyst for the founding of the Gaelic League. That speech, entitled 'The Necessity for De-Anglicising Ireland', was delivered to the Irish Literary Society on 25 November 1892. In this address, a hard-hitting one, he criticised the contradictory nature of the contemporary Irish: 'the Irish race is at present in a most anomalous position, imitating England and yet apparently hating it'.[8] He made an attack on 'this constant running to England for our books, literature, music, games, fashions, and ideas'.[9] He bemoaned in particular 'the greatest stroke of all in our Anglicisation, the loss of our language',[10] and set out a vision for its revival amongst all Irish people, whether Unionist or Nationalist. Declan Kiberd in his excellent sweeping tome on Irish Literature, *Inventing Ireland: The Literature of the Modern Nation*, claims this speech was the signal for the rebirth of cultural and literary criticism in Ireland.[11]

In a number of other speeches, he made reference to the success of the GAA including a speech in Cork in early 1893 where he said that the Irish 'would have lost their games completely only for the Gaelic Athletic Association which had done more for Ireland in a few years than all the platform orators for fifty years'.[12]

The Gaelic League came into being on 31 July 1893. Many people had 'an eye but not an ear knowledge of the language'[13] and the primary objective of this new movement was to go to the country and get people speaking Irish again. The task ahead of the Gaelic League was formidable. It had to influence people from historically Irish-speaking areas to retain their native tongue that they were now seeing as 'an impediment to wordily [sic] success, and that a knowledge of the tongue of "the stranger" is essential, if they wish to make their way in the world'.[14] Reminiscent of the founding of the GAA nine years previously, there were few people in attendance at the first meeting and also somewhat reminiscent of the GAA, the Gaelic League, after an initial solid but unspectacular start, spread like a prairie fire.

The Gaelic League succeeded beyond all hopes and expectations of its original founders. The 'Parnell Split' and his premature death in October 1891 were still raw in people's minds and the Gaelic League filled the vacuum caused by people's loss of faith in politics. Parnellites, anti-Parnellites and even a few Unionists supported the League.[15] It was different to the great Irish movements in the nineteenth century organised by Daniel O'Connell, Thomas Davis, Isaac Butt and Charles Stewart Parnell – it was not overtly political. The organisation it was most similar to was the GAA, an organisation on its knees at the time primarily due to its involvement in politics.

By the turn of the century, the Gaelic League was soaring in popularity. In 1899, Hyde claimed there were over 92 Gaelic League branches, ranging in membership size from 50 to 400.[16] Others claim the League grew to 600 branches with over 20,000 members.[17] It had branches in every town and village of the country.[18] According to Declan Kiberd, there were only six books in print in Irish at the time the League was started. Yeats would claim that there were 50,000 textbooks sold in one year alone due to the League. 'A civil rights agitation was mounted.'[19]

There are a number of reasons for this extraordinary success. The language that had been abandoned as the language of the peasant and the no-hoper for the bulk of the nineteenth century was now a source of pride for people. The Gaelic League called up feelings that Sir Horace Plunkett described as 'sentiments and thoughts which had been developed in Gaelic Ireland through hundreds of years, which no repression had obliterated entirely, but which remained a latent spiritual inheritance in the mind'.[20]

The Gaelic League's non-political stance provided a good neutral ground for people of differing viewpoints to meet; it provided an alternative means for nationalistically inclined people to express their patriotism.[21] Father O'Growney's recently published simple lessons in Irish made it easier for people to learn the language and its weekly journal, *The Leader*, helped spread the Gaelic League philosophy effectively.[22] External factors such as a comprehensive settlement of the Land Question through the Wyndham Act of 1903 and the dogged effort made by the Boers in fighting the once almighty British Empire in the Boer War of 1899–1902 were all beneficial to the League.[23]

It had a very simple structure that also contributed to its early success. Employed organisers and travelling teachers went around the country and in areas where ten or more people expressed an interest in Irish, a branch was set up. Branches were self-governing and were merely obliged to make a contribution to the central organisation. This entitled a branch to a vote in elections of the Gaelic League.[24] In many ways the branch structure of the Gaelic League was similar to the branch structure of its sister organisation, the GAA.

Another major factor for its success was its leader. Hyde was president of the Gaelic League from its inception in 1893 up to 1915. This coincided with the years of its greatest success and popularity. He, more than anyone else, insisted on its politically neutral stance. Hyde was also a very personable man who people were willing to support. Comments from those who were his friends and those who had fleeting interactions with him all paint the same picture. A hard to read man, yes, but a man who was engaging, courteous to everyone he met, a man with a clear vision in knowing what he wanted the Gaelic League and Ireland to progress towards and a man who had the exceptional communication skills necessary to deliver his vision effectively.

An early battle of the Gaelic League involved a campaign led by Hyde to have Irish accepted as a subject on the school curriculum. The issue came up for discussion at the Committee of Intermediate Education in 1899. The campaign was fought by professors of Trinity College, including former tutor of Oscar Wilde, John Pentland Mahaffy, who argued that the language was a basic one with no academic credentials. They stated that it was 'almost impossible to get hold of a text in Irish which is not religious or that is not silly or indecent'.[25] They came up against a formidable opponent in Hyde who, whilst remaining courteous and dignified throughout the very public debate, dissected their arguments by producing evidence from many eminent Celtic scholars throughout Europe. Scholars from universities in Leipzig, Greifswald, Berlin, Liverpool, Copenhagen, Rennes and Oxford provided citations supporting the Irish language as well as demonstrating its merits as a language with a deep scholarly history.[26] It was a resounding success for Hyde and the League with Irish being accepted as a subject on the curriculum, and Hyde receiving the plaudits from a public now firmly behind him.

By the beginning of the twentieth century, the Gaelic League was seen as the strongest and most popular organisation in the country[27] and Hyde was a man much in demand. He was asked to join and write a play for the new Abbey Theatre which had been established by W. B. Yeats, Edward Martyn and Lady Gregory. He wrote the first play ever written and performed in Irish, *Casadh an tSúgáin* (*The Twisting of the Rope*), in which he was also the leading actor. He was the one person who 'straddled the two developments of Gaelic revivalism and Anglo-Irish literary developments' according to historian R. F. Foster.[28] Ironically, as Hyde was imploring his fellow Irish people to speak their native tongue, a raft of Anglo-Irish literary greats were starting to craft their trade in the English language; people such as Yeats, Joyce, and J. M. Synge. Hyde's literary output up to this date had included his folktales in Irish *Leabhar Sgeulaigheach*, *Love Songs of Connacht* and *Religious Songs of Connacht*. Arguably his magnum opus was his *Literary History of Ireland* published in 1899. These works introduced many people to Irish and the rich folktales of the past.

John Redmond, leader of the Irish Parliamentary Party, recognising the popularity of the Gaelic League, offered Hyde a seat in parliament at Westminster. Hyde declined.[29] In November 1902 he was offered another honour that he had no hesitation in accepting: patron of the GAA.

4

The GAA Reborn

After the trauma of the 'Parnell Split' and the criticism the GAA received as a result of its support for Parnell, the GAA made a concerted effort to disassociate itself from politics. A clear sign of a commitment to all things nationalist and political were the bans. Under the new leadership the bans on the RIC and 'foreign games' were seen as liabilities. Once the RIC ban was removed in 1893, it was only a matter of time before the ban on 'foreign games' would also come under scrutiny and it was rescinded in 1896. The man responsible for this move away from politics was Richard Blake who was GAA general secretary from 1895 to 1898. A Meath man, Blake was a controversial figure who made as many enemies as he did friends in the GAA. He was convinced that the reason for the GAA's spectacular decline in fortunes was due to its meddling in politics and he was firmly opposed to the IRB's control over the Association. As a self-confessed admirer of rugby and cricket, Blake, in particular, was against the ban on 'foreign games'. After he was forced to resign as general secretary in 1898 he went on to become a member of Bective Rugby Football Club and the Meath county cricket team, and for most of his subsequent journalistic work he covered rugby and cricket.[1] When the ban on 'foreign games' was removed in

1896, the following directive was issued to all affiliated clubs, 'That the Gaelic Athletic Association shall be a strictly non-political and un-sectarian association; no political questions of any kind shall be raised at any of its meetings …'[2] The decision to remove the Ban was condemned by the GAA founder, Michael Cusack, who called the new ethos of the GAA 'a miserably Arctic condition of things' where people who 'support the Anglicising party which Dr Douglas Hyde is so strenuously opposing' were now allowed to be members of the GAA.[3]

Blake can be credited with stemming the downward spiral of the Association. Numbers started to creep up again during his tenure – clubs affiliated to the GAA went from 114 to 358 – and the GAA's income increased considerably. He was responsible for bringing the All-Ireland finals to Jones' Road in Dublin (which became Croke Park in 1913) and was instrumental in codifying Gaelic football, giving it the shape it has largely kept to this day.[4] It could be argued that he went too far in his opposition to GAA involvement in politics and nationalism, though, and it was for this reason that he was forced to resign as general secretary. In 1897 the GAA was invited to become a member of the '1798 Centenary Committee' to play a role in remembering the revolution of that year. Blake opposed involvement in this body which he saw as IRB controlled. This was a step too far for many GAA members, including future president James Nowlan, and it was not long before Blake was removed from office.[5]

The GAA subsequently played a large part in the 1798 commemorations. According to Brendan MacLua, author of the pro-Ban book, *The Steadfast Rule*, 'the G.A.A. was reborn. It emerged a completely changed and tremendously revitalised organisation. It immediately took its place at the forefront of the new national resurgence and was never again to relinquish that position.'[6]

The GAA reverted back to its links with Irish nationalism, joining other new groups, including the Gaelic League, in

James Nowlan was GAA president from 1901 to 1921, serving for longer than any other president in GAA history. He was instrumental in placing the organisation on a sound financial footing and overseeing the massive expansion the GAA experienced after the turn of the twentieth century. He openly identified with separatist nationalism and was fully behind a renewal of the lapsed bans. *(Courtesy of the GAA Museum, Croke Park)*

promoting a Gaelic Ireland ideal. Funds for memorials to nationalists such as Kickham, Nally, and the Manchester Martyrs were raised by the GAA, motions to revive Irish industries and the Irish language were passed at GAA meetings and it was agreed that all GAA medals were to be of Irish manufacture and design and to be inscribed in Irish.[7] The GAA formed a particularly strong bond with the Gaelic League. Many GAA members and officials were also Gaelic League activists. 'It never overlooked an opportunity, whether at local or central council level, of supporting the Gaelic League. It took a major part in the annual cultural (and later industrial) parade held under League auspices every St Patrick's Day – which, in 1903, became a public holiday following a campaign in which the GAA took part'.[8] The Gaelic League had led the campaign to have St Patrick's Day made a public holiday, persuading most Irish businesses to close on that day to apply maximum pressure for the British Government to bring about that change.[9] The Gaelic League played its part too in constantly promoting the

GAA over every other sport, with regular calls from its president, Douglas Hyde, for closer co-operation between the two bodies. In fact, the sport of camogie came about through women members of the Gaelic League playing their own version of hurling; it was soon registered as a GAA sport.[10]

The 1901 Annual Convention was a hugely significant one for the GAA. At that convention, James Nowlan was elected president with Luke O'Toole as general secretary. Both served in their respective positions for over twenty years, bringing much needed stability to the Association as well as steering the organisation on an administrative path that would be the envy of many others. A Kilkenny native, Nowlan (the main GAA ground in Kilkenny is named in his honour) had a long association with the Gaelic League, dating from its foundation in 1893. He was also a member of the IRB, serving for a period on its Supreme Council. He would remain GAA president until 1921, the longest serving president by a considerable length of time. A Wicklow man, Luke O'Toole defeated Michael Cusack for the position of general secretary and remained in that role until his untimely death at his desk in 1929,[11] guiding the GAA through the most turbulent period in its history including the First World War, the Easter Rising, the War of Independence and the Civil War. O'Toole started the extraordinary trend of general secretaries serving for lengthy periods in the GAA throughout the twentieth century. Only three more men would hold the office of general secretary after O'Toole for the rest of the century, providing crucial stability as the Association grew and changed along with the country.

Both men were instrumental in reorganising the Association into four provincial councils, placing the organisation on a sound financial footing and overseeing the massive expansion the GAA experienced after the turn of the century. They also openly identified with separatist nationalism and they were fully behind a renewal of the lapsed bans.

The ban on 'foreign games' was reintroduced on the same day Nowlan and O'Toole were elected in 1901. It was introduced on a voluntary basis, leaving it to the discretion of the county boards to enforce it – more of a plea than a demand.[12] T. F. O'Sullivan from Kerry, who later wrote a history of the GAA, put forward the motion:

> That we the Representatives of the Gaels of Ireland in convention assembled hereby pledge ourselves to resist by every means in our power the extension of English pastimes to this country, as a means of preventing the Anglicisation of our people: that County Committees be empowered to disqualify and suspend members of the Association who countenance sports which are calculated to interfere with the preservation and cultivation of our own national pastimes: that we call on the young men of Ireland not to identify themselves with rugby or Association football or any other form of imported sport which is likely to injuriously affect the national pastimes which the G.A.A. provides for self-respected Irishmen who have no desire to ape foreign manners and customs.[13]

At the Annual Convention of 1902, the same convention that selected Douglas Hyde as patron, a compulsory ban was introduced. A decision was also made to sanction the use of vigilance committees to monitor the activities of GAA members.[14] Members of these vigilance committees were sanctioned to attend 'foreign games' to 'spy' on GAA members who were in breach of the Ban. In 1903, the compulsory nature of the Ban was removed and county boards were again allowed discretion to implement the Ban or not. It was to be made compulsory again at the 1904 Annual Convention (held in 1905).[15] This version of the Ban would remain in place until 1971.

The Ban was reintroduced in the first few years of the twentieth century for a different reason. It was reintroduced due to a renewed sense of nationalism in the country, a sense of pride in all things Irish. It was deliberately political. Douglas Hyde claimed that the GAA paved the way for the Gaelic

League. The GAA was the first of the Irish-Ireland movements that sprang to life in the latter part of the nineteenth century and it certainly was an inspiration for the other Irish-Ireland bodies that were to be formed. However, by the start of the twentieth century its popularity had decreased greatly from its initial heights. The 'Parnell Split' had very nearly seen the Association disappear altogether. A great deal of credit must go to the Gaelic League and Hyde himself for the GAA's reinvention and subsequent popularity. It could be argued that, at the turn of the century, the Gaelic League was the most popular movement in Ireland and Hyde, as leader, was the person most instrumental in changing people's minds and getting support for the concept of de-anglicisation. The Gaelic League did not just reinvent the Irish language, it reinvigorated the Irish spirit and could justifiably claim to be the driving force behind this renewed sense of pride in everything Irish, be it the language, Irish industry or, indeed, its native pastimes. There is strong evidence to suggest that the Gaelic League was the body that reinvigorated and set up many new GAA clubs around the country. According to David Hassan, 'an active Gaelic League division in Strabane, County Tyrone led directly to the foundation of four GAA clubs in the town in the late nineteenth century'.[16] Conor Curran in his book *Sport in Donegal: A History* demonstrates the active role Gaelic League branches in Donegal played in setting up and participating in GAA clubs.[17] Tom Hunt ascertains that the Gaelic League was directly responsible for the establishment of GAA clubs in many counties, including Longford, Westmeath, Derry, Fermanagh and Dublin.[18] It was no surprise that Hyde would be named as the sixth patron of the GAA in 1902, considering the help he had given to the Association both directly and indirectly over the previous ten years.

5

Hyde Becomes Patron of the GAA

Hyde had been friends with Michael Cusack, the founder of the GAA, from his early days in Trinity College in 1880 through their involvement in the Gaelic Union. Both were among the most active members of the Gaelic Union. Hyde remarked that Cusack was the most fluent Irish speaker he had ever met.[1] W. F. Mandle in his book, *The Gaelic Athletic Association and Irish National Politics 1884–1924*, claims that Hyde offered Cusack advice on setting up a national pastimes body before the meeting of 1 November 1884 in Thurles that established the GAA.[2] Hyde was certainly one of the earliest members of the new body[3] and Cusack was one of the earliest members of the Gaelic League.[4] Hyde was never shy in his praise for the GAA and was a firm advocate of the two bodies forming close links with each other. As a follow up to his famous De-Anglicising Speech of November 1892 at the Irish Literary Society, Hyde spoke to the same body in January 1894, where he remarked that one of the first steps for people to take to de-anglicise themselves was to wear 'that most national and comfortable of garments, the striped garments of the Gaelic Athletic Association, and for their home-spun frieze and tweed in preference to the cast off garments of the Manchester and London shop boys which were bought at fairs

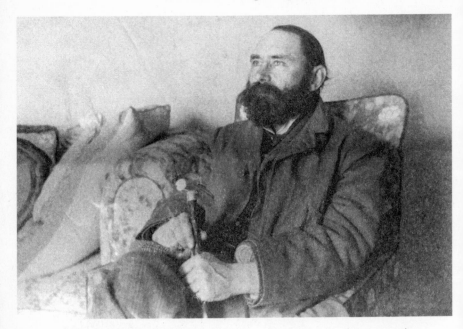

Douglas Hyde at the turn of the twentieth century. By that stage the Gaelic League had become 'the strongest and most popular organisation in the country'. There was little surprise when he was honoured by the GAA to become a patron in 1902. *(Courtesy of the James Hardiman Library, NUI Galway)*

and markets by their peasantry'.[5] In 1896, Hyde made another speech, calling for greater links between the two bodies:

> The Gaelic Athletic Association and the Gaelic League have much in common, seeing that the latter pursues the literature of Ireland and the former pursues the games of Ireland, both tending to de-Anglicisation. The League and Association ought to be drawn into closer communion, and branches of the League established in connection with every branch of the Association. Some thing [sic] like this was done some years ago in Waterford when Irish by choice was the language used in the hurling field.[6]

He concluded with what has turned out to be a somewhat prophetic comment, 'We can always have an organisation like

Advanced nationalist, political activist, and subject of most of W. B. Yeats' love poetry, Maud Gonne McBride was proposed as patron of the GAA on the same day as Hyde was made patron in 1902 but was ruled out as no notice proposing her had been received. To date, no woman has been made GAA patron. *(Courtesy of the National Library of Ireland)*

the GAA, but we may not always have a Gaelic League'.[7] At the first national annual event organised by the Gaelic League, known as the Oireachtas, held in 1897, there were calls for Irish to be the language used at GAA gatherings.[8]

Even though the GAA has bestowed the honour of patron on very few people, there can be little doubt that Hyde was seen as an appropriate and popular choice amongst its members. He was made patron at the Annual Convention held in November 1902.[9] The new Archbishop of Cashel, Dr Terence Fennelly, successor to Dr Croke who had died earlier in the year, was made patron on the same day.[10] It was reported that Maud Gonne was also proposed as a patron on that day but was ruled out as no notice had been received.[11] Another motion passed at that convention that would lead to future ramifications for Hyde was a resolution to suspend any members of the GAA who played or encouraged in any way the sports of rugby, association football, hockey or any imported game which could harm the national games.[12]

Hyde was, at that time, deeply devoted to the Gaelic League and made many personal sacrifices to ensure its growth. He had no steady income, as the only teaching job he had was in New Brunswick from 1890 to 1891. His devotion to the Irish language was seen as an obstacle when he applied for posts in Trinity College Dublin, Queen's University Belfast and the University of Chicago. His wife Lucy Cometina Kurtz, who he had married in 1893, the same year the Gaelic League was founded, was eager to move from Frenchpark in Roscommon. She urged Hyde to move to Dublin and was somewhat resentful of the Gaelic League and the demands it made on her husband.[13] Although based in Roscommon, Hyde travelled to any part in Ireland or England to address meetings, settle disputes, or give advice.[14]

The biggest trip he made on behalf of the League was a fundraising one to the United States in 1905. He went there at the behest of leading Irish-American philanthropist and lawyer, John Quinn, who organised the trip. Lucy accompanied him. Hyde was given a rousing send off in November 1905 with processions held in Dublin, Tipperary and Cork in his honour. GAA members were prominent at those gatherings. Hurlers formed a bodyguard for Hyde in Dublin whilst singing 'The Marching Song of the Hurling Men' which was composed by Hyde himself[15] at the suggestion of Ellen O'Leary, sister of fellow GAA patron John.[16] Its first verse was evocative:

> We the numerous men of Eire,
> Born beneath her pleasant skies,
> To our gatherings from her mountains
> In our thousands we arise.
> See the weapons on our shoulders,
> Neither gun or pike we bear,
> But when Ireland calls upon them,
> Ireland soon shall find them there.[17]

Members of various different GAA clubs as well as the Executive of the GAA were there to wish their patron a safe and successful journey. Hyde himself 'thanked, above all, his old friends of the Gaelic Athletic Association'.[18] He went on to say:

> I was one of the original members of the Gaelic Athletic Association when it was started and [sic] when I was a Trinity College boy. From that day I have followed closely the fortunes of the Gaelic Athletic Association, and I felt that any body of men that was engaged in the physical development of Irishmen was, to use a mathematical phrase, the complement of what the Gaelic League was doing to build up the intellectual side of Irishmen; and the two bodies had so much in common, and were doing so much for the production of the finest race type, that I have often wondered we were not more closely knit together.[19]

Hyde received a warm welcome too when he arrived in America later that month. He met the American president, Theodore Roosevelt, on his arrival (the first of two meetings) and was impressed with Roosevelt's knowledge and support for Irish literature and the language.[20] He also garnered the support of the presidents of Harvard and Yale, prominent businessman Andrew Carnegie, and the daughters of American literary giants Ralph Waldo Emerson and Henry Wadsworth Longfellow[21] as well as John F. 'Honey Fitz' Fitzgerald, the grandfather of future Irish-American president, John F. Kennedy.[22] In an editorial devoted to Hyde on his arrival, *The New York Times* commended the work Hyde was doing for the Irish language movement and the impact this would have on all other languages in danger of extinction.[23] At a gathering in Carnegie Hall, New York, Hyde was announced as a 'missionary from Ireland'. 'He informed his audience that Ireland was no longer an old and poor woman but a beautiful woman who had begun to move and to play, she has begun to sing'.[24] Hyde crisscrossed the country in seven months, travelling some 19,000 miles, visiting over sixty cities, some on two or three occasions, and speaking to around 80,000 people. At one engagement he remarked, 'The Gaelic League is teaching Irishmen to know themselves ... It is transforming Irishmen from imitators into independent producers, teaching them to initiate, not imitate.'[25] He raised $30,000 (approx. €500,000 today) which put the League on a solid financial footing for the coming years. He gave $5,000 back to the citizens of San Francisco who had experienced a devastating earthquake in April 1906 that killed over 3,000 people. He was offered a gift of a new motor car worth $2,500 on his departure from New York but he declared 'that he could not depart from the rule of his life – not to accept any personal reward for his services to the Gaelic League and on behalf of Irish unity'.[26] The car was returned to the contributors.

When Hyde returned to Ireland in June 1906 he was greeted with a rousing reception and again prominent in that reception were members of the GAA.[27] Hyde was at the height of his popularity. Dunleavy and Dunleavy in their biography on Hyde, *Douglas Hyde: A Maker of Modern Ireland*, even claimed the Thurles branch of the GAA hailed Hyde had replaced Parnell as the new 'Uncrowned King of Ireland'.[28] He was granted the Freedom of the City in Dublin, Cork and Kilkenny. He was subsequently offered the Freedom of the City of Limerick in 1909.

In 1906 he was appointed to the Fry Commission, which recommended the establishment of a National University for Ireland and he would lead the charge to make sure Irish was an essential prerequisite for anyone interested in entering the new university. Meetings were held throughout the country with Hyde speaking to over 100,000 people at one gathering.[29] He received the support of the county councils who promised to withhold scholarships if Irish was not accepted as an essential subject. He was also supported by John Redmond's Irish

Parliamentary Party. Hyde and Gaelic League co-founder, Eoin MacNeill, were made professors of the new university. Hyde served as first professor of Irish Studies in University College, Dublin from 1909 until his retirement in 1932.

This was to be the apex of the League's and Hyde's success. Hyde had been playing a delicate juggling act for years to keep the League non-political and had succeeded admirably in keeping the League available to every man and woman of any class, creed or age. He was warned by novelist James Hannay (alias George Birmingham) in 1907, 'I think the movement you started will go on, whether you lead it or take the part of a poor Frankenstein who created a monster he could not control'.[30] And Hyde did lose control eventually. Advanced nationalists like Pádraig Pearse were becoming more and more active. Pearse acted as editor of the League's newspaper *An Claidheamh Soluis*. Eoin MacNeill set up the Irish Volunteers in 1913 in response to the formation of the Ulster Volunteers and funds for the League were diverted to this new militant body. The moment when Hyde decided that the League had gone too far towards politics came at the Árd Fhéis of the Oireachtas held in Dundalk, County Louth, in 1915. A resolution was passed by the League that one of its objectives would be to ensure Ireland's freedom from foreign domination. The new Coiste Gnotha (Executive Committee) was formed of people who were more associated with politics than the language movement and Hyde decided his time with the League had come to an end. On resigning he said, 'I slipt away about 1 o'clock p.m. the following day after appearing as usual and talking to everybody, and arranging with Peadar MacGinley to take the chair at 2 o'clock. I got out my baggage from the hotel without anyone noticing it, got into the hotel bus and got to the train and was soon on my way to Dublin with a lighter heart than I had known for years'.[31]

What Hyde had achieved with the Gaelic League was an extraordinary accomplishment. By the late nineteenth century the Irish language was on its knees. It had either been abandoned or neglected by the leading Irish figures of that century such as Daniel O'Connell and Charles Stewart Parnell and had become a stigmatism for people to be associated with. Hyde, more than anyone else, was responsible for resurrecting it. On his achievements, Declan Kiberd commented, 'Of Hyde, it could justly be said that he rescued the Irish element from absorption and made it, for a brilliant generation from 1893 to 1921, conscious of itself'.[32] Gerard Murphy, in an obituary after the death of Hyde in 1949, sums up Hyde's impact succinctly:

> He had a vision of something great which was a personal discovery of his own. He had the power too of communicating that vision to others. And his life-long fidelity to that vision was such that, long before he died, what was once personal to himself had become the common property of all his countrymen and changed the national outlook in a way that would have seemed incredible in the late 1890s of the last century.[33]

Hyde was not embittered by the direction the Gaelic League had taken although he did not agree with it personally. In later years he acknowledged the League's ultimate role in politics and in bringing about the Irish Free State, 'The Gaelic League grew up and became the spiritual father of Sinn Féin, and Sinn Féin's progeny were the Volunteers who forced the English to make the treaty. The Dáil is the child of the Volunteers, and thus it descends directly from the Gaelic League, whose traditions it inherits.'[34] León Ó Broin, writing in 1938, went as far as to say that Hyde could 'justly be styled the principal architect of the new Irish State'.[35]

6

The Ban – A Fundamental Principle
of the GAA

Support within the GAA for the Ban on 'foreign games' steadily increased from 1905 onwards. In 1905 the margin to retain the Ban was by only forty-six to thirty-two votes.[1] However, a year later a motion to make the Ban rule optional was defeated heavily, by fifty-one votes to fifteen.[2] At that same Annual Congress the RIC ban was reintroduced with the added exclusion of British military personnel for the first time. A motion to rescind this ban in 1907 was heavily defeated, by seventy votes to nineteen.[3] Over the following years, new measures were brought in, strengthening the ban on 'foreign games' as well as the introduction of new bans. It was confirmed in 1908 that the phrase 'encouraging in any way' which was incorporated in the article on the Ban, included spectators at 'foreign games',[4] a decision which would have major repercussions for Hyde some thirty years later. Jail wardens were added to the list of excluded professions in 1909 and in 1911 a motion was passed prohibiting GAA members from attending dances or other forms of entertainment organised by the RIC or British soldiers.[5] A motion in favour of removing the Ban received only four votes that same year,[6] a clear sign that opposition to the Ban was, to all intents and purposes, dead.

Luke O'Toole, GAA general secretary, (centre) with Michael Collins (left) and Harry Boland (right) in Croke Park. The GAA has looked to portray itself as centrally involved in the struggle for independence that engulfed the country from 1912 to 1921. The ban on 'foreign games' played its part in creating that impression. *(Courtesy of the GAA Museum, Croke Park)*

The opposition to the removal of the Ban became even more pronounced after the onset of the independence struggle which engulfed the country from 1912 to 1921. As events transpired, the Ban played its part in portraying a picture of the GAA as being centrally involved in that struggle for independence. Senior officials within the GAA have, throughout the years, been quick to add to this impression even though the truth is not so clear-cut and green-tinted as they would like. It has been a widely-held view that the GAA were as responsible for the founding of the Irish Volunteers as the Gaelic League. The Irish Volunteers were a military organisation set up to offset the founding of the Ulster Volunteers, a group that vowed to use any means necessary to stop Home Rule from coming into Ireland. Luke O'Toole, the GAA general secretary, a man not known for his public pronouncements, was one of the platform speakers at the Irish Volunteers' inaugural meeting held at the Rotunda in Dublin on 25 November 1913, urging 'all Irishmen to join the organisation'.[7] The GAA president James Nowlan, a member of the IRB, is reported as advising GAA members to join the Volunteers and to 'learn to shoot straight' – it was suggested that rifles could be offered as prizes instead of medals for future competitions.[8] In reality, the GAA's support for the Irish Volunteers was more lukewarm. Within weeks of the formation of the Irish Volunteers, it was decided at a Central Council meeting of the GAA not to endorse the group officially, and Croke Park was not offered as a venue for drilling purposes to the Volunteers.[9]

Another widely-held view is that the GAA played a significant role in the Easter Rising of 1916. There can be no doubt that many GAA members participated. Records show that over 300 out of an estimated total of 1,500 to 1,800 participants of the Rising in Dublin were members of the GAA.[10] Five of the fifteen men executed after the Rising had GAA connections – Pádraig Pearse, Seán McDermott, Eamon Ceannt, Con Colbert and Michael O'Hanrahan. Many other Easter rebels who became considerably more prominent in the following years were active GAA members. They included Michael Collins, Harry Boland, Austin Stack and the GAA president himself, James Nowlan, who was arrested and interned in England for alleged involvement in the Rising,[11] highlighting the belief amongst the British authorities that the GAA was one of the instigating bodies of the Rising. The reality, again, would suggest the GAA's involvement was not as significant as first meets the eye. Although many GAA members from Dublin took part in the Rising, the vast majority of participants were not involved in the GAA. Members from fifty-three GAA clubs in Dublin fought in the Rising, many other clubs had no member involved whatsoever.[12] Officially, the GAA was slow to endorse the Rising too. Drawing parallels with St Peter denying all knowledge of Christ, the GAA was swift to issue a statement to the British authorities renouncing all involvement in the Rising and 'drawing attention to the Association's constitutional ban against political activity by the GAA, although it was conceded that individual members had exercised their rights to join any number of nationalist organisations, ranging from the moderate United Irish League to the breakaway Volunteers'.[13] The GAA even went one step further than required by stating the Association had not objected to the visit to Dublin in 1914 of the British Prime Minister, H.H. Asquith,[14] to remove any doubt of their good faith towards the crown.

The British authorities played a vital role in bringing the Ban into focus just a few months after the Easter Rising, and gave the Ban a new momentum as a fundamental principle of the GAA. This came about through an attempt by the British government to bring in an entertainments tax on sports and other recreational bodies. An amendment was added to exempt organisations 'which had been founded with the object of reviving national pastimes'.[15] The GAA, believing it fell into that remit, was told by the Chancellor of the Exchequer that it was a decision for the Customs and Excise department to make.[16] The GAA then decided to make a deputation to the British Commander-in-Chief in Ireland, Sir John Maxwell, to seek exemption from this tax. Considering what had happened in the aftermath of the Easter Rising and the subsequent public outcry at the perceived heavy-handedness of the British authorities, this was an extraordinarily ill-conceived idea by the GAA, a body purporting to be anti-British. It clearly showed there was a price to the GAA's nationalism at times. Maxwell was not interested in exempting the GAA from the Entertainments Tax unless the Association was willing to remove its ban rules.[17] There was no chance the GAA would or could agree to this. The Revenue tried, without success, to enforce the tax: the GAA refused payment and by the end of 1917 the Revenue had given up even trying to get payment from the GAA.[18] The GAA received a moral boost and the Ban was the instrument that provided it. According to Paul Rouse, this 'victory for the GAA would be vital for the future of the Ban. Firstly, in offering financial concessions in return for removal of the Ban, Dublin Castle conferred a degree of importance on the rule which it had never achieved in its own right. This would be interpreted by GAA officials as implicit recognition that the Ban was a significant element in the nationalist armoury'.[19] This is echoed by MacLua, 'The British authorities saw the Ban and its kindred rules as the nationalistic emblem of the G.A.A. It was this that gave the Association a precise sense of being part of the national endeavour.'[20]

The hardening of people's attitudes against the British that developed from the Easter Rising permeated the GAA too. In 1918, magistrates were added to the list of banned professions and the GAA added its voice to those in opposition to the proposed conscription of Irish people to the British First World War effort.[21]

British attitudes and measures hardened too and they were determined to curb the GAA. In July 1918, Dublin Castle issued an order banning all hurling or Gaelic football matches from being played without an RIC permit. The GAA Central Council counteracted by prohibiting anyone within the GAA from seeking such a permit, on pain of suspension from the GAA.[22] The GAA also organised a 'Gaelic Sunday' in open defiance of the RIC permit order, urging all clubs to hold matches on Sunday 4 August 1918. It is estimated that over 1,000 matches took place on that Sunday[23] with numbers of players ranging from over 50,000[24] to 100,000[25] participating. The Oireachtas of the Gaelic League opened on the same day in Killarney, also without a permit from Dublin Castle.[26]

In the build-up to the commencement of open hostilities with the British that would become known as the War of Independence, the GAA looked to further its nationalist credentials. In the beginning of 1919, days before the first shots of the war were fired in Soloheadbeg, County Tipperary, and the meeting of the first Dáil took place in the Mansion House, the GAA proposed debarring members of the civil service who took the oath of allegiance to the crown.[27] This was a controversial decision within the GAA with many in its ranks opposed to the move. It took all the persuasive powers of Harry Boland to convince members that whilst some were willing to sacrifice their lives for Ireland, it was not too much to ask for members of the civil service to lose their jobs for the cause. The motion to ratify the ban was passed by fifty votes to thirty-one.[28]

Unsurprisingly, the issue of the Ban was not up for discussion during the years of the War of Independence. However, after the Anglo-Irish Treaty was signed in 1921, it came under close scrutiny again. Once the treaty was signed there was a belief that the Ban would no longer be necessary to retain as Ireland, or at least part of Ireland, had attained a degree of independence from Britain. The early to mid-1920s were dominated by debates on the Ban within the GAA with MacLua claiming that most people in favour of removing the Ban came from the pro-treaty faction of the Civil War that followed the War of Independence and those opposing it from the anti-treaty side,[29] an assertion backed by de Búrca.[30] This is disputed by Rouse who claims that there were people from both sides of the divide who were for and against the removal of the Ban with a strong element of each faction showing they were more devoted to the Irish-Ireland cause than the other.[31] Dan McCarthy, who was president of the GAA and a pro-treaty supporter, sponsored the early efforts to remove the Ban in the 1920s. One of his fiercest opponents was Eoin O'Duffy, also a prominent member of the pro-treaty side, who considered the attempt to remove the Ban as 'an outrage on the living and dead'.[32]

Members who supported the removal of the Ban argued that the primary reason for its existence had now disappeared with the departure of the British from Ireland. They also contended that the Ban was retarding the growth of the GAA, particularly in schools and the cities and that the majority of the players were against the Ban.[33] It was also mentioned that the ban rules were not being enforced rigidly, a point that would be raised time and time again during the Ban's lifetime. It was felt that removing the Ban would open the GAA's doors to new members who would like to play Gaelic games as well as rugby and soccer.[34]

Those who opposed the Ban's removal argued that although the British may have left, the country was still deeply anglicised. De Búrca contended that an anglophile wave affected the country directly after the treaty and 'in the civil service, in the National Army and at most official functions it became fashionable to adopt British social habits and even to imitate British customs. Little or no effort was made to evolve or even to support distinctively Irish ways or customs'.[35] Many within the GAA felt the time was not right to remove such an important principle. Another argument put forward by pro-Ban supporters related to the three key founding members of the GAA – Michael Cusack, Archbishop Croke and Maurice Davin. They argued that these three men were firmly pro-Ban and would not countenance any opposition to the Ban, a rather jaundiced viewpoint considering the contradictory messages and outright opposition demonstrated by some or all of the three on different occasions. It was also argued that the Ban was the primary nationalist emblem of the GAA, something it should be very proud of and its support for the nationalist cause was a key factor in the Association's popularity and continued growth.[36]

Despite considerable opposition to the Ban within the GAA, all motions seeking its removal were heavily defeated with the exception of 1922 when the vote count was twenty-one to twelve to retain the Ban.[37] In 1923, the vote in favour of the Ban was fifty to twelve[38] and in 1924 it was fifty-four to thirty-two.[39] In 1925 there were two ban motions up for debate:

one, banning members from playing 'foreign games', was passed by sixty-nine votes to twenty-three; and the other, banning members attending 'foreign games', was passed by fifty-nine to twenty-five votes.[40] That year, 1926, was a decisive one for the ever growing body of members supporting the Ban. The vote to retain the Ban was given its most resounding endorsement to date with a vote of eighty to twenty-three.[41] There was also another ruling passed, based on a motion put forward by Jerry Beckett of Cork, 'That it be decided, after disposing of motions to this Congress concerning foreign games, that all future considerations of this Rule be deferred for three years and triennially thenceforth; and that an addendum to this effect be inserted in the Official Guide.' This motion was carried by seventy-two votes to twenty-three.[42] This, a sensible move in many ways, stopped this most divisive of issues coming up at every Annual Congress. It did mean that the Ban would not be threatened for a long time; in fact, it would be more than forty years before the Ban would come under serious pressure again. The ruling stopped the possibility of any momentum being gained by those opposed to the Ban.

The GAA made other moves in the 1920s to cement the Ban's position. At the request of the GAA, Gaelic games were the only sports played by the Free State Army. This decision would lead to conflict with a Fianna Fáil government soon after the furore caused by the removal of Hyde as patron, when the government sought to overturn this position. Vigilance Committees were reactivated in 1924 despite disbanding when they were attempted previously.[43] In 1924, organisers of the reinvigorated Tailteann Games had to withdraw hockey from its list of events after the GAA threatened to boycott the tournament and GAA clubs were ordered by the Central Council to offer immediate counter-attractions where 'foreign games' were played.[44]

The end to the yearly wrangling on the Ban also heralded the beginning of a five-year period during which the GAA grew hugely, something not seen as a coincidence by Ban supporters.[45] Member and club numbers doubled, attendances at matches increased, with over 50,000 people going to All-Ireland finals from the 1930s. Consequently, increased gate receipts led to more secure finances for the Association, enabling the GAA to acquire grounds up and down the country.[46]

The man most responsible for overseeing this change in the GAA's fortunes was the general secretary from 1929 to 1964, Pádraig Ó Caoimh. The previous incumbent, Luke O'Toole died suddenly at his desk at the age of fifty-six on 17 July 1929.[47] For the first time in almost thirty years, the GAA had to look for a new general secretary and undertook a comprehensive process to find O'Toole's successor. 'The Central Council decided applicants must have been members of the association for at least five years, must be under 40 and would face an examination consisting of Irish (oral and written), English, arithmetic and book-keeping. The chosen candidate would act as both secretary of the GAA and manager of Croke Park; be paid a salary of £300 (rising in annual increments of £10 to a maximum of £400), and be provided with a free house and electric light'.[48] Eleven people applied for the post with Ó Caoimh eventually defeating Frank Burke, a dual All-Ireland winner with Dublin, by eleven votes to ten. Ó Caoimh would go on to be recognised as 'the architect of the modern GAA'[49] and 'the GAA's most devoted servant'.[50]

Born in Roscommon in 1897, Ó Caoimh moved as a young child to Cork, the county he would be associated with for the rest of his life. He played hurling as well as Gaelic football for the Nils club, became a founder member of the Nemo club and was involved in the union with the Rangers club in 1922 to form the now famous Nemo Rangers club; he was its first secretary.[51] A fervent nationalist, Ó Caoimh joined the Irish Volunteers in 1916 and became prominent in the Sinn Féin movement. He also played an active role in the Gaelic League from an early age,[52] his passion for the Irish language remained with him for the rest of his life. As GAA general secretary he was responsible for the publication of the

Pádraig Ó Caoimh, GAA general secretary from 1929 to 1964, seen by many as the architect of the modern GAA, was an unbending advocate of the Ban. (*Courtesy of the GAA Museum, Croke Park*)

bilingual magazine *An Camán*,[53] a joint venture between the GAA and the Gaelic League that lasted from 1932 to 1934,[54] and after that magazine's failure he was responsible for another bilingual effort started in 1936, *An Ráitheachán*, which had Hyde as one of its contributors.[55] A teacher by profession, he left his full-time teaching post in 1919 to devote his energies to the struggle for independence as an IRA officer. He also became manager of the Dáil (the first Dáil) employment bureau in Cork. 'He took part in many engagements against the British in Cork. Arrested in December, 1920, he was sentenced to 15 years' penal servitude.'[56] Upon release from Parkhurst Prison on the Isle of Wight, off the coast of England, in 1922 after the signing of the Anglo-Irish Treaty, he opposed the treaty and fought on the republican side during the subsequent Civil War.[57] Ó Caoimh was provided with the ideal training ground for the national position of GAA general secretary in his role as secretary of the Cork GAA board from 1920 until 1929.[58] He was a prominent referee who took charge of Munster, Inter-Provincial and All-Ireland finals.[59] He was also a manager at a tobacco factory in Cork before taking on his new role in Croke Park in 1929. His first major test as an administrator came in 1932 with the organisation of events for the Tailteann Games and the Eucharistic Congress in Croke Park – there were 2,000 stewards to manage at the Eucharistic Congress.[60] He would go on to prove himself an exceptional organiser for the GAA who 'felt that he was serving a national movement rather than filling the post of chief executive of a sports organisation'.[61] Another key achievement for Ó Caoimh was the staging of the 1947 All-Ireland football final between Cavan and Kerry in the Polo Grounds of New York. This logistical challenge was overcome with great zeal in the space of five months to see the first All-Ireland played off the shores of Ireland with a simultaneous radio broadcast back home. During his thirty-five-year reign as general secretary the numbers of members and attendees at GAA events soared and there also was a significant increase to the Association's coffers. In 1929 the Central Council income was £9,000. By 1964, it was £70,856. Assets had grown from £20,000 to £571,188.[62] Alf Murray, GAA president at the time of Ó Caoimh's death in 1964, remarked in a tribute to Ó Caoimh, 'in 1929 there were 1,500 clubs, in 1963 there

were more than 3,000 … the number of grounds owned in
1929 must have been very few, there are now close on
400 grounds owned and properly invested in the association'.[63]
Ó Caoimh desired to have a GAA ground in every parish in
Ireland and he took greatest pride in the construction of
Croke Park, overseeing the building of the Cusack, Hogan and
Nally Stands during his time. Three major competitions – the
National League, the Railway Cup and the All-Ireland minor
championships – were established due to his efforts. He also
supported the Association at club level, realising the heart of
the GAA was based in the local communities.[64] Ó Caoimh
worked diligently throughout the last years of his life on behalf
of the GAA even though he suffered ill health: he had to
undergo four major operations between 1944 and 1963.[65] On
his death in 1964, *The Anglo-Celt* commented, 'the genial
Corkman had guided the GAA from strength to strength and
led it from comparative modesty to make it the proud vital
force in the life of the nation that we know it to-day. He has
left it behind, unchallenged, the most powerful amateur
sporting organisation in the world'.[66] The primary GAA
ground in Cork city, Páirc Uí Chaoimh, is named in his
honour.

Ó Caoimh was also an unbending advocate of the Ban,
although some would claim his views on the Ban thawed in
the latter years of his life.[67] For most of his long years as the
administrator-in-chief of the GAA he firmly promoted the
Irish-Ireland movement and he saw the Ban as a cornerstone
of that cause. He played a central role in the most controversial
decision involving the Ban, the removal of Hyde as GAA
patron.

7

Hyde Becomes Ireland's First President

After resigning as president of the Gaelic League in 1915, Hyde was able to devote himself full time to his teaching at UCD. Many observers felt that he did not teach Irish in the proper way, that he did not demand exacting standards. He was more interested in people enjoying speaking Irish than knowing the intricate details of its grammar. 'We must not be purists' and 'Keep them amused' were oft-quoted remarks attributed to Hyde.[1] Some Irish language purists worried about the amount of laughter coming from his classroom in UCD – as far as they were concerned, order and grammar were more important. Hyde was more interested in fluency, 'to provide students with an ability to use Irish as a living language and to postpone concern about the niceties of grammar to a later time'.[2] Perhaps the new Irish Free State should have heeded Hyde's advice. Irish became the first language of the new state and became an integral part of its educational curriculum. But instead of bringing Irish to more people, in many ways it acted as its death knell. People were forced to learn Irish, to learn its grammar and, as a result, it became a chore for people who abandoned it as soon as they left the classroom. Hyde, as a teacher, realised this danger, and students who were taught by him recalled his passion for the language that he, in turn, instilled in them.[3]

The Minister for Education with responsibility for the teaching of Irish in schools, Eoin MacNeill, was one of the founding members of the Gaelic League. W.T. Cosgrave, the first president of the Executive Council of the Free State, entrusted MacNeill with 'the Gaelicisation ... of our whole culture ... to make our nation separate and distinct and something to be thought of'.[4] MacNeill pessimistically commented on his task that 'you might as well be putting wooden legs on hens as trying to restore Irish through the school system'.[5] He was right though this did not stop the government, or subsequent governments, in their quixotic bid to have everyone speaking Irish as their primary language enforced through the school system. Despite the Gaelic League's trojan efforts, most people still connected Irish with poverty and social inferiority and the Department of Education not only had to teach the teachers of Irish in schools the language so that they, in turn, could teach the pupils but they also had to convince the people of Ireland *that Irish pays*.[6] The government made huge efforts to introduce Irish as the primary language of the school system with teachers being sent on crash courses and all instructions being taught through the medium of Irish for the first two years of primary school. This was extended when Tomás Derrig became Fianna Fáil Minister for Education in 1932. Although the governments of the Irish Free State went to extraordinary lengths to prioritise Irish in the education system, they only played with the language when people went looking for jobs; there was no real tangible benefit to speaking the language. The first governments of the state failed to make Irish pay and, as put in a way only J. J. Lee could:

> The results of all this fertilising was a luxuriant crop of weeds, and a pervasive stench that offended all but the coarsest nostrils. The essential hypocrisy occurred less in the area of compulsory Irish in the schools than in the

failure to provide opportunity, or obligation, for the regular use of Irish subsequently. The refusal of all governments since the foundation of the state to practise what they preached alerted an observant populace to the fact that the revival was a sham.[7]

In February 1925, Hyde was co-opted unanimously to the Senate of the Irish Free State,[8] a position he held for only a few months. He put his name forward for re-election in the autumn of that year but was decisively defeated, receiving a meagre total of 1,721 first preference votes, compared to the more than 14,000 first preference votes achieved by the leading candidate.[9] Hyde fought a lacklustre campaign but one of the primary reasons he lost so heavily was because Catholics were urged to vote against him as he was alleged to have voted in favour of divorce legislation, something he denied.[10] Other commentators believed it was due to the unpopularity of the Gaelic League, the chief proponents of making Irish compulsory in schools.[11] There were a number of comments on the poor performance of the Irish language enthusiasts[12] that reached even as far as New Zealand.[13] From being the most popular movement in Ireland before nationhood had been achieved by the twenty-six counties, the Gaelic League now experienced a deterioration of its position. The Gaelic League ideal had become government policy and this, ironically, led to its own decline as well as that of the language itself. *The Irish Times* claimed the Gaelic League had become 'moribund' because 'that curse of our *perfervidum ingenium* – politics – assailed the League' and the first step it should take was 'to forget the years the locusts have eaten' and reappoint Hyde as president.[14]

On New Year's Day in 1926, Hyde received the honour of being asked to launch officially the Irish Free State's first radio station, 2RN. His was the first voice heard by listeners from Ireland's new broadcasting service. Speaking primarily in Irish, Hyde spoke of the components that make a nation a nation, stating: 'A nation cannot be made by Act of Parliament; no!

not even by a treaty. A nation is made from inside itself: it is made first of all by its language, if it has one; by its music, songs, games, and customs. These make it an entity different from others, and give it meaning and an individuality.'[15] In 1927 the Academy of Letters presented Hyde with the Gregory Medal, the other recipients were W. B. Yeats, George Bernard Shaw and George Russell, for the 'great creative, intellectual and cultural movement he had founded'.[16]

Hyde retired from UCD in 1932. During his tenure as Professor of Irish Studies he had added significantly to the body of works in Irish. Upon his retirement he moved permanently back to Ratra in Roscommon to look after Lucy: Lucy had suffered chronic debilitating illnesses for most of their marriage and this became more marked as the years went by. He became Senator again in 1937 under the new Constitution but his brief stint did not end, as it had before, in electoral defeat. In this instance, he was asked to leave the Senate in order to accept a much more important job, first President of Ireland.

In the 1930s, the main opponents of the Anglo-Irish Treaty came to power: republicans under the name of Fianna Fáil, led by Éamon de Valera. Once de Valera took power in 1932, he went about dismantling the treaty: the oath of allegiance to the King of the British Empire was removed; land annuities, which formed part of the treaty, were withheld from the British, a decision which would lead to the costly Economics War with Britain; and a mockery was made of the office of Governor General – the King's representative in Ireland. The position of Governor General was offered to Domhnall Ó Buachalla by de Valera in 1932. Under instructions from de Valera, Ó Buachalla 'used the title an seanascal (chief steward); lived in modest houses in the Dublin suburbs rather than in the vice-regal lodge; cycled rather than use an official car; received a reduced annual stipend of £1,200; refused to receive deputations or accept addresses of welcome; did not host receptions; never appeared at official functions; and was rarely seen in public'.[17] The office was abolished in 1936. The culmination of the dismantling of the treaty came with the new Constitution, Bunreacht na hÉireann, introduced on 1 July 1937. Under the new Constitution there would be a President of Ireland, Uachtarán na hÉireann, directly elected by the people of Ireland for a term of seven years, a person 'who shall take precedence over all other persons in the State'.[18] The person could be any citizen of Ireland over the age of thirty-five.[19] The President would not be permitted to leave the State during his/her term of office without the consent of the government,[20] the President could not be a member of the Oireachtas or hold any other position of employment and could be impeached from office for stated misbehaviour.[21] The President would have a largely formal role with a few limited powers such as the dissolution of the Dáil if the government did not command a majority support of the Dáil. The President could also seek advice from the 'Council of State' before signing bills into law if the need arose, and could also refer a bill to the Supreme Court if it was felt it was repugnant to the Constitution (something Hyde did twice in his term as President[22]). The President's signature would be required on all bills before being passed into law.[23] Before the Constitution came into being, there were real fears that the new President could become a dictator.[24] 'No aspect of the draft constitution received so much time or was examined in such minute detail as those articles relating to the presidency, with three of the five days at committee stage devoted to it.'[25] The *Irish Independent* claimed the powers of the President were 'far in excess of those exercised by the ruler of the British Empire; they flavour more of Fascism or Hitlerism than of a "democratic state" which Eire is declared to be'.[26] Many opposed to de Valera believed it would be a vehicle to impose a de Valera dictatorship or to implant a de Valera puppet to carry out his wishes. This view may seem somewhat hysterical now; in the 1930s, when Europe was enveloped by totalitarian states, it was a genuine fear. Dermot

Keogh and Andrew J. McCarthy in their book, *The Making of the Irish Constitution 1937: Bunreacht na hÉireann*, attest the opposition need not have feared as de Valera was no dictator, 'How did a document so protective of citizens' rights emerge from a decade so heavily influenced by anti-democratic ideas rooted in Catholic authoritarianism, vocationalism, corporatism, fascism and Nazism. Perhaps, or indeed, de Valera was far more complex a political thinker and constitutionalist than may have yet been realised.'[27] Many who debated the constitution in 1937 would be surprised 'that Presidents have been so docile, either in exercising their discretionary powers or accumulating new ones'.[28] It was thought succeeding Presidents would increase their authority and develop the power and prestige of the role.[29] The reality would turn out to be very different.

There was widespread speculation as to who the new 'Chief Citizen'[30] would be. The two frontrunners were Sean T. O'Kelly, Fianna Fáil vice-president of the Executive Council, and Alfred 'Alfie' Byrne, the popular Lord Mayor of Dublin. It was even speculated that de Valera might run for the position himself.[31] The main political parties decided it would be damaging to the new office if the first President was elected along party political lines. Meetings between senior members of Fianna Fáil and Fine Gael were held to reach an agreement on a unified candidate. The meetings in April 1938 did not last long for one name stood out as acceptable to all, Douglas Hyde. Lauding this decision by the main parties, coupled with a boast of having suggested Hyde initially in 1937, *The Irish Times* wrote:

> Dr Hyde is a man to whom Ireland owes a great deal ...
> All parties in Saorstat Éireann owe their titles, and largely their existence, to him; that the new Constitution can be promulgated in Irish is the result of his life-work, and he has the supreme advantage of being 'above the battle' ...
> The President of the New Ireland must be a man who is

Hyde's inauguration ceremony as President of Ireland on 25 June 1938 in Dublin Castle. Hyde was elected unanimously as Ireland's first President under the new Constitution of 1937, Bunreacht na hÉireann. *(Courtesy of the National Library of Ireland)*

unsullied by the mud-slinging of the hustings, a man who can command the respect and admiration of all citizens, irrespective of their political or religious beliefs, and will carry out his important functions in a dignified and impartial manner. Douglas Hyde is such a man.[32]

Time Magazine believed the main reasons the '78-year-old, tall, erect, walrus-mustached Gaelic scholar' was selected were due to his age and he would therefore be inclined to serve only seven years to make way for younger men afterwards, like de Valera. He was a Protestant and such a selection could be enticement for the '1,290,000 inhabitants of stubbornly independent, strongly Protestant Northern Ireland' to abandon partition and re-unite Ireland. His non-political views were also seen as a reason.[33] It was reported in Nazi Germany that

Hyde's election was a 'far-reaching' plan to bring about a union between northern and southern Ireland,[34] something Hyde's wife Lucy felt would be 'a fitting finish to his lifework'.[35]

On a visit to Dublin later in the year, Joe Kennedy, American Ambassador to Britain and father of future American president, John F. Kennedy, described Hyde's election as President as 'an act that is eloquent of that brotherhood and tolerance which remain the hope of mankind in an angry world'.[36]

The President-Elect was welcomed home to Roscommon with a procession in his honour in early May 1938, and the chance to throw in the ball at a Gaelic football game in Ballaghaderreen. Quoted at the match, he said he, 'was proud ... to receive such an honour from the Gaels of Ballaghaderreen, and it was a source of pleasure to him to be amongst the young Connacht Gaels'.[37]

Hyde was inaugurated on Saturday 25 June 1938 in a ceremony lasting just fifteen minutes in Dublin Castle. He arrived to a fanfare of trumpets, was administered the oath of office by the Chief Justice who then proceeded to offer him the great seal of office.[38] Taoiseach de Valera then made a speech, addressing Hyde:

> Mr President, on behalf of the Irish nation, on behalf of the living, those who dwell at home as well as our kin beyond the sea, on behalf also of the dead generations who longed to see this day but have not seen it, I salute you. You are now our President, our Head freely chosen under our own laws, inheriting the authority and entitled to the respect which the Gaels ever gave to those whom they recognised to be their rightful chief, but which for centuries they denied to those whom a foreign law would enforce upon them. In you we greet the successor of our rightful princes, and in your accession to office we hail the closing of the breach that has existed since the undoing of our nation at Kinsale.[39]

Crowds watch Hyde's presidential inauguration party drive down O'Connell Street in Dublin on 25 June 1938. A lucky few (at the top right of the photograph) are using the vantage point of Nelson's Pillar, which was subsequently destroyed by the IRA on 8 March 1966. *(Courtesy of the National Library of Ireland)*

In Hyde's first speech he vowed to be a President for 'all creeds and classes'[40] of Irish people. This commitment would lead him into conflict with an organisation he had a long affiliation with, the GAA, in a matter of months.

8

Jazzing Every Night of the Week

The pattern of extending the ban rules continued unabated within the GAA in to the 1930s when a ban was imposed on GAA members from organising any forms of entertainment with 'foreign dances', which was extended in 1932 to include the banning of GAA members from attending any 'foreign dance'. GAA members were also prohibited from writing on GAA matters for any foreign newspaper from 1930.[1] The Association had gone full circle from the ban debates of the early 1920s when there was a significant body of people within the GAA who openly called for the Ban to be removed, to an implacable position just a few short years later where the ban rules were sacrosanct. The GAA genuinely believed the Ban was one of the primary reasons for its increase in popularity. This belief is reinforced by GAA scholar Marcus de Búrca: 'by demonstrating that alone of the pre-1922 national bodies it was as strong as ever, above party politics and inflexible in adhering to its fundamental aim of fostering native games to the exclusion of foreign games, the GAA in the 1920s gained in prestige among supporters and attracted thousands of new members. This was its reward for the fact that, as Michael Collins remarked some months before his death, the GAA was "the one body ... which ... never failed to draw the line between the Gael and the Gall".[2] Others saw the GAA as too unyielding and inward looking, more concerned with the past than with the future. Prominent politicians in the new Free State were amongst this group and the Ban was the issue that caused the most discord.

The GAA has, to a large extent, received preferential treatment from most governments since the foundation of the State. This has often come in the forms of grants or tax exemptions. The Cumann na nGaedhael government, in its Finance Act of 1927, exempted the GAA, and no other sporting body, from income tax on profits it earned.[3] This could be considered quite an achievement, considering the Finance Minister at the time was Ernest Blythe, a man who has achieved legendary status as one of the most frugal Ministers for Finance the country has seen.

The GAA came up for discussion again during a debate in the Dáil to discuss the Finance Bill in 1931. Myles Keogh TD sought an amendment to include other forms of sport in the exemption from income tax on profits. What followed was a fascinating debate on the GAA, its contribution to the nation-alist cause and views from TDs on the Ban. Blythe, opposing the amendment, recognised the role the GAA had played in Ireland's fight for freedom and the disadvantages it had over rugby or soccer which benefited from their international outlook. He did, however, take a more hard-line view on the GAA than before and particularly on its ban on 'foreign games'. He stated, 'I must say that I have not a bit of sympathy with the sort of boycott policy that is carried on by the G.A.A. – policy of branding a man as a bad Irishman or a bad citizen if he happens to play a particular game of football. I disagree entirely with that.'[4] Due to Éamon de Valera's past as a rugby player with Blackrock College, many people were interested in his views on the matter. He felt there should be no tax on any game. He did suggest a special encouragement for the develop-ment of hurling in particular and Gaelic football as well, considering it was recognised as a national game. He added the caveat that hurling, in his opinion, was much more important than Gaelic football from the national point of view.[5] Fianna Fáil TD Sean MacEntee, who would succeed Blythe as Minister for Finance less than a year later, believed the GAA had earned its right to preferential treatment because of its conduct during the War of Independence, unlike the Irish soccer and rugby bodies who had remained loyal to the crown. He also claimed 'to have very little esteem or regard for' Gaelic football, having played rugby and soccer himself and he was also critical of the Ban, stating, 'I would like every Irishman to play the game that most appeals to him and I have no sympathy with the policy of exclusion pursued by the Gaelic Athletic Association'.[6] Others commented on the paltry coverage the national press gave to Gaelic games compared to other sports. Richard Walsh claimed, 'I saw matches here in Dublin at which there were 40,000 people present, matches under the Gaelic code, and they scarcely got two or three inches in some of the daily papers, while matches under the other codes at which there might not be a dozen people present got a column and the reports were lavishly illustrated with photographs'.[7] This was addressed just a few short months later with the founding of the Fianna Fáil backed newspaper, the *Irish Press*. According to Mark O'Brien in his book, *De Valera, Fianna Fáil and the Irish Press – The Truth in the News?*, the *Irish Press* 'largely made the Gaelic Athletic Association what it is today through reporting GAA games that at the time were downplayed by the other two papers in Dublin, *The Irish Times* and the *Irish Independent*. Its first edition was deliberately timed to coincide with the 1931 All-Ireland hurling final'.[8] Fortunately for the *Irish Press*, that final would live long in the memory, with three games needed to separate Cork from Kilkenny attracting almost 92,000 people to the matches.[9] In the same first edition there was a plea from Hyde urging people to speak Irish.[10]

Richard Walsh, in the same Dáil debate, also criticised some of the main secondary schools and colleges who discriminated against the GAA by their exclusion of playing Gaelic games and he condemned the Irish Rugby Football Union's (IRFU) reluctance to embrace the new state by refusing to fly the Tricolour at matches at Lansdowne Road. They had, he claimed, 'designed a bastard flag before they would agree to recognise the national flag'.[11] The IRFU (unlike the Irish soccer body which had split into the Irish Football Association (IFA) in Northern Ireland and the Football Association of Ireland (FAI) in the south) had remained a thirty-two county body after partition. It was agreed that the Union Jack would be flown at international matches played in Ravenhill, Belfast, to appease the Northern Ireland members of the IRFU. It was also decided, however, to fly a 'Rugby Union' flag that included the coats of arms of all four provinces instead of the Tricolour at matches held in Lansdowne Road. This decision came in for heavy criticism from many quarters, including members of the IRFU who felt this was a clear example of an anti-national bias.[12] In early 1932, the Connaught branch of the IRFU started a campaign to reverse this decision and to have the Tricolour flown at all Irish international matches. Initially the IRFU refused to alter its position,[13] until pressure from the government forced it to fly the Tricolour at the next international match between Ireland and England.[14] The Minister for External Affairs, Patrick McGilligan, sent a letter to the secretary of the IRFU recognising that the IRFU was 'not an exclusively Irish Free State institution', but he could not 'see why the international practice of flying the flag of the country in which international matches are played should not be followed at Lansdowne Road'. He advised the union to fly the 'National flag on the principal flagstaff at Lansdowne Road' at the upcoming international match against England.[15] If ever motivation was needed for the GAA to retain its ban on 'foreign games', this saga involving the IRFU undoubtedly helped. The IRFU was criticised in 1934 by the Gaelic League for offering the first toast of the evening to the King of Great Britain at a banquet it held,[16] driving a further wedge between it and people devoted to all things Irish.

Sean MacEntee, Fianna Fáil Minister for Finance, was accused of 'jazzing every night of the week' for allegedly supporting the playing of jazz music by Irish Free State broadcasting radio stations. *(Courtesy of the National Library of Ireland)*

The amendment to exempt other sports as well as Gaelic games from taxation was defeated by forty-nine votes to fifty-nine in the Dáil in 1931. Fianna Fáil came into power the following year and the new Minister for Finance, Sean MacEntee, decided to raise revenue by bringing in an entertainments tax on people attending sporting events with one exception: patrons attending Gaelic games would not be taxed. This decision led to further heated debate in the Dáil and Senate on the GAA's preferential status in the Irish state with the game of Gaelic football coming in for particularly severe criticism. Professor Alton stated that Gaelic football was not more national than rugby; rugby had a longer history in Ireland.[17] Senator Oliver Saint John Gogarty went a step further saying that Gaelic football 'should be double taxed, because it was a bastard of soccer and Rugby … I am not really saying that Gaelic football should be taxed, but surely its ingredients should be released from taxation'.[18] Most people who criticised the proposed bill felt it would have a negative impact on the health of people in the country. One TD, Mrs Collins-O'Driscoll, seeing that all other arguments to change MacEntee's mind were failing, decided to deploy the use of flattery, stating that the lady hockey players of Ireland, on viewing photographs of politicians during the recent election, believed MacEntee was the best looking of them and they subsequently voted for him. For this reason, she proposed, hockey should also be exempt from the tax.[19] This ploy failed too and the bill was passed by sixty-three to fifty-eight votes.

On that occasion MacEntee would certainly have pleased the GAA. He received stinging condemnation, however, from the GAA's sister organisation, the Gaelic League, in 1934 for his alleged support for jazz music being aired on the Free State broadcasting radio stations. Seán Óg Ó Ceallaigh, secretary of the Gaelic League, claimed, 'Our Minister for Finance has a soul buried in jazz and is selling the musical soul of the nation for the dividends of sponsored jazz programmes. He is jazzing every night of the week.'[20]

Since the foundation of the Irish Free State, the Gaelic League had seen a massive haemorrhaging of numbers. With the Irish language now the remit of the government, the need for the Gaelic League had dissipated. With the huge loss of numbers it was only natural that the Gaelic League struggled financially during the 1930s and, in many ways, became dependent on the GAA for funding. This reliance would continue over the coming decades with the GAA a dependable source of much needed funds that allowed the Gaelic League to continue in its quest for the language revival.[21] There was, at times, a cost to this generosity; with the two organisations no longer considered equal partners, the GAA exerted its influence in more ways than financially.

In the early 1930s, the Gaelic League took a more extreme outlook, aping the GAA in many ways by introducing bans and condemning all that was not Irish. The Gaelic League was particularly outspoken on 'foreign dances' such as 'contortionate jazz dancing', with one member declaring that 'they might as well hang their harps on the willow tree', claiming the 'cancer at the heart of Ireland to-day is the cinema, literature and the dance hall'.[22] Jazz music was seen by some opponents as 'music with abominable rhythms … borrowed from Central Africa' and 'the dance of negroes'. It was also believed to be 'far more sexual than a reel or a jig or most European music'.[23] The Catholic Church, which saw its power increase considerably with the birth of the new state, was also vehemently against jazz and all foreign dances to the point of obsession, blaming such dances on the moral decadence it saw as prevalent in Ireland and the startling increase in illegitimate births – there was an increase of 29 per cent between 1912 and 1927.[24] This fear and outrage of jazz music was not an exclusively Irish reaction. Across Europe, there was alarm at this music that originated in the United States which was becoming more and more popular in Europe. In France it was claimed that jazz has 'ruined Paris and driven Parisians sex-mad'. When jazz was broadcast on radio stations in France, announcements were made at the start stating they would be playing jazz 'so that listeners susceptible to be shocked by such modern syncopation can plug out'.[25] In Hungary, jazz was accused of 'being immoral, inartistic, unpatriotic, and godless'.[26] Jazz had many detractors in the United States too. One leading American academic, Dr Henry Van Dyke from Princeton University, said jazz was 'invented by demons for the torture of imbeciles'.[27]

The Gaelic League decided, in 1932, to introduce a ban on 'foreign games and dances', however, this was not as widespread as the GAA bans, as it affected only those who wished to be a member of any of the committees of the Gaelic League and not normal members.[28] There was widespread opposition to this move within the Gaelic League from some senior figures who believed the Gaelic League was 'passing rules which are against a lot of things … and the individual member of the organisation has less freedom as a result'.[29] In January

1934, Fr Peter Conefry, parish priest of Cloone parish in Leitrim, organised an anti-jazz demonstration under the auspices of the Gaelic League held in Mohill, Leitrim, which was attended by over 3,000 people 'bearing such slogans as "Down with Jazz" and "Out with Paganism"'.[30] It received the support of the Primate of All Ireland and Archbishop of Armagh, Cardinal Joseph MacRory, who was also a patron of the GAA. He stated:

> I heartily wish success to the County Leitrim Executive of the Gaelic League in its campaign against all-night 'jazz' dancing. I know nothing about 'jazz' dances, except that I understand they are suggestive and demoralising; but 'jazz' apart, all-night dances are objectionable on many grounds, and in the country districts and small towns a fruitful source of scandal and of ruin, spiritual and temporal. To how many poor, innocent young girls have all-night dances not been the occasion of irreparable disgrace and life-long sorrow? Nobody, I am sure, wants to deprive our young boys and girls of legitimate pleasure and recreation or of the opportunity of meeting each other, but all this they can have in an evening dance, lasting three or four hours.[31]

Éamon de Valera also sent a message expressing his backing for the Gaelic League's efforts as did another patron of the GAA, Douglas Hyde, who stated that 'all games and dances should be Irish, as well as the language'.[32] This sentiment would come back to haunt him in ways he would not have foreseen just four years later. The Gaelic League's anti-jazz campaign saw its efforts come to fruition with the passing of the Public Dance Halls Act of 1935. 'The act was draconian, making it practically impossible to hold dances without the sanction of the trinity of clergy, police and judiciary.'[33]

9

Hyde the Committed Patron

Marcus de Búrca in his comprehensive study on the GAA, *The GAA: A History*, claimed that before Hyde was removed as patron, it was known by very few, perhaps one in a hundred, that Hyde was a patron of the GAA.[1] The evidence would suggest otherwise. With the possible exception of Archbishop Croke, it could be argued that Hyde was the most active of all patrons right up to the time he became President of Ireland. As Gaelic League president, Hyde was the one person, whether from the Gaelic League or the GAA, who constantly called for closer co-operation – even union – between the two bodies. When he resigned from the Gaelic League he never wavered in offering his support for the GAA and advising the two Irish-Ireland bodies to work more closely with each other. Hyde wrote an article entitled 'Games and Nationality' that appeared in the *Nenagh Guardian* in 1924, in which he called for an amalgamation between the GAA and the Gaelic League. He spoke in language that would have been manna to the supporters of the Ban, saying that Ireland as a new nation must be stopped from becoming 'a second rate English county, and her men from becoming second-hand imitation Englishmen'.[2] He went on to say: 'Both bodies have so much in common that it has been a perpetual source of astonishment to me that there has not been anything of real

In 1934, the *Irish Independent* marked the GAA Golden Jubilee with a souvenir booklet, honouring the GAA patrons. In the same booklet, Hyde claimed the GAA paved the way for the Gaelic League. GAA president, Sean McCarthy, thanked Hyde for the sterling work he had accomplished for the Gaelic movement. *(Courtesy of the* Irish Independent*/GAA Oral History Project)*

union or drawing together between them'.[3] He continued with what could be construed as implied support for bans on 'foreign games and dances' by stating:

> No Gaelic Leaguer that ever I knew of cared to lend his support to foreign games in preference to the native ones encouraged by the GAA. Have the members of the GAA reciprocated to anything like the same extent in aiding the ideals of the Gaelic League, or in running clear of foreign songs, dances, music and language?[4]

Bemoaning the lack of promotion of the Irish language by the GAA, Hyde declared that neither the GAA nor the Gaelic League were:

> ... complete without the other. The Gaelic League recognised this from the first. Has the Gaelic Athletic Association recognised it equally? Well-developed brains in well-developed bodies is the true ideal of the Gaelic League. Well-developed bodies with well-developed Irish brains ought to be the ideal of the GAA. I am sure it is too, only that it does not unfortunately show itself in action as one should expect that it would do. Thousands of Irishmen will go to see a hurling match because it is the national game who would not go to look at a cricket match. Yet very often the players never think of any other aspects of the question than that of the match alone. The idea that they are really and powerfully contributing to the revival of Irish nationality has I believe, never occurred to thousands of them. If this is true, it is a real misfortune for Ireland, and it robs the game of half its zest and significance for the unthinking players.[5]

He ends on a note of optimism, believing, 'as Ireland becomes more Irish, the GAA will aid in reviving Irish nationality all along the line, and become a great, a powerful and an enlightened ally of the Gaelic League in its secondary work'.[6]

Speaking at a lecture in Trinity College in 1930 on Irish culture, Hyde made the claim that Irish music, more than anything else, helped to draw Irishmen closer together around the world. In the same lecture, he said of the GAA, 'The *camán* (hurling) and Gaelic football have done more for Ireland of my time than almost any other agency I know'.[7]

In 1934, to celebrate the Golden Jubilee of the GAA, the *Irish Press* and the *Irish Independent* produced souvenir booklets to commemorate the Association achieving the fifty-year milestone. The booklets included contributions from Cardinal MacRory, Primate of All Ireland, Dr Harty, Archbishop of Cashel (both men patrons of the GAA), Sean McCarthy, then president of the GAA, and Hyde. In a glowing tribute to the GAA written in Irish, Hyde reiterated his oft made remark that the Association paved the way for the Gaelic League.[8] McCarthy, in turn, thanked Hyde for the sterling work he had accomplished for the Gaelic movement.[9]

The Irish Times, in an article, published in 1935, that overflowed with gushing praise for Hyde, made the observation that Hyde 'never contemplated a State in which the Gaelic language would have degenerated into a field for bans and boycotts, and in which the Gaelic League, with its proud charter, would be obsessed with the iniquity of attendance at Rugby football matches'.[10] Based on some of Hyde's previous utterances, it could be argued that *The Irish Times*' assertion was not accurate. He supported the Gaelic League anti-jazz movement of 1934 and he had previously written on the importance of supporting native games over foreign ones. On the other hand, there was some evidence to suggest that he was not intolerant of 'foreign games'. His son-in-law, married to his daughter Una, was Judge James Sealy. Sealy was a well known rugby international who also served as president of the IRFU in the 1920s.[11] It would be argued by many that Hyde's personal views were not important the moment he became first citizen of Ireland, representing all of the people of Ireland, regardless of their beliefs.

Croke Park on the day of the All-Ireland football final 1938: Hyde was an attendee at the match. The Cusack Stand had been erected that summer with the aid of a rugby club, Old Belvedere. *(Courtesy of Gaelic Art)*

After Hyde became President of Ireland in June 1938, he still enjoyed very cordial relations with the GAA. In 1938, Michael Cusack, another man who had had his own troubles with the GAA previously, was given the posthumous honour of having a stand named after him in Croke Park. Ironically, the GAA needed the help of a rugby club, Old Belvedere, to construct the Cusack Stand. According to *The Irish Times*, in a move the newspaper called 'classic absurdity', the GAA needed a few yards from the Old Belvedere rugby ground adjoining Croke Park to complete the construction of the stand. Old Belvedere obliged the GAA and, in return, the GAA built the rugby club a small stand, a stand GAA members would, of course, be unable to visit for fear of suspension.[12] In a letter dated 9 August 1938, Ó Caoimh invited Hyde to the opening of the Cusack Stand on 21 August 1938, the occasion of the All-Ireland football semi-final between Kerry and Laois,[13] saying in the letter, 'We know that you always did your best for the Gaelicisation of Ireland, and we greatly desire that, as Patron of the Gaelic Athletic Association, you should be with us in order to participate in the joy we all feel at the erection of this stand.'[14] This appreciation expressed for Hyde's efforts towards the Gaelicisation of Ireland would not save him a few months later. Hyde was unable to attend that event to honour his former friend but he was in attendance at the All-Ireland football final between Galway and Kerry held just a few short weeks later on Sunday 25 September 1938.[15] It was reported in the *Connacht Tribune*: 'He was accorded a great ovation on his arrival. He was welcomed in the name of the GAA and conducted to his seat in the Hogan Stand as the Irish Transport and General Workers' Union band played the National Anthem'.[16] The secretary to President Hyde, Michael McDunphy, however, did not write in such glowing terms regarding this reception:

> His arrival (the President) passed unnoticed. There was no announcement from the loud speakers, and although the Anthem was played its significance was not realised by the spectators … Arrangements should be made in future to ensure that the President's arrival at such events will be marked in a more fitting manner. He should be conducted to his seat in such a way that:
> 1. His arrival is visible to the spectators. If necessary his car should be driven across the field:
> 2. An appropriate announcement should be made over the loud speakers in Irish and in English so that the people are aware of his arrival.
> 3. The National Anthem should be played as soon as he appears.
> 4. In addition, a separate enclosure should be provided for the President where he may be free from troublesome attention.[17]

McDunphy was seen as Hyde's most important member of staff. The family name was originally Dunphy, however, after his father joined the Gaelic League, he added the 'Mc'.[18] McDunphy had a long association with the civil service dating back to pre-independence when he joined the Department of Education in 1911. He was dismissed from the British civil service in 1918 for refusing to take the oath of allegiance to the crown and he returned to the Irish Free State civil service in 1922. He served as assistant secretary to the Provisional Free State government from January to December 1922 and in the same position for the executive council for the Free State government until 1937. In 1936 he was appointed a member of an ad-hoc committee tasked with defining the language for the proposed new constitution. He was subsequently appointed as secretary to the President of Ireland in December 1937, a new role created after the passing of the new constitution.[19] McDunphy was recognised for his strong organisational skills and his commitment to protocol; he kept meticulous files on everything remotely associated with the Office of the President, a much needed exercise in establishing the new office and a valuable source of information today. He wrote a book in 1945 on the President's role, which he dedicated to Hyde, entitled *The President of Ireland: His Powers, Functions and Duties.* As well as serving Hyde, he also worked for the second President, Sean T. O'Kelly, before retiring in 1954. He died in Dublin in 1971.

At the 1938 All-Ireland football final, the President arrived at the same time as the Lord Mayor, Alfie Byrne (a person also seen as a potential candidate for President a few months previously) which, according to McDunphy, 'tended to obscure the arrival of the Head of State'.[20]

The game itself ended in a draw between Galway and Kerry and the replay took place on Sunday 23 October 1938. According to McDunphy, Hyde did not attend the replay because 'The President is not particularly interested in football and will not attend the replay. In any case the season is very late and it is thought that he should not be exposed to the inclement weather.'[21] The 'inclement weather' did not stop Hyde from going to a soccer match between Ireland and Poland a few weeks after the replay. McDunphy mentioned that he informed Ó Caoimh of Hyde's decision not to attend the replay but he did not say if he included the reasons why Hyde was not interested in attending. Perhaps, it would have been wise not to.

These minor issues resulting from the All-Ireland football final, however, would pale into insignificance compared with the next interaction between the GAA and the President.

10

1938 – The Year of Ban Controversies

By 1938, the GAA had much to be proud of. It had reached the significant milestone of fifty years in 1934 to much fanfare and celebrations. Each year the Association went from strength to strength in terms of number of members and attendances at GAA events. In 1938, Michael O'Hehir, one of the great icons of the GAA, made his first radio broadcast of a match, the All-Ireland football semi-final match between Galway and Monaghan.[1] The Ban itself had achieved 'a resilience and an in-built shock-absorption all of its own. It was accustomed to the buffeting of battle … it had survived many an assault in the past and was to survive quite a few more in the years which lay ahead.'[2] This year provided the GAA with a number of trying incidents that would test the Ban's strength to its core, culminating with the decision to remove Hyde as patron.

The first major incident to receive considerable attention in the media that year involved a case that would bear a considerable amount of similarities to the episode affecting Hyde. George Ormsby, a highly decorated Gaelic footballer for the great Mayo team of the 1930s, had attended a soccer match on 6 February in Sligo. The Sligo County Board suspended him for being in breach of the ban rule on 'foreign games'. It was revealed, however, that Ormsby had been on duty as a garda on the day in question and the Connaught Council of the GAA reinstated him as a result.[3] Galway still objected to Mayo being awarded a National Football League tie against them due to the fielding of Ormsby as one of the Mayo players, stating the Ormsby case was still being investigated when the match was played.[4] The Central Council of the GAA, after they were asked to get involved, decided to write a letter to the Garda Síochána Commissioner to verify if Ormsby was on duty at the soccer match. The Commissioner replied, stating Ormsby was on duty thus leading to his reinstatement; however, the Central Council still decided to award Galway the two points for the match, even though Mayo had won the actual game.[5] Mayo, who were going for a record fifth National League title in a row, were rumoured to be considering withdrawing from the National League for that season, such was their anger with the Central Council's decision.[6] In the end, Mayo did not withdraw from the National League and went on to win their fifth title in a row later that year. (This success was continued the following year with a sixth title, a record that stands to this day.) The main finding that could be construed from the Ormsby Case was the difference the GAA deduced from members attending 'foreign games' in an official capacity as opposed to attendance on personal grounds.

In April 1938, at its Annual Congress in Limerick, the Gaelic League decided to remove the ban, installed since 1932, prohibiting committee members from attending or promoting 'foreign games and dances' by a margin of just two votes.[7] The resolution came in for severe criticism from many members of the Gaelic League with the secretary of the Meath County Committee resigning in protest.[8] However, it was the GAA who provided the Gaelic League with the most vehement opposition. The two bodies had been genuine sister organisations in the past and mutual respect for each other was the predominant sentiment. Their respective fortunes had changed greatly since the foundation of the Irish Free State: the GAA had never been more popular or successful whilst the Gaelic League was fighting for survival, reliant on the GAA for much needed funding. Pádraig Ó Caoimh would go on to claim, in 1960, that the GAA had made contributions to the Gaelic League of £50,000 for the previous twenty-five years.[9] Many GAA county boards, club boards and provincial councils reacted by withdrawing their support for the Gaelic League including, Cork,[10] Belleek in Fermanagh,[11] Meath,[12] Laois, Galway and Munster.[13] Other GAA outlets decided to hurt the Gaelic League financially by refusing to submit teams to the Thomond Feis Competition, a competition organised by the Gaelic League that included Gaelic games: Tipperary and Cork GAA county Boards responded in this fashion.[14] Some GAA clubs which had run local 'feis' competitions for the benefit of their local Gaelic League branches decided to discontinue their support as a protest.[15] Relations became so strained between the two bodies that it was suggested the former Gaelic League president and then President-Elect of the country, Douglas Hyde, should intervene 'to use his powerful influence to restore the ban'.[16] The president of the Gaelic League, Peter Toner McGinley (known as 'Cú Uladh'), began to waver on the League's decision and hinted to an *Irish Press* journalist that a revision of that outcome was a possibility.[17] The Gaelic League decided to seek a meeting with the Central Council of the GAA,[18] a meeting that was granted on the recommendation of the Gaelic League activist and GAA president, Pádraig McNamee, on the basis that the GAA could not tolerate the Gaelic League removing its bans.[19] The Gaelic League meekly acquiesced to the demands of the GAA at its Annual Congress the following year and the bans were re-imposed by a margin of forty-two votes to thirty-five.[20] Many Gaelic League members felt the pressure being exerted on them by the GAA, and as the considerably weaker body they felt they had no other option but to reverse the decision on the bans. Others felt the bans were not needed by the

Gaelic League; they had only been introduced in 1932 and did not affect grass-roots members. It was also highlighted that some within the GAA were responsible for the promotion of foreign dances, thus hampering traditional *céilithe* organised by the Gaelic League. Many felt it galling for the GAA to take such a hypocritical stance when many of its members were openly flouting its 'foreign dances' ban (see page 99) [21]. This episode revealed an ugly and sinister side to the GAA, a body that would use its financial and personal resources to bend its so-called sister organisation to its will. The stance the GAA took against the Gaelic League would also have implications for Hyde for attending the soccer match between Ireland and Poland in November that same year. It would mean the GAA would have to take a hardened stance on anyone who broke its 'foreign game' rule, regardless of who they were.

One of the most notorious incidents involving the Ban was discussed at the same GAA Central Council, held in June 1938, that agreed to accept a deputation from the Gaelic League to resolve their differences.[22] That incident involved James (later Colonel) Cooney, an engineering student from UCD who hailed from Tipperary. Cooney, playing in midfield, was a central figure of the Tipperary team that won the previous year's All-Ireland hurling title. He attended an international rugby game in Dublin in February 1938 and was duly suspended for three months. Believing his ban was over in May – before the start of the Championship season in the summer – the Tipperary GAA board looked to field Cooney in their first championship outing against Clare.[23] Clare objected and brought the issue before the Central Council. (In a strange quirk of fate, a Galway referee named Jimmy Cooney denied Clare a victory over Offaly in an All-Ireland hurling semi-final of 1998: Clare were leading by three points but Cooney blew the full-time whistle too early and when the game was replayed, Offaly emerged as the victors.[24]) Each player must declare the county with which they intend to play for the season but the Central Council ruled that the relevant date was not the one signed by the player but the date the declaration was received by the Central Council. As the Central Council had received Cooney's declaration before Easter when he was still suspended, it was considered invalid and Cooney could not be selected for the Munster Championship that year. Tipperary decided to defy the Central Council and fielded Cooney against Clare anyway. Tipperary won the game but were disqualified and the game was awarded to Clare, thus ending Tipperary's defence of their hurling title.[25] The episode was confusing for many people to grasp, including many officials in the GAA, and it appeared that the GAA was being overly pedantic as well as being completely intransigent.

11

The Soccer Match

On 13 November 1938 Hyde, along with An Taoiseach Éamon de Valera; Oscar Traynor, Minister for Posts and Telegraphs; Paddy Lynch, Attorney General; and Alfie Byrne, the Lord Mayor of Dublin, went to an international soccer match at Dalymount Park in Dublin between Ireland and Poland,[1] a game which Ireland won by three goals to two. Ireland had played Poland in May that year in Warsaw and had been routed by six goals to nil.[2] (The following June, Poland lost five–six to Brazil in a thrilling World Cup match, held in France, that is famous because one of their players, Ernest Willimowski, and a Brazilian player, Leonidas, became the first two people to score four goals in a single World Cup finals game.[3] An Irishman, Paddy Moore was the first person to score four goals in a World Cup qualifying game, against Belgium in 1934.[4]) There was huge interest in the match because Ireland had beaten Switzerland in September, their most recent international. The match against Poland broke the previous attendance record at a soccer match in Ireland by 1,000 people,[5] with over 34,000 packed into Dalymount Park to see Ireland beat Poland after both teams had been presented to the President. Both Hyde and de Valera received standing ovations on their arrival and departure, and were seated in reserved seats in a box on the grand stand.[6] There was no need

An Taoiseach Éamon de Valera, President Douglas Hyde and Oscar Traynor watch as Ireland beat Poland by three goals to two in Dalymount Park, Dublin, on 13 November 1938. Hyde's attendance at this match saw him removed as patron of the GAA. *(Courtesy of Getty Images)*

for any Vigilance Committee member of the GAA to be in attendance to spy on Hyde as he certainly was not an inconspicuous attendee. McDunphy was very happy with the reception accorded to Hyde by the FAI: comparing the receptions Hyde received at both sporting events, McDunphy said, 'In marked contrast with his reception at the All-Ireland Football Final in Croke Park on 25 Sept. 1938 ... were the arrangements made for the reception of the President at Dalymount Park ... He was received at the gate by the senior officials of the Football Association. A private room was placed at his disposal. His arrival was announced in Irish and in English. A special box was placed at his disposal, in fact in every way the utmost respect was accorded to him as Head of the State.'[7]

Since becoming President in June, Hyde had received a number of invitations from many groups and societies throughout the country, including numerous sporting bodies. Naturally, he was unable to attend all of the functions he was invited to, so he made a rule 'that in his official capacity he will be present only at functions of a State or national character, or of such a special nature as to make it desirable, in his opinion, that he should attend'.[8] The President had received an invitation from the FAI to attend the game against Poland; 'This was the first occasion on which the Head of State attended a Match played under Association Rules.'[9] He also received invitations from the rugby[10] and cricket[11] bodies of Ireland.

The President's Office was aware, long before the GAA Central Council meeting of 17 December, that there could be potential repercussions with the GAA as a result of the President's attendance at the game. A decision to attend was made regardless of the consequences as, according to McDunphy, soccer was seen by the President as being a popular sport amongst 'a very large section of the Irish people, a big number of whom are and have been earnest workers in the National Movement'.[12] One of the guests at the soccer match with Hyde who agreed with that sentiment was Oscar Traynor. The Dublin-born Minister for Posts and Telegraphs was a keen soccer enthusiast, having played as goalkeeper in his youth for Frankfort and Strandville in Dublin before distinguishing himself at Belfast Celtic from 1910 to 1912. He toured Europe with Belfast Celtic, visiting places such as Hungary, Austria, Germany and Czechoslovakia.[13] He became president of the FAI in 1948 and remained in that position until his death in 1963. As FAI president, he suffered the wrath of the Archbishop of Dublin, John Charles McQuaid, for walking on to the pitch in Lansdowne Road in 1955 to welcome the 'Iron Curtain' soccer team of Yugoslavia who were in Dublin to play the Irish international team in a match the powerful clergyman actively sought to ban.[14] Traynor was of great assistance to Hyde and de Valera at the soccer match against Poland, explaining the rules of the game to two soccer novices.[15] Today, the Oscar Traynor trophy is awarded annually to the winners of a countrywide junior league competition by the FAI. Nobody could doubt his commitment to the national movement either. He was a member of the Volunteers from that body's outset as well as a member of the IRB. He fought in the Easter Rising of 1916, playing a prominent role as commander of the last headquarters outpost in O'Connell Street,[16] and was interned in Knutsford and Frongoch afterwards. He took a leading role in the War of Independence, including commanding the attack on the Custom House in May 1921, an attack that led to many casualties on the Irish side. He was an opponent of the Anglo-Irish Treaty and fought for the anti-treaty side in the subsequent civil war before being arrested in July 1922 and imprisoned in Gormanstown camp until 1924.[17] Initially opposed to de Valera's decision to leave Sinn Féin and found Fianna Fáil in 1926, he eventually joined the party in 1929. He was elected TD in Fianna Fáil's breakthrough election of 1932 and served continuously in Dáil Éireann until his retirement in 1961. He was appointed by de Valera as Minister for Posts and Telegraphs in 1936, a position he held until the cabinet reshuffle following the outbreak of the Second World War in 1939. Traynor was then promoted to the role of Minister for Defence and was responsible for the country's defences for the duration of the war. 'He was thus faced with the heavy responsibility of reorganising the entire Defence Forces in as short a time possible and equipping the biggest force of men ever under arms in the history of the State.'[18] Aside from a period in opposition from 1948 to 1951 he would serve as Minister of Defence up until 1954. On Fianna Fáil's re-entry into government in 1957 he was appointed Minister for Justice, a position he held until his retirement in 1961. He died of cancer two years later. It was as Minister for Defence that he would also become embroiled in a conflict with the GAA in 1943 when he was responsible for

Fianna Fáil minister Oscar Traynor (standing in the car). Traynor, an advanced nationalist who played a key role in Ireland's struggle for independence, was also a former professional soccer player. He took great umbrage at the assertion that only GAA members were 100 per cent Irishmen. As Minister for Defence in 1943, he was at loggerheads with the GAA for opening the Irish Army to sports other than Gaelic games. *(Courtesy of the National Library of Ireland)*

ending the army's policy of special treatment for Gaelic games being played by its soldiers and officers, allowing them to choose whichever games they wished to play, a decision that caused outrage within the GAA.[19] Other notable advanced nationalists who had a preference for non-Gaelic games included Cathal Brugha, 'a first class cricketer who bowled for Belvedere and Pembroke cricket clubs', and Todd Andrews, another soccer enthusiast.[20]

McDunphy disputed the assertion from members of the GAA that soccer was a British game, stating, 'It is a truly International game which is played throughout Europe. Teams representing their countries have been sent abroad by, inter alia, Germany, Spain, Hungary, Czech-Slovakia, Austria, Holland, etc.'.[21] Although the rules of soccer originated in Britain in the late nineteenth century, the game had become a truly global one by 1938. The third World Cup organised by the Fédération Internationale de Football Association (FIFA) had taken place earlier that year in France with more and more countries looking to participate as the tournament grew in popularity. FIFA was founded in Paris in 1904[22] and had fifty member countries in 1938, including Ireland.[23] The Football Association of England lived in splendid isolation of the FIFA World Cup, despite its success, until 1950, when it competed for the first time, at a World Cup tournament. McDunphy also expressed the view that the President did not want 'to ally himself with the narrow parochial outlook of those who regard it as an offence against nationality to play or even look at any healthy game of which they do not personally approve'.[24] Regardless of Hyde's personal views, he was now President of Ireland and favouring one sporting body over another would have been perceived as a political decision, something the new President, the first President under the new constitution, was keen to avoid. It is hard to see how the President could have come to any other conclusion. Did the GAA expect the President of the State to refuse every invitation received for every event organised by one of the 'foreign games' for his seven years as President? For the President to do so would have been a gross dereliction of his duties. He could not have called himself impartial and above politics. It would also have been hugely damaging to the new office, which was very much in the teething phase of acceptance as a legitimate and important function of the state.

The attendance of Hyde and de Valera at the match was widely reported in the media. Some newspapers reported on the possible implications for the GAA. The *Daily Mail* wrote 'Dr Douglas Hyde, the President of Eire, and Mr de Valera, the

Prime Minister, lifelong patrons of Gaelic games and culture, will on Sunday attend a 'foreign' game … According to the code of the Gaelic Athletic Association, any person who attends a non-Irish game such as Association football, Rugby, hockey, or cricket, is automatically banned from taking part in Gaelic football or hurling'.[25] *The Sunday Times*, in an article headlined 'Gaelic Ban Defied By Mr De Valera To See "Foreign" Game', commented that Hyde would also be attending rugby matches later in the year.[26]

Sinn Féin held its Árd Fhéis on the same day Hyde and de Valera attended the soccer match. Both came in for criticism at the proceedings. Sinn Féin president, Margaret Buckley, in her address, made an extraordinary claim about Hyde, one that she certainly would have difficulty backing up with evidence: 'Dr Hyde is the right man in the right place. He has always been a staunch supporter of the British connection, and it is not surprising that when closer relations with the British Empire were contemplated, a figure-head acceptable to that Empire should have been selected.' She continued, 'A new label had been put on the office of Governor-General, but Douglas Hyde is successor to all the Lords Lieutenant, and is, as they were, the King of England's representative in this British dominion now called "Eire."'[27] This was one of a number of comments referring to Hyde as successor to Donal Ó Buachalla, the last Governor General. Attacking 'the crime of partition' which she said, 'was assuming the aspect of an incurable disease, and the plight of the Nationalist population in the "robbed territory" was appalling. Economically, they were being starved out, and while they fought for the right to live the Free State super-statesmen wined and dined with those who held the key to the problem.'[28] At the same Árd Fhéis, Hyde and de Valera were chastised for attending a soccer match whilst previously ignoring GAA games in aid of republican prisoners.[29]

At a dinner held in honour of the Irish and Polish teams: 'Mr W. T. Dobrzynski, the Polish Consul-General, expressed appreciation of the honour that had been shown them by the attendance of President Hyde and Mr de Valera at the match'.[30] The same sentiments were expressed by Miss 'Jackie' Rotwandowna, correspondent with Polish sports paper, *Start*, who wrote in the *Sunday Independent*: 'We feel greatly honoured that Poland's match with Ireland to-day will be the first Soccer game attended by the President, Dr Douglas Hyde, and by Mr de Valera, and we thank them for their kindness in accepting the invitation of the F.A.I. – not only on behalf of the team, but also on behalf of the entire Polish nation.' She was effusive in her praise for de Valera in particular, remarking, 'Our officials and players experienced the greatest thrill of their lives when introduced to Ireland's Prime Minister, Mr de Valera. His popularity in Poland is due chiefly to the fact that our country, too, had to fight for its independence, and we always admired the same fighting spirit in the Irish.'[31] The Polish interest in de Valera would also have been helped by his prominent international role as president of the Assembly of the League of Nations. We can see from these remarks that the Polish soccer team and its delegation were deeply grateful to Hyde and de Valera for their attendance at the soccer match. Poland's history shared many similarities to Ireland's. It too had only recently gained independence, an independence that would be cruelly taken from it just ten months later when Nazi Germany invaded Poland on 1 September 1939, signalling the start of the Second World War. Hyde's act of courtesy, bestowed on a foreign nation, would be cited as a justification for his attendance at the game by many members of the GAA once Hyde was removed as patron.[32]

At the same dinner, representatives of the FAI sought to demonstrate that the GAA was not the only sporting body in Ireland with nationalist tendencies and beliefs. Dr W. F. Hooper, FAI president, toasting the Polish team in Irish, said, 'There was a close similarity between Ireland and Poland, for both had been subjected to foreign rule and both had survived it … I am not quite sure if you are satisfied with your position … but we are not. One part of our country is partitioned and we will not be satisfied until we get that.'[33] The FAI secretary, Myles Murphy, commented on Ireland's membership of FIFA, 'They [Ireland] had now a record in the Federation of which any country could be proud. They were also playing there as a distinct and separate nation. He could assure them that they would not go back to any association, in Britain or anywhere else, if by doing so, they had to give up their membership of the Federation.'[34]

In the days following the match more newspapers commented on Hyde and de Valera's attendance and the possible ramifications for the GAA's Ban rule.[35] The *Daily Express*, in an article entitled 'Ban On Players May Be Lifted' that would prove to be way off the mark, went so far as to predict that the GAA's Ban was likely to be rescinded as a result of their attendance.[36] This certainly would have added to the pressure on the GAA Central Council to take some action against Hyde. To do nothing would have posed many questions on the retention of the Ban.

Letters on this topic started to appear frequently in newspapers, with some people agreeing with the President and the Taoiseach, others not. One correspondent called 'Lily White', who claimed to have won two All-Ireland football titles with Kildare, wrote: 'It's very poor encouragement for me trying to make them [his two sons] Irish and keep away from foreign games when I read in the *Independent* that our President and Mr de Valera were present at the match with a German as referee. Thank God we have still 250,000 in our ranks that would not go to Dalymount last Sunday.'[37] Another person in a rather tongue-in-cheek letter said:

> The pictures in the newspapers depicting our beloved Tay Shock watching (and even applauding!) a foreign game were too much for my nerves, and I felt compelled to rush forthwith to see a doctor, who told me I was

suffering from oopoozodoc lynphangitis, brought on by extreme distress. I have been confined to bed all the week, and nothing but whisky will stop in my stomach. Can nothing be done to save us from such humiliating displays in future? It is to be sincerely hoped that that sterling and very broadminded body of sportsmen, the Central Council of the G.A.A., shall take this matter up without delay, for it amounts to a national disgrace, and would be tolerated nowhere outside that Orange compound known as the Six Counties.[38]

Most people who wrote to newspapers agreed with Hyde and de Valera attending the soccer match on the primary basis that both men represented all the people of Ireland, and not just the members of the GAA.[39]

Their attendance at the soccer match did, in effect, reopen the debate on the Ban which had been dormant for some time, not necessarily within the GAA but certainly in the general domain. *The Leader* devoted an article to evaluating the merits and de-merits of the Ban on 26 November. Written by 'a Young Gael', the article favoured a removal of the Ban, fancifully suggesting collaboration between the GAA and the FAI, 'I suggest that the GAA and the Football Association of Ireland combine to form an Irish Sports Federation to take control of all field games in the 32 Counties, including Hurling, Gaelic Football, Soccer, Rugby, Tennis, Golf, Hockey and Cricket.'[40] The same article claimed the Ban was in place as a deterrent against English games as 'no good can come out of England', the extreme measures were adopted to 'speed the Gaelic revival' and declared that GAA members may not have had a problem with the games themselves but had 'a strong objection to the West British cliques that control them'.[41] There may have been some justification in having this perception regarding members of the IRFU. The FAI and many prominent soccer players, including Oscar Traynor, certainly took issue with this viewpoint.

As a sign of what was to follow from some GAA clubs around the country, the Armagh GAA County Board, at a meeting held on 18 November, expressed disapproval at Hyde's and de Valera's attendance suggesting: 'their action can bear no other interpretation than that the traditional standpoint of the Gaels has been abandoned'.[42]

The GAA laid a considerable amount of criticism at de Valera's door for attending the match. There was, however, little the GAA could do as de Valera was not a member of the Association. In contrast, Hyde was patron of the GAA and it was this fact that was raised by the Patrick Pearse GAA Club in Derry on 4 December 1938 who put down a motion to remove him as patron.[43] In a lively debate, they claimed that the same rules should apply to patrons as well as to everyone else. Others said that Hyde was just showing courtesy to Poland. It took the carrying vote of the chairman to have the motion passed. The club also attacked the FAI for accepting partition by refusing teams from the six counties. Yet, Pádraig McNamee, GAA president at the time, was a public servant in employment as an examiner of the Northern Ireland Education Board,[44] a fact that could be construed as a personal acceptance by McNamee of partition. There would be two more GAA presidents – Seamus McFerran and Alf Murray – who worked in the civil service of Northern Ireland while serving as GAA president before the Ban was removed in 1971.[45] People working in the Civil Service of Northern Ireland were obliged to take the oath of allegiance to the crown. This was picked up on in a letter to the *Irish Independent* after Hyde was removed as patron where the writer, 'Disgusted', suggested that GAA officials taking the oath of allegiance to a British king deserved the same punishment as Hyde if the GAA was to be fair.[46] There can be no doubt that none of these individuals had any choice but to take the oath, in order to continue working in the place where they had chosen to live. They could, however, be placed in the same category as the FAI in accepting the reality of their situation.

Only a few years before, in 1919, the GAA banned those civil servants who took the oath of allegiance to the crown from becoming members of the Association (see page 50). A similar ban was not imposed on GAA members who worked for the Northern Ireland civil service once the Northern Ireland state came into being, a decision that allowed people like McNamee to participate in the GAA.

The *Evening Mail* strongly denounced the decision taken by the Patrick Pearse Club, stating: 'It is an act of discourtesy that will be deplored all over the country. It shows an inability to distinguish between the man and his office … No high functionary of the State can allow his private opinions to interfere with his official duties.' The pedigree of Hyde as an Irish-Irelander was also pointed out: 'The mere suggestion that the President of the State, who has done more for the revival of the Irish language than any other man alive or dead, is "unpatriotic" is a proposition that will cause a ripple of laughter throughout the country.'[47]

Other GAA clubs and county boards soon followed the Derry club's lead, calling for the removal of Hyde as patron, including Offaly[48] and East Kerry[49] who drew attention to the perceived persecution GAA members in Northern Ireland were experiencing at the time. These arguments were in reference to the bombing of a GAA hall in County Tyrone[50] and GAA matches being stopped by the Royal Ulster Constabulary (RUC) in Fermanagh[51] and Tyrone,[52] with one member from Kerry stating, 'It is a national disgrace that while Gaelic games are being banned and Gaelic halls blown up in Northern Ireland, President Hyde and Mr de Valera should attend a soccer match in Dublin.'[53] The bombing incident took place in Gort, Brantry, South Tyrone, where some bombs went off (more failed), partially destroying a GAA recreational hall that had just been constructed and was due to be opened formally less than a week after the bombing.[54] There were other reports of incidences of intimidation used by the RUC to stop Gaelic games from being played, such as in early 1939, when uniformed and plain-clothes RUC officers went to the inaugural game of a newly-formed GAA team, Thomas Russell in Downpatrick, just days after uprooting the posts at the new grounds of the team.[55] The prohibition of GAA matches in Northern Ireland by the RUC helped to inflame further the argument brewing between those on both sides of the Ban debate. Speaking after a Gaelic football match was stopped in Newtownbutler in Fermanagh, Father Maguire, parish priest of the town, said: 'Coercion has now definitely made its appearance in Northern Ireland. The whole position reminds me very vividly of the days of the Black and Tans, when we were hardly allowed freedom to attend our duties of public worship ... The prohibition of this match is a direct insult to the whole national body of the GAA.'[56] Ulster was the most vociferous province in its call for the removal of Hyde as patron. With matches being abandoned and some GAA halls destroyed, members of the GAA in the six counties of Northern Ireland were certainly experiencing trying times. It is little wonder that they adopted a more hard-line approach on the 'foreign games' ban rule.

There were further calls from South-West Donegal GAA Board,[57] Wexford GAA County Board[58] and London GAA County Board[59] to have Hyde removed as patron of the GAA. At the Wexford County Board meeting, an opinion was expressed that if Hyde 'in his official capacity, found that he was called upon to do certain things not in keeping with the rules, the thing for him to do was to hand in his resignation as patron'.[60] At the Annual Convention of London GAA County Board, the chairman called Hyde and de Valera's attendance at the soccer match 'the greatest blow the Association has suffered ... Their action has rocked the foundations of the national pastimes.'[61] There was a strongly held belief that the Ban and the prosperity of the GAA were interlinked. Some people were genuinely concerned that the leaders of the State, by attending 'foreign games' for the very first time, could bring about an end to the Ban and the continued success of the Association.

A judge in Monaghan made an interesting observation relating to the furore caused by the criticism of Hyde by certain GAA bodies. He was dealing with an application from a GAA club to be granted a license to hold a dance on their premises in early December 1938. The judge in question, Justice Goff, asked if the GAA club would be holding 'foreign' as well as Irish dances at the event. On hearing that they probably would, he criticised the hypocrisy of the GAA in looking to remove Hyde for going to a soccer match and yet flouting its own rule on 'foreign dances'. He described it as 'the worst type of foreignism, the dirtiest type'.[62] This incident was discussed on 17 December, at the same GAA Central Council meeting during which Hyde was removed as patron; Pádraig McNamee requested that Monaghan County Board investigate the matter.[63] The GAA came in for extensive and consistent criticism from many quarters for the alleged incidences of flouting the 'foreign dances' rule.

The *News Review* mockingly attacked the whole Irish-Ireland movement and, as it saw it, its extremism; stating:

> Dr Douglas Hyde came unstuck last week with his country's 'Irish-Irelanders'. An Irish-Irelander is a super-patriot who tries to eat only Eirish food, wear only home-produced clothes, read only his countrymen's books, and be entertained solely by local amusements. Everything whose Eirish origin is unproved he regards as 'foreign' and therefore in the worst of taste. At the invitation of the Eire Football Association whiskery President Hyde last week attended a soccer match between Poland and Eire, beamed over players and fans. To the Gaelic Athletic Association, an out-and-out 'Irish-Irish' organisation which bitterly eschews the Anglicising influence of such 'foreign' games as soccer, this was treason.[64]

The run up to the final meeting of the Central Council of the GAA was dominated by Hyde's attendance at the soccer match on 13 November. Newspapers seemed to cover little else since that date and many clubs and county boards called for Hyde's removal as patron. There was little chance of the issue not being discussed at the meeting.

12

The Banned Patron

When the Central Council met on 17 December, GAA president Pádraig McNamee was faced with a dilemma: if he chose to ignore Hyde's 'indiscretion' it would not go unnoticed. There had been too many arguments and counter-arguments within the media, and many GAA clubs had called for action to be taken against Hyde. If he sanctioned Hyde's removal he was removing the Head of State as patron of the GAA, someone who had done so much for the Irish-Ireland cause, an issue to which McNamee was deeply devoted.

Born in Armagh in 1896, Pádraig McNamee was a passionate Irish-Ireland advocate who dedicated himself to this cause. He was a teacher by profession and taught on the Falls Road in Belfast before moving to Holywood, County Down, where he served as principal for over twenty years.[1] The GAA ground in Holywood is named after McNamee. He also served as examiner of Irish for the Northern Ireland Ministry for Education.[2] McNamee's two main passions in life were the GAA and the Gaelic League. He was a founder member of Comhaltas Uladh in 1926, the Ulster Council of the Gaelic League, and served as secretary for over twenty-five years.[3] Comhaltas Uladh, at times, had a fractious relationship with the Gaelic League in Dublin, being in many ways

Pádraig McNamee, GAA President from 1938 to 1943, was the first Ulsterman to hold the position. He was president when Hyde was removed as patron in 1938. *(Courtesy of the GAA Museum, Croke Park)*

independent of the central organisation.[4] At a gathering to promote the Irish language in Ireland's 'Alsace-Lorraine'[5] (the six counties) in 1944, the following remarks were made about McNamee:

Mr Pádraig McNamee's work for the games of the Gael and the tongue of the Gael is well known in every home in Ireland. At very great personal inconvenience he has had to make a long and arduous journey to be with us to-day … I know however, that inconveniences of any sort are no account with Mr McNamee whenever an opportunity offers of helping on a cause he has most at heart – the restoration of the Irish language.[6]

Ironically, on his retirement as secretary of Comhaltas Uladh in 1957, he received the Dr Douglas Hyde medal for outstanding work for the Irish language, nineteen years after he made the decision to remove Hyde as GAA patron.[7] He devoted most of his life to the GAA and was the first Ulsterman to be elected president of the Association in 1938. He would go on to serve for five years, two years more than the standard term served by presidents. He is the second longest serving GAA president, after James Nowlan. He was chairman of the Ulster Council of the GAA from 1935 to 1937 and, once he finished his presidency, he served again from 1943 to 1945. He was centrally involved in organising the All-Ireland football final of 1947 between Cavan and Kerry held in the Polo Grounds, New York. He sacrificed all of his annual leave that year to visit New York and prepare the way for the final to take place. Along with Ó Caoimh, McNamee must take great credit for organising this mammoth logistical undertaking. In 1969, he became chairman of the 'McNamee Commission', a body that produced a highly praised report in 1971 outlining the future direction of the GAA just months after the removal of the ban on 'foreign games'.[8] The 90,000-word report recommended changes covering organisation and structure under the categories of financial management, youth, grounds, communications, hurling, discipline and sponsorship.[9] Commenting on the findings of the Commission on his retirement from the GAA Central Council in 1972, McNamee said, 'I learned more about the strengths and weaknesses of the Association during the three year period I served on the Commission than I ever thought possible or even existed'.[10] Alf Murray, ex-president of the GAA, proclaimed at the same meeting honouring McNamee on his retirement that he 'had been an inspiration to me and all in Ulster'.[11] McNamee died in 1975, having devoted himself selflessly for decades to the GAA and the Gaelic League. His efforts were recognised by the GAA a year later when they named the new annual GAA communication awards after him.[12]

At the Central Council meeting of 17 December, McNamee moved, with little debate, that Hyde had ceased to be a patron of the GAA by his action of going to the soccer match.

McNamee and the general secretary, Pádraig Ó Caoimh, as well as most members of the Central Council, were firm believers of the traditionalist viewpoint within the GAA. They had dedicated their lives to the pursuit of an Irish-Ireland. As both men would go on to state at the Annual Congress of 1939, there could be no wavering in the quest for that Irish-Ireland; that 'Gaelic Front'.[13] They believed they were taking the only course open to them after Hyde attended the soccer match. They argued that the rules were absolute and no one could breach them, regardless of their station in life. They felt that although twenty-six counties of Ireland had achieved independence, there still were six under British rule and the rest of the country was as far away as ever from being free of British influence. The Ban was the GAA's most potent tool in its war against the Anglicisation of Ireland. In some ways, it could be argued they were following a similar policy to the government of the day. When Fianna Fáil entered government in 1932, their aim was to dismantle the Anglo-Irish Treaty, to make Ireland self-sufficient. In essence, they wanted Irish industry to be self-reliant and in no way dependent on external factors. Although it may have been a noble dream for Fianna Fáil and the GAA to pursue, it was just a dream. In 1938, Fianna Fáil ended the Economic War with Britain, a debilitating battle that had stifled economic growth for most of Fianna Fáil's first years in power. *The Irish Times* described it as an 'economic policy which had its virtues, but threatened to run mad, has been slowed to a discrete pace by the trade agreement'.[14] De Valera negotiated three separate agreements with Prime Minister Neville Chamberlain's British government on finance, trade and defence: Ireland would pay a lump sum of £10 million to resolve the land annuities dispute which signalled the start of the Economic War; trade between the two countries was freed up to degrees not seen since before 1932; and, importantly for the looming European war, the defence ports of Spike Island, Berehaven and Lough Swilly were handed back to Ireland ('Every inch of the soil of the twenty-six counties now is independent'[15]), an act crucial for Ireland to remain neutral in the event of any war. This thaw in relations between the two governments would have been seen as further evidence of a deteriorating commitment by de Valera and Fianna Fáil to the Irish-Ireland cause by many people in the GAA.

There can be little doubt that there was no personal malice against Hyde in the Central Council's actions. Very few people ever demonstrated malice towards Hyde. The Central Council's decision, however, was an extraordinary one to make. The decision appears as a knee-jerk reaction to the furore that was caused after Hyde's attendance at the soccer match. It would have been advisable for McNamee to consult more widely than he did, instead of making a rash decision that, inevitably, led to huge amounts of criticism outside the Association. Aside from the fact that Hyde was the first citizen of the country, he also was the person most identified with the Irish-Ireland movement and could be described as the father of that movement. His work for the Gaelic League was his primary concern but he also supported the GAA. It was Hyde and his colleagues in the Gaelic League who played a decisive role in turning around the fortunes of the GAA when it was at its lowest ebb. The *Irish Press*, in a concise and reasoned article, best summed up the general sense of bewilderment at the GAA's decision by stating:

> Like everybody else, they [the GAA] are aware that Dr Douglas Hyde was chosen as Head of the State principally because he had done more than any other man living for the revival of Gaelic culture and, like everybody else, they welcomed the choice. Now, because in the ordinary exercise of the duties of his office, the President attended the international football match between Ireland and Poland, he has come under their ban. To complete the Gilbertian situation would only require an official reproof from the Gaelic League to the GAA because the proceedings at which the ruling was made were conducted in a foreign language.[16]

The storm that had been brewing now reached a crescendo. The GAA's decision received widespread national and international media coverage, and was analysed in newspapers such as the *Sunday Dispatch*,[17] the *Sunday Independent*,[18] the *Irish Press*,[19] *The Irish Times*,[20] the *Irish Independent*,[21] the *Irish Daily Telegraph*,[22] the *Daily Express*,[23] the *Daily Sketch*,[24] *The Times*,[25] *The Manchester Guardian*,[26] the *Glasgow Herald*,[27] the *Calgary Daily Herald*[28] and the *Windsor Daily Star* from Canada, *The New York Times*,[29] the *Christian Science Monitor*[30] in Boston, the *Chicago Daily Tribune*,[31] as well as newspapers around the country. The reaction was generally one of outrage and condemnation. The *Glasgow Herald* described it as 'a studied and calculated insult' and said it would be difficult for the GAA to find another patron because no one 'who has the least regard for his personal freedom of action would accept such a questionable honour'.[32]

In its editorial, *The Irish Times* commented:

> A connection of thirty years' standing is to be broken by a display of intolerance which it would be difficult to

parallel even in those countries in which party zeal passes for patriotism. A name which shed lustre on the GAA for the greater part of its history will do so no longer. The loss will be to the GAA. Misplaced zeal cannot go farther; the zealots, at least, might have the decency to feel ashamed. Their little victory over President Hyde will be Pyrrhic, because the Head of the State will continue to be the representative of all the people, and not of any clique, however large it may be.[33]

The *Limerick Leader*, in its editorial 'Things That Matter', called for an end to the Ban, stating:

'An Craoibhín' is not merely the present distinguished head of the State but is easily one of the greatest Irishmen of this or any age. He has done more to Irishise this country and assert and preserve its individuality than any man living, and it is simply shocking that a body of his own countrymen should virtually declare him unworthy of recognition and respect. The shameful and small-minded action taken is the result, of course, of keeping the foreign games 'ban', which was decided upon for a specific purpose when the circumstances were altogether different from what they are at present. In the Ireland of to-day this 'ban' is an insult to the games it is supposed to protect, and its continuance is nothing more than a degrading manifestation of the slave mind ... at least nine out of every ten Irishmen will regard this decision with feelings of utter humiliation mixed with disgust.[34]

In Hyde's native county, the *Roscommon Herald*, drawing parallels between the fascist regimes rampant in Europe at the time and the GAA, was also scathing in its condemnation of the GAA: 'Hitler and Mussolini might do that sort of thing; the GAA should not try to do it. The serfs of the Dictators have no choice but to obey, but the people of Ireland have fought to free themselves from serfdom. We say that the GAA has covered itself with ridicule by "banning" the President of Eire.'[35] The same paper also stated that the GAA was 'more an heir of Cromwellian Puritanism than it is of the modern healthy spirit of sport'.[36] *The Manchester Guardian* also drew comparisons between Nazi Germany and the GAA saying they both had peculiar methods of either staying away from events or forcing other people to stay away from functions.[37]

Members of the clergy also got involved. The parish priest of Boyle, County Roscommon, Canon O'Beirne, condemning the 'short-sighted policy' to remove Hyde, commented that they should also remove members who played bridge or attended foreign dances if they were to be consistent.[38] The GAA's somewhat loose adherence to the 'foreign dances' ban rule, introduced in 1929, was the one issue that was constantly raised by opponents of the Central Council decision as demonstrating inconsistencies and an element of hypocrisy within the Association.[39] The Monaghan court ruling granting a license to a GAA club showed that this rule was clearly being flouted, and there seemed minimal conviction in implementing the rule strictly. The *Tuam Herald* commented on GAA members going to jazz dances.[40] One delegate at a GAA meeting in Tipperary even commented that the GAA openly advertised dances that were clearly in breach of the 'foreign dance' rule.[41] One day after the decision to remove Hyde was ratified at the Annual Congress of 1939, the GAA was criticised for its holding of 'foreign dances' at a Gaelic League meeting. Pádraig McNamee, in attendance at that meeting, said rather sheepishly: 'he would do his best to see that only *céilithe* were held by the GAA';[42] not a very strong commitment from the GAA president.

Some members of the Oireachtas were also outraged at the GAA's decision to remove Hyde. Prominent veteran General Richard Mulcahy contacted the President's Office just days after Hyde was removed as GAA patron to discuss 'proposals which he and some other persons had in mind for the termination of the absurd position in which it was not possible for the Head of the State to be Patron of a Body which was founded for the promotion of National Games'.[43] The request to meet was turned down by Hyde, through McDunphy, on the basis that the President could not involve himself in an act where 'there were bound to be differences of opinions' and that 'any movement which was likely to be successful on its merits should not require the President's intervention'.[44] The issue also came up in a Dáil Debate on the Offences Against the State Bill held in March 1939, when Laois Labour TD William Davin questioned if the GAA 'could be brought under the powers contained under Section 7 of the Bill, charged and found guilty of intimidating the President in the exercise of his normal duties'.[45] The Ceann Comhairle's response to Davin was a request for him to take the bill seriously. Incidents of involvement from politicians were rare, however, which is surprising, considering the attention the controversy received.

The secretary to the President, Michael McDunphy, kept a lot of press cuttings relating to Hyde's removal from the GAA, commenting on the extent of coverage the issue was receiving: 'The press cuttings in connection with this matter are so numerous that ... they have accordingly been made the subject of a separate file'.[46] There are, in fact, two large files that can be viewed in the National Archives of Ireland devoted solely to the press coverage Hyde's removal received. McDunphy also commented on the conversations he had, expressing the consensus viewpoint that the GAA's decision had 'caused considerable and growing dissatisfaction'.[47]

W. F. Hooper, president of the FAI, contacted Michael McDunphy on 21 December to see if the President would be interested in becoming patron of the soccer body. McDunphy wisely declined on behalf of the President as the 'time was not opportune'[48] with his removal as GAA patron having taken place just days previously. The FAI was clearly being opportunistic and Hooper and his colleagues agreed that the

The first Council of State Meeting is convened by Douglas Hyde. Michael McDunphy, secretary to the President's Office, is seated third to the right (to Hyde's left). McDunphy was seen as the most important member of the President's staff and took meticulous care in recording all correspondence relating to Hyde's removal as GAA patron. *(Courtesy of the National Library of Ireland)*

best decision for the President to make was to decline their invitation.

The President decided to remain silent on the matter,[49] a silence he maintained up to his death. Hyde's first public engagement after the Central Council meeting was a significant one, a radio broadcast to the United States, a Christmas message to over 160 radio stations in the United States.[50] He made no mention of the GAA. Instead, he gave a positive address reminiscing on his fundraising trip to America over thirty years previously and the progress the Irish language had made since then. Accepting that there was a lot more still to do, he expressed pride for the Irish language reaching the status of the official language of the Irish State under the constitution.

He also said, 'Although the struggle for national self-expression has been long and intense, the people of Ireland have never become embittered',[51] comments that many people could be forgiven for believing were extraordinary, considering what had happened to him at the hands of one of those bodies so devoted to national self-expression. His decision to remain silent is all the more understandable considering the personal tragedy that he experienced just days later. His wife Lucy, who had suffered from poor health for many years, died on 31 December 1938. It was described by the *Irish Press* as the 'joy of mid-summer inauguration' being 'changed to gloom'.[52] She had been confined to bed for some time before her death and was therefore unable to take up residence in Áras an Uachtaráin when Hyde became President, remaining instead in Ratra, Frenchpark, County Roscommon.[53] She had even been too ill to attend Hyde's inauguration in June.[54] At the behest of de Valera, flags were flown at half-mast at most public buildings and some private ones dear to the Hydes.[55] The funeral was a simple ceremony, with only immediate family members invited to the service.[56] De Valera and other government ministers expressed a desire to attend, but it was Hyde's explicit wish that the funeral be a private affair.[57] It was probably just as well considering the embarrassing episode of senior Irish Catholic politicians waiting outside St Patrick's Cathedral, a Protestant ground, at Hyde's own funeral in 1949. Hyde had been suffering with a severe cold since Christmas and, under doctor's orders, was unable to attend his wife's funeral.[58] The people in the local area drew the blinds of their windows out of respect and the local post office was inundated with 'little green packets with the words of sympathy' for Lucy.[59] There was a huge outpouring of condolences for Hyde's bereavement from all quarters in Ireland and beyond, including from the GAA president[60] and from various county boards and councils within the Association.[61] One of the messages of sympathy was from King George VI and Queen Elizabeth of Britain. This created a minor incident in government circles. Thanking the monarchs for their message, McDunphy, due to the insistence of Hyde, described Lucy as Hyde's 'beloved wife'. The Department of External Affairs contacted McDunphy, commenting that it was an inappropriate use of the word 'beloved' and advising him not to be so informal in the future.[62]

The year 1938 had started as a memorable one for Hyde, with the ultimate honour of being elected as first President of Ireland, and had ended on a sour note with the severing of relations with a body he had personally helped to reach its level of prominence and popularity and one he was always proud to be associated with. It finished even more dreadfully when, on the last day of the year, he was beset with the deeply tragic loss of his wife to whom he had been married for over forty-five years. The following year would not bring much respite for Hyde with his status as GAA patron the main topic for debate at GAA club, county and provincial conventions at the start of the year, culminating with the Annual Congress in April where a number of motions on Hyde's removal as patron were the centrepiece items on the agenda.

13

GAA Conventions Debate Hyde's Removal

The timing of Hyde's attendance at the soccer match in November 1938 coincided with convention season for the GAA, with all club, county and provincial conventions needing to be held before the Annual Congress in April 1939. This process, in some cases, started just days after the soccer match. Unsurprisingly, the main topic discussed at almost all of these conventions around the country was Hyde's attendance at the soccer match and his subsequent removal as patron. With each new discussion at each GAA meeting came a report and an opinion from most of the national and provincial newspapers. It would mean the Hyde incident would dominate the news for the first few months of the year until the Annual Congress took place during Easter Week 1939.

Ulster

Ulster was in a very different position to the rest of Ireland, with six of the nine Ulster counties making up Northern Ireland. This would lead to many divergent views to the rest of Ireland, with a tendency for most county boards in Ulster to be against any conciliatory measures towards Hyde. The GAA had taken longer to develop in Ulster than in any other part of the country. Representatives from Ulster first attended an Annual Congress in 1888 and Ulster GAA was even harder hit than everywhere else after the 'Parnell Split' of 1890, with the GAA becoming almost extinct in the province after supporting Parnell.[1] By the turn of the twentieth century, Ulster GAA still lagged behind the rest of the country – the Ulster Council was established in 1903, the last provincial council to be set up. The Gaelic League greatly assisted the GAA in gaining a foothold in Ulster and was directly responsible for the setting up of a number of GAA clubs.[2] Hyde offered his support to the GAA in Ulster by frequently attending Gaelic games in the province.[3] When the Government of Ireland Act was enacted in 1920, separating the six counties from the rest of Ireland, the GAA was directly affected. It lost thousands of its potential membership base, Irish nationalists, who moved to southern Ireland after partition.[4] The events, as discussed in Chapter 11, of the RUC cancelling GAA matches and GAA halls being bombed were an all too regular occurrence from 1920 onwards. In 1922, the B-Specials arrested the whole Monaghan Gaelic football team on their way to a match against the home team in Derry.[5] There were numerous instances of clashes between the GAA and the RUC from the inception of the Northern Ireland state and as David Hassan, in his study 'The GAA in Ulster', comments, 'the GAA in Ulster encountered problems again in the early 1930s as the full extent of British cultural hegemony became even more apparent … Under law the government of Northern Ireland had the right to block transmissions if it believed this to be in the public interest. Understandably wary of internal dissention and keen to distinguish itself from the Free State, "all events south of the Border were studiously ignored; even the results of matches played by the Gaelic Athletic Association were refused air time".'[6] Based on this experience, there can be little wonder why Ulster would be the most zealous of all provinces in upholding the Irish-Ireland cause.

The GAA Central Council's decision was made on 17 December 1938: the South Donegal Divisional Board held its convention just one day later, on Sunday 18 December, one of the first bodies to hold its annual convention following the controversial decision. They were fully behind the Central Council's decision to remove Hyde as patron, a stance taken by nearly all clubs within Ulster. At the same meeting, the Northern Ireland government was condemned for banning Gaelic games.[7]

The West Tyrone Division was one of the few exceptions in Ulster. At a meeting held shortly after the Central Council meeting, representatives stated, 'President Hyde attended a foreign game in his official capacity and as a matter of courtesy to visitors, and it was strange that he should be penalised by the GAA ... Dr Hyde ... was chiefly responsible for the promotion of the Irish language and culture, while people North and South posing as Gaels were allowed to attend foreign games and foreign dances without any serious notice being taken.' The chairman at the same meeting conceded that there was a 'looseness in the rule in relation to foreign entertainments, and there should be a tightening up by Congress'.[8] Coalisland Fianna Gaelic Football Club, in a book commemorating their history, claimed they too were opposed to the removal of Hyde, stating, 'Fully cognizant of the good work that Hyde had done for the Gaelic Movement, the Fianna were among the many clubs which protested loudly at this shabby and ungrateful treatment and called for Hyde's reinstatement'.[9]

A lone voice from Tyrone would also question the Central Council's decision at the following Ulster GAA Council meeting held in Omagh, County Tyrone, on 14 January 1939, saying that Hyde should have been notified before he was suspended. The consensus at the meeting was that Hyde had removed himself by going to the soccer match and if they could have removed de Valera as well, they would have.[10] At the same meeting, letters were read out 'urging the Council [Ulster GAA Council] to impress on the Central Council the

Sir Basil Brooke, Northern Ireland Minister for Agriculture in 1939 and future Prime Minister, commenting on the Hyde Incident, said, 'Supposing by some mischance we happened to be included in Eire, and we wanted to sing "God Save the King", fly the Union Jack, or attend 12th of July or 12th of August celebrations, do you think the only punishment we would get would be erasing our names from citizenship in Eire?' *(Courtesy of the* Belfast Telegraph*)*

importance of standing firmly by the Gaels of the Six Counties in resisting any attempt to impose a ban on the National Games'.[11]

Sir Basil Brooke, Northern Ireland Minister for Agriculture and future Prime Minister of Northern Ireland, offered his opinion on Hyde's removal, saying: 'that they might laugh at such action, but he would point out another aspect. Supposing by some mischance we happened to be included in Eire, and we wanted to sing "God Save the King", fly the Union Jack, or attend 12th of July or 12th of August celebrations, do you think the only punishment we would get would be erasing our names from citizenship in Eire? This is a just pointer to the attitude which exists among certain citizens of *that country* [emphasis added]'.[12] A rebuke from the GAA was quick in coming, with one member responding, 'One of these "Brookes" ... has been babbling rather badly of late. He had a dig or two at the G.A.A., and then he said that the posts on the border merely typified the significant divisions existing between ourselves and the people of Eire. We are in the happy position to-day of telling Sir Basil Brooke that he is not correct when he says that we are divided from our brethren in Eire.'[13]

Acknowledging the criticism received and defending his actions, the GAA president Pádraig McNamee said in an address to students at St Columb's College, Derry, that: 'they were, however, merely adhering to the standing rules of the Association, and they had acted in the way they thought would cause least hurt to Dr Hyde'.[14] This viewpoint of 'least hurt' which McNamee would go on to claim on a number of occasions was something with which the President's Office certainly did not agree. Commenting on the Central Council's decision, Michael McDunphy commented: 'It is noteworthy that at no time was a communication received by the President from the GAA or any person purporting to represent that Body, regarding the President's attendance at the Irish-Polish Match on the 13th November, 1938, or the subsequent action taken by the GAA itself.'[15] At the heart of the debate was not just any President of Ireland. It was Hyde, a man who was widely respected for his work for Irish culture and the Irish language in particular, the individual credited with instigating the foundation of the Gaelic League. As one critic of the decision said, 'It is a case of the child turning on his father'.[16] McDunphy claimed that the GAA made no attempt to contact Hyde for his entire duration as President after he was removed as patron. At the very least, the GAA could have corresponded with the President to explain the reasoning behind its decision. Instead it chose to ignore Hyde, an act that can only be viewed as extremely discourteous to him. Most of the senior figures of the GAA met Hyde at Croke Park for the All-Ireland football final of 1938.[17] This would have provided them with ample opportunity to discuss his role as patron of the GAA and as President of the State, an office he had taken up just a few months earlier. No such conversation is recorded as having transpired. The GAA could also have communicated with the President, offering a protest before he went to the soccer match or, at the very least, explained to him why they had taken the action to remove him once he did go to the match. He was also, as some members claimed, entitled to the same due process granted to members accused of attending 'foreign games', an explanation within five days of alleged attendance to the Central Council.[18] McNamee, at a Gaelic League meeting in 1944, would go on to claim that no officer had been removed from the GAA without an opportunity to defend themselves.[19] This obviously did not apply to patrons; Hyde was afforded no forum to justify his presence at the soccer match in November 1938.

Most of Ulster was, however, fully behind fellow Ulsterman McNamee. At the Armagh GAA County Board Annual General Meeting, held on 29 January 1939, the chairman stated, in a hard-hitting, uncompromising speech:

> At the present moment in two parts of Ireland one saw two different methods being adopted to weaken the national games. The great national daily newspapers were doing their utmost to cause a split in the ranks of the players, and some papers were working might and main to give foreign games equal stature and further more to make British games sport in this country. One saw two chief men of Ireland, Leaders of the State, openly patronising foreign games. They were not going to be misled by what politicians had done. The Gaels of Ireland would not take the insult lying down; they would fight against this treachery from within as they would attacks from without.[20]

This fiery language was supported by a motion, passed unanimously, praising the Central Council for their consistent attitude in dealing with those who infringed the 'foreign games' rules. The Linnanog GAA club in Armagh also passed a resolution supporting the Central Council in its decision to remove Hyde.[21]

By the time the Ulster GAA Annual Convention came around on 25 February in Enniskillen, County Fermanagh, there was no doubt as to where Ulster's loyalty lay. At that meeting the president of the Ulster Council of the GAA, Fr Michael Collins, supporting the Central Council, stated:

> However much we love Dr Hyde for his work for the Gaelic cause, we love the Gaelic cause still more. Whilst in this part of the world we have had a considerable amount of opposition to contend with, we think it was not too much to expect that the Government, and the members of the Government, one and all, in the other part of the country should have thrown their full weight behind the cause of the GAA, instead of for the first time in their history, throwing their weight in the opposite direction.[22]

He went on to say that the cause they were fighting for, an Irish-Ireland, did not receive adequate support from people like Hyde and de Valera, an incredible statement, which, in essence, dismissed Hyde's entire career in one fell swoop. Gerry Arthurs, in his more measured address as secretary of the Ulster Council, claimed that it was 'sad to find prominent persons who rendered noble service to the cause associating themselves with functions which, if not exactly hostile, are at least at variance with the Irish-Ireland programme'. He also made the reasonable assertion that the 'foreign games' rule, like any other rule, could be removed by democratic means and until that happened; it needed to be adhered to loyally.[23] He then made the bold assertion that 'Ulster to a man, woman and child, were behind the Central Council in its decision'[24] to remove Hyde.

Also speaking at the Ulster Convention, McNamee criticised the newspapers for being unfair and a nuisance to him, and for making the Hyde incident an issue, particularly the English newspapers who: 'did not care three farthings about what they did with Dr Hyde or anyone else'.[25] He reiterated his assertion that the GAA had taken a course of action that, in his opinion, had caused least hurt to Hyde.[26] McNamee's criticism of the newspapers for causing the controversy must also be questioned. McNamee was the one who removed Hyde as patron, even though he claimed Hyde had removed himself for attending the soccer match. Hyde was President of Ireland and a man who was known the world over for his dedication to Irish culture, the GAA being an integral part of that culture. It was extremely naive for McNamee to think there would be no repercussions or reporting of Hyde's removal as patron. Of all the people the GAA could have offended, Hyde was the last person who would have expected such a snub. And naturally, the ensuing criticism was more severe as a result. It would be fair to say that many newspapers were not fans of the GAA or of Irish culture in general, including some indigenous titles, and with such ammunition provided to them, they were extremely critical of the GAA. On the whole, most of the journalism on this issue was fair; the facts themselves were astonishing enough to sell newspapers. In the same speech, McNamee expressed his admiration for Hyde's work and even claimed he did not think it was Hyde's fault, blaming instead 'the people who forced him, or enticed or encouraged him to go there',[27] a patronising comment that could be construed as suggesting that Hyde was incapable or unable to make independent decisions.

With Northern Ireland's unique political position compared to the rest of the country, the Ban was seen as crucial for the GAA to survive. One of the primary reasons that had been advanced to remove the Ban was that Ireland had attained a

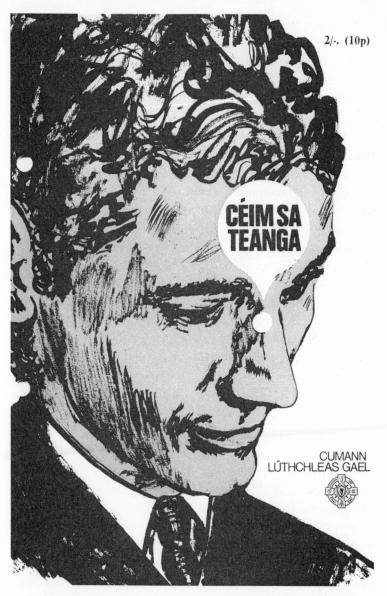

Céim sa Teanga was an Irish language book published by the GAA. The GAA financially assisted Irish language movements, such as the Gaelic League, and espoused the use of Irish as the primary spoken langauge in Ireland. The GAA was accused, on many occasions, of paying mere lip service to the Irish language cause. *(Courtesy of the GAA Oral History Project)*

large degree of independence. This was not the case for the six counties of Northern Ireland. GAA enthusiasts were living in a more perilous position than they had been prior to 1920. Their rights, including their rights to express themselves through Irish culture, were severely curtailed, with the GAA, in particular, targeted by the Northern Ireland authorities. The Ban was seen as paramount to allowing them to retain their Irishness and to oppose the authorities of the North. It was almost inevitable that they would take a hard-line approach to Hyde, and considering the circumstances they faced in the North, it was, in many ways, understandable.

Connacht

There was a great deal of support in Hyde's home county for the President. Fr Mahon, president of Roscommon GAA County Board, unable to attend the annual convention, had a letter read out at the Annual Convention of Roscommon GAA County Board. In the letter he stated: 'Personally, I think that this motion [to remove Hyde] should never have been brought forward. Even when it was brought forward, a distinction could have easily have been made between Dr Hyde as President of this country and An Craoibhín Aoibhinn [Hyde's nom de plume, meaning 'Pleasant Little Branch'], founder of the Gaelic League.'[28] Claiming Ireland was now emerging as a 'World Power' (it is hard to see how he came to such a conclusion), he was more concerned with the Irish language being promoted than the Ban on 'foreign games'. Fr Mahon also went on to reiterate the complaint that was repeated throughout the country; the GAA was not being rigorous in ensuring only traditional dances were performed at GAA events.[29]

The Irish language was seen by many in the Irish-Ireland movement, most notably Hyde, as the most important issue to promote, yet the GAA appeared to be less than zealous in its approach to adopting the language. In the past, Hyde had bemoaned the efforts made by the GAA in supporting the Irish language, saying the GAA had not gone far enough.[30] Most meetings and correspondences conducted by the GAA were done so in English. In contrast, according to a claim by Hyde, whenever he met with either the Taoiseach, de Valera, or the Tánaiste, Sean T. O'Kelly (who would succeed Hyde as President in 1945), their meetings were conducted *as Gaeilge*.[31] There were many GAA activists, including McNamee and Ó Caoimh, who were also active in the Gaelic League, which makes it all the more surprising that the GAA's efforts could be so lukewarm towards the native tongue. Some efforts to rectify the situation were taken in 1938 following meetings between the GAA and the Gaelic League at which they agreed to work closer together. At the Central Council Meeting of 17 December 1938, the same meeting where Hyde was removed as patron, the following resolutions were passed with regard to the language: 'That delegates at the various Conventions should use as much Irish as possible, the revival of Feiseanna throughout the country, that as far as possible that Minor games should be conducted in Irish, and that notices in Cinemas should be in Irish, and that there should be better news items in the Cinemas from the Irish-Ireland point of view.'[32] This still suggested only minimal effort was being paid to the Irish language. De Búrca argues that the GAA has done more than pay minimal heed to the language, stating:

> Critics of the GAA who argue that it merely pays lip-service to the language overlook the fact that there is a limit to the contribution which a sports body can make to a cause such as the revival movement. They also ignore the very substantial material assistance that has been provided for many years by the Association to the language bodies, including in particular the proceeds from the annual Oireachtas hurling competition and the provision of Gaeltacht scholarships.[33]

There are some valid points in those comments raised by de Búrca. However, the GAA was not, and has never been, just a sports body. It has prided itself on being a national organisation dedicated to the revival of an Irish-Ireland. This was particularly pronounced from the 1930s until the Ban was removed in 1971. For a body espousing to promote everything that was good in Ireland as Irish, more substantial attempts to promote the language could have been made: a few token gestures were not enough. Presidential addresses from people like McNamee, Sean McCarthy and Seamus Gardiner, throughout Annual Congresses held in the 1930s and 1940s, were littered with calls for greater efforts to promote the Irish language within the GAA,[34] yet very little in the way of tangible means to achieve this goal were put forward. An obvious measure that would have offered a real boost to the language would have been an insistence that all GAA meetings be conducted in Irish. Or, perhaps, the GAA like everyone else realised the attainment of Irish as the primary language spoken in the country was a mere pipe-dream and an exercise in futility. De Búrca is also correct in saying that the GAA did help Irish language organisations financially. We have seen, however, another side to this assistance when the GAA refused to aid the Gaelic League once the Gaelic League decided to remove their bans in 1938.[35] It could be argued that the GAA's commitment to the Irish-Ireland cause was an à la carte commitment, picking aspects it liked and ignoring the ones it found too difficult to impose. A perfect example of the GAA's flexibility in its commitment to the language revival movement can be seen in a letter that appeared in the *Irish Independent* on 31 December 1938 when a correspondent pointed out:

> Only a comparatively short time ago a player was suspended for being present at a 'foreign' game. He was called before a meeting of his executive to explain his delinquency. He appeared, and conducted his defence entirely in Irish. Unfortunately, there was no interpreter,

and the matter had to be put off *sine die* [without a date fixed]. It is only a few years back that posters for GAA events appeared bi-lingually – a sop to the language revival.[36]

Another person maintained that the GAA had become a powerful force for the English language by conducting all its meetings in English.[37] Breandán Ó hEithir in his fine memoir on the GAA, *Over The Bar*, gives an example of a debate on the Ban that took place whilst he was a student in University College Galway. The suggestion of the debate being conducted solely in Irish received the most vehement opposition from supporters of the Ban. Their 'thin skin of pretence came off – like so many tomatoes dipped in boiling water'.[38] On the one hand, the GAA was proclaiming it was at the vanguard in promoting an Irish-Ireland and, on the other, it was doing only a minimal amount to secure the Irish language as the primary language in the country, arguably the most important element of the Irish-Ireland movement. A former president of the GAA, Peter Quinn, admitted in 2002 that the GAA could have done more for the language saying that 'the GAA had never realised its potential … in relation to the Irish language'.[39]

Fr Mahon shared the views of most Roscommon GAA members who supported Hyde. Dan O'Rourke, renowned Roscommon footballer, Fianna Fáil TD and future president of the GAA, in his address as chairman of Roscommon GAA County Board, was critical of some actions of the Central Council, in particular on the extreme nature in how it dealt with Hyde, but supportive of the Ban and an expansion of additional bans, claiming the GAA would not be the power it was without the Ban.[40] O'Rourke conceded that more effort was needed to promote the Irish language and Irish dances, stating, 'Twenty or thirty years ago there was a much greater inclination for Irish dances and for speaking the Irish language outside the schools. I feel if we are to Gaelicise this country and bring about Pearse's ideals, Irish both free and Gaelic, there will have to be a greater effort to practise the language as well as Irish games.'[41] O'Rourke also emphasised the important role the GAA played in the national struggle for independence, making the bold claim (and demonstrating a rose-tinted view), 'that the majority of those who take part in the framing of the laws in this country, or in the fight for the freedom of this country, were members of the GAA or are to-day members of the GAA. I think the GAA has done a great deal for the freedom of this country.'[42] One commentator, in disagreeing with the GAA's decision on Hyde, questioned the GAA's lofty view on its past nationalist efforts, asking, 'Is it or is it not a fact that shortly before Easter Week, 1916, when the bravest hearts and brains in Ireland were thinking and plotting and planning the complete destruction of British rule and setting up of an Irish Republic the GAA Central Council of that time were sending a deputation to the British House of Commons and begging the British Chief Secretary to remove the entertainments tax on GAA games?'[43]

It was no surprise that Roscommon would be supportive of its most famous son – it was one of three counties that brought forward a motion to Annual Congress calling for the reinstatement of Hyde as patron.

Another county to do so was Mayo. At the Castlebar Mitchell GAA Club annual meeting (chaired by Eamon Mongey who would, years later, become one of the leaders of the anti-Ban movement led by Tom Woulfe),[44] the Castlebar Club annual meeting,[45] the East Mayo GAA Annual Convention,[46] the West Mayo GAA Annual Convention[47] and at the North Mayo GAA Annual Convention[48] there was widespread condemnation of the Central Council's act of removing Hyde as patron. It was mentioned at the Castlebar Club annual meeting that the Ban was 'a farce as far as 90 per cent of the Gaels were concerned'.[49] The North Mayo GAA Board 'decided that the Central Council should have asked President Hyde for an explanation of his attendance at the Ireland-Poland Association Football match in November, before removing his name from the roll of patrons'.[50] It was claimed that there were glaring inconsistencies in the GAA; on the one hand, the Central Council victimised Hyde, who had given his all for Ireland and, on the other, they ignored the flouting of the 'foreign dance' rule by allowing Gaelic football clubs to run 'foreign dances' throughout the country without making any effort to sanction such offenders. The men who made the decision to remove Hyde consistently claimed they were only doing what they had to do, to uphold the rules of the Association. Yet another rule was clearly being abused to add to the GAA coffers, and there is practically no evidence to suggest that anyone was suspended for organising a 'foreign dance'. To critics of the GAA and supporters alike, this was surely the most frustrating aspect of this sorry episode. The GAA was being disingenuous in proclaiming that anyone in breach of its rules would be punished. The North Mayo GAA Board also raised the issue of Hyde not being offered due diligence by the GAA.[51] Others suspended under the 'foreign games' rule were, at least, afforded the opportunity to defend themselves before a committee. There is little doubt that Hyde would not have availed of such a hearing, as it would have impacted upon the dignity of the office he held. He still should have been offered the same protocol if he was to be treated the same as everyone else. Based on the club board meetings held in Mayo leading up to the county convention, at that meeting, there was a unanimous resolution asking for the name of Hyde to be restored as patron.[52]

Motions dealing with the Hyde incident were also on the agenda at the Galway GAA County Convention.[53] No motion was passed calling for Hyde's reinstatement, not surprising considering it was a Galway motion at the Central Council meeting of 17 December which led to Hyde's removal in the first place, something, according to the *Connacht Tribune*, Galway GAA should not be very proud of.[54] At the Galway GAA County Convention, the chairman, Fr O'Dea, said that, 'the GAA were strong enough to ignore their enemies, but their greatest danger was from the disloyal critics within their own ranks' who were attacking the GAA in recent weeks for merely upholding the rules as they stood.[55]

At the Connacht GAA Annual Convention, held in Castlebar, County Mayo, on 26 February 1939, Patrick Kilduff was chairman. In his address, he condemned 'members of the Association who were not carrying out the rules – members who attended foreign games ... The foreign dance was another smaller menace and it was to be deplored that clubs were running dances.'[56] The *Roscommon Herald* reported Kilduff as also saying he 'deplored that Irishmen would allow themselves to have the filth of the foreigner fostered ... and urged that the Gaels of Connacht and Ireland to stand loyally together until they saw realised the unity of their country and the foreigners driven from their shores completely'.[57] There is no recording of any discussion at this provincial convention on Hyde or the motions put forward by the Roscommon and Mayo County Boards to have him reinstated as patron.

There was one contemporary incident that people from Connacht could have highlighted as almost a direct replica of the incident involving Hyde: the suspension of Garda Ormsby from the GAA for attending a soccer match in Sligo earlier in 1938 and his subsequent reinstatement once it was proven he had attended the match in his official capacity. The Ormsby Case demonstrated that there was precedence for people in an official capacity to attend 'foreign games' and not be subjected to Rule 27. Surely, Hyde should have fallen into this category too. The soccer match was the first occasion Hyde attended such an event, a 'foreign game'. He was the most recognisable Irish-Ireland advocate of all. In what other capacity would he have attended the match other than as President of Ireland? It is inexplicable that the GAA ignored this considering the amount of embarrassment the whole incident caused the Association. Both Ó Caoimh and McNamee expressed regret at having to remove Hyde as patron.[58] They also said they were left with little option. And yet, the Ormsby Case, an incident so glaringly similar and one that had been the cause of fractious debate within Connacht GAA at the start of 1938, one that made it as far as the Central Council to be ruled on,[59] just months before the Hyde incident, was not used as a perfectly acceptable precedent in allowing Hyde to remain as patron. What is almost as incredible is that, despite two letters to the *Irish Independent* in 1939 alluding to the similarity of the cases, almost no one seems to have put forward this argument at the time.[60] There seems to be little, if any, mention of the Ormsby Case and the obvious connection with the Hyde incident amongst GAA circles anywhere and particularly in Connacht where it was still a very raw issue.

Munster

In Munster there was also a large divide between those who supported and those who opposed the Central Council's decision. In Clare, the chairman of Clare GAA County Board, Monsignor Michael Hamilton, came out in favour of the Central Council's decision, saying that, although the GAA had been heavily criticised for removing Hyde, 'Perhaps every member of the GAA had more respect for that person that any of their critics, but the action they had taken was due to their adherence to the principles of the Gaelic movement.'[61] Monsignor Hamilton would later claim that de Valera and Kevin Barry were not 100 per cent Irishmen because they played 'foreign games'.[62] The GAA had even abandoned the idea, in 1923, of funding a memorial to the martyred Kevin Barry when it was realised he played rugby.[63] Clare brought forward a motion to Annual Congress, 'That the ban on foreign games be strictly enforced'.[64]

The Fianna Fáil cumann in Ennis expressed their disapproval at Hyde's removal.[65] It just so happened that Clare was the constituency of the Taoiseach, Éamon de Valera, and it would come as no surprise to many that such comments from the Fianna Fáil Ennis cumann were instigated by the former

Blackrock rugby player himself. In a letter to *The Irish Times*, a correspondent remarked that many members of Clare GAA were disgusted by the Central Council's decision, claiming that Hyde was 'gratuitously insulted'.[66] The same correspondent highlighted the stupidity of banning certain 'foreign games' without other games not originating in Ireland being banned also, such as golf and tennis. Only soccer, rugby, cricket and hockey were banned games. A GAA member could still play golf, even though it had been invented in Scotland, or tennis, which originated in France. Soccer, in particular, was seen as an international game as could be seen by the popularity of the French-founded soccer organisation, FIFA, which had fifty member countries. The GAA even helped to promote other sports originating outside of Ireland. A baseball game was played in Croke Park in 1948 even though baseball was founded in America. The irony was not lost on the *Nenagh Guardian* who said even Hyde, deep in retirement at the time, might be invited to the baseball game in Croke Park.[67] An American football game was held in Croke Park in 1953 in aid of the Irish Red Cross society.[68] There was also confusion from certain quarters in the GAA on which 'foreign games' were banned and which ones were not, with some believing golf was banned too.[69]

North Kerry called for the restoration of Hyde's name to the list of patrons of the GAA 'because of the sterling services rendered by Dr Hyde to the cultural advancement of Gaelic Ireland' and because Hyde as President would be expected to welcome foreign visitors to the country. Others made the point that Hyde could have welcomed the Polish team at Áras an Uachtaráin (in one letter, it was still called the Viceregal Lodge) without also attending the match and, in that way, he would not have offended the GAA.[70] It was decided to bring the motion to reinstate Hyde forward to the Kerry County Convention in Dingle,[71] but the motion did not make it any further.

The chairman of Waterford GAA County Board, M. V. O'Donoghue, supporting the Central Council, said: 'It was a thousand pities that Dr Hyde had allowed himself to be a pawn in a dirty game of political chess.' Gaels had learned, he concluded, from bitter experience to recognise desertion when they saw it. He called on Waterford Gaels to close their ranks and not to be sabotaged in their loyalty to the Gaelic creed.[72] There was also support for the Central Council in East Cork[73] and in North Cork.[74] One commentator derided the East Cork decision, saying it would 'make any Irishman with decent instincts burn with shame and indignation ... To ingratitude we add uncouthness and boorish behaviour. Even in the midst of the revered President's bereavement we must check the gracious impulse and emphasise our rudeness and injustice.'[75] At the Literary and Philosophical Society of University College Cork a motion was carried disapproving of the GAA's attitude towards Hyde. At the same debate, another motion was passed condemning Germany's treatment of Jews.[76]

At the Cork County Convention, the chairman, H. J. O'Mahony said:

> I hold there is every reason to be despondent when we find that we are asked to believe that, in order to prove to the world that the Irish people understand the laws of hospitality, it is necessary that a lifelong member of our Association should jeopardise his connection with it, and when we find that the head of this State is compelled to act in a manner which we hold to be a negation of all he stood for during his long and honourable career, truly we might exclaim: 'Something is rotten in the State of Denmark'.[77]

At the East Cork GAA convention held in Cloyne in January 1939, a number of references were made by some of the clergy present to the role of the Catholic Church within the GAA. One priest, Rev. T. O'Brien, said 'the national games ... formed a very important part in the Catholic Action movement in this country'.[78] Another clergyman, Canon O'Connell, the parish priest of Cloyne, commented on 'a deeper motive in the movement [the GAA] – the spirit of loyalty to the Church and the friendship with the clergy which the GAA had always fostered from the days of the Most Rev. Dr Croke'.[79] These comments were condemned by some observers, with one person stating, 'Religion in any sectarian sense ought never to be introduced in connection with the GAA any more than with the Gaelic League itself, or the Feis Ceoil'.[80] The GAA, from its outset, always saw itself as a non-sectarian body. One of its founding patrons was a Protestant, Charles Stewart Parnell. Douglas Hyde, of course, was also a Protestant. Historian John A. Murphy, in an article he wrote for *The Irish Times* marking the centenary of the GAA in 1984, questioned the decision to remove Hyde on sectarian lines. 'Was the GAA true to its non-sectarian constitution? Was it, in fact, the Catholic Church at play?'[81] It is true that the Catholic Church did play a large role in the GAA and the Association did not have a track record of attracting many Protestants to its folds. The question could also be asked, what Irish body did? Only a handful of Protestants have played Gaelic games, most famously Sam Maguire of Cork and London, after whom the All-Ireland senior football trophy is named. Prior to Jack Boothman of Wicklow becoming president in 1994, no Protestant had held senior office within the GAA and, in truth, little effort had been made to combat this.[82] The GAA honoured every Archbishop of Cashel after Croke and also made the Primate of Ireland, Cardinal MacRory patron of the GAA. In fact, Hyde was to be the last non-Catholic person to be made patron of the Association. The hierarchy of the clergy took pride of place at All-Ireland finals, as described by Murphy:

> It was on the GAA's great national occasion that the Catholic dimension was strikingly evident. In 1945, Bishop Browne of Galway spoke approvingly of All-Ireland days at Croke Park when 'a mighty concourse rises to honour Faith and Fatherland ... a spontaneous manifestation of the Irish traditional way in which

religion, nationality and life are in harmony.' On such occasions, church luminaries ranked as large in the protocol as state eminences. A special anthem greeted the Primate of All-Ireland: a soulful rendering of 'Faith of our Fathers' – ironically an English hymn – preceded the national anthem: and out on the pitch, captains and officials genuflected before bishops and annular osculations were performed.[83]

Special treatment for the clergy was not reserved for All-Ireland finals alone. Up and down the country the clergy were offered 'soft seats and great views' at matches they attended.[84] Prominent figures of the clergy were also awarded the honour of throwing in the ball at the start of each match. De Búrca claims that there was a marked increase in participation from the clergy from 1929 onwards with many priests being frequently elected to positions on county boards and provincial councils.[85] There is, however, little evidence to suggest that there was any sectarian link to the removal of Hyde. Although some members of the clergy were in favour of Hyde's removal, many others were outraged by the decision. No evidence exists to suggest that Hyde was removed as GAA patron because he was a Protestant or that the decision was approved by other members for sectarian reasons.

Tipperary was one county that had suffered more than most under the Ban. Only a few months earlier, Tipperary had been suspended from the Munster Hurling Championship for fielding James Cooney against Clare, thus disallowing them from defending their All-Ireland title from 1937.[86] Coupled with the Hyde incident, the Ban was a contentious topic during convention season in early 1939. At the West Tipperary GAA Convention, there was support for Hyde who 'had dedicated his whole life to the herculean task of resuscitating the soul of Ireland by saving the language ... to make "*Tír agus Teanga*" a glorious reality and not an empty shibboleth'. At the same meeting, the chairman expressed regret 'if the necessity arose to wound the heart of this fine old man in the evening, almost the night, of a life given unreservedly to Ireland'.[87] Archdeacon Slattery, parish priest of Nenagh, condemned the GAA for the insult thrust upon Hyde and suggested that GAA members in the future would find it difficult to hold government positions for fear of breaking the ban rules of the GAA.[88] The incident was also viewed at the Mid Tipperary GAA Convention as 'a chapter of history that is best forgotten'[89] with the chairman, Fr Fogarty, maintaining that the Ban 'is making the G.A.A. a source of humiliation for its friends and the laughing stock of its enemies'.[90] The *Nenagh Guardian*, in a reasonable article, stated the GAA Central Council, with the rule being what it was, had little choice but to remove Hyde. The paper called for a change, though, to the ban rules to exclude spectators from Rule 27.[91]

At the Tipperary GAA County Convention, there was a vigorous debate on the Ban with many people questioning the governance of the Ban as well as the 'stain of hypocrisy' of 'dances advertised under the name of the GAA and whist drives were being organised under the auspices of the GAA, all adherence to the foreign rule ... they inside in the ranks of the GAA were out for purity of purpose from the national point of view, and yet they allowed in foreign dances and games'.[92] Many members and people outside the Association claimed it was an open secret that many members were breaking the 'foreign games' rule on a regular basis, a point illustrated in Breandán Ó hEithir's memoir *Over The Bar*. He gave examples from his childhood of how schoolboys used pseudonyms when playing 'foreign games' to circumvent the ban rules.[93] He gave examples of pupils who went on to have sporting careers of distinction in both hurling and rugby who circumvented the Ban rule at school with the complicit help of their teachers, the Patrician Brothers, and played both native and 'foreign games' under different names. He also described how people looked to avoid members of the Vigilance Committees at 'foreign games' who were:

There trying to spot their straying sheep among the graceless goats. A peak cap pulled down over the eyes, a scarf worn high across the face, the loan of a friend's gaberdine or crombie over-coat, were some of the recommended disguises of the period for those who chose to run the gauntlet.[94]

The Central Council was being dishonest in saying no one in breach of the rules would go without sanction. This was simply not the case. Some believed the GAA did not apply the ban rules as rigorously on people they considered 'too important' for the Association. There has been a persistent rumour throughout the years that the legendary Limerick hurler Mick Mackey was a keen fan of rugby, like many fellow Limerick people. To sacrifice a pre-eminent player like Mackey to the Ban would damage the GAA, so it was allegedly decided to offer him a position on a Vigilance Committee. He was then allowed to attend rugby matches to 'spy' on GAA members to see if they also were attending 'foreign games' and contravening Rule 27, a job it is believed he did not carry out assiduously.[95]

The *Limerick Leader* embarked on a campaign to remove the Ban after Hyde was removed as patron, devoting a number of its editorials to the topic. Its centrepiece article was on the Ban for its issues of 19 December 1938,[96] 21 January 1939,[97] and on 28 January 1939.[98] It claimed the Ban was 'serving no useful purpose, as every intelligent and broadminded person knows'. It reserved unconditional condemnation for the way in which Hyde had been treated, calling it 'shameful and insulting'.[99] The *Limerick Leader* also felt that the Hyde incident had 'focussed a great deal of fresh attention on this whole question [the Ban]. From discussions all over the country it is quite clear that there is now among the rank and file of the Gaels a very large and steadily growing volume of opinion in favour of removing the Ban.'[100] The paper was attacked by Fr Michael Purthill, chairman of Limerick City GAA Board, who claimed that:

No one would dare to dictate to any powerful organisation what it should or should not do, especially if this organisation has shown over a long period of time that it has been successful. If any change in the rules is needed that change should come from the inside, and people not connected with the Association should be very slow to propose changes in its constitution or in its rules.[101]

In reply, the *Limerick Leader* lambasted Fr Purhill for his arrogance and the 'extraordinary claim that the GAA is above the people and should be altogether immune from their criticism'.[102] Others in Limerick reverted to the national card as the reason for keeping the Ban, with the chairman of South Limerick GAA claiming 'the day the ban on foreign games was lifted was the day their grand Association was gone. Their unity of purpose in that respect was the key of the golden storehouse of the Association' and if the Ban was removed, 'their own games would be swallowed up and the foreigner would turn around and sneer at them when they were gone'.[103] Motions were put forward at Knockainey GAA Club[104] and Ballingarry Club[105] expressing disapproval of the Central Council's decision to remove Hyde, and yet again, as with all counties in Munster, no motion got through the county convention in Limerick seeking Hyde's reinstatement as patron.

Leinster

The conventions in the counties of Leinster were to follow a similar trend to the conventions of Connacht and Munster, with opinions divided within the province. Kildare was one of three counties that put forward a motion calling for the restoration of Hyde as patron. It was believed by GAA members of Kildare that McNamee had acted too hastily and beyond his power in removing Hyde: Hyde was just showing courtesy to a foreign country; there was no more need for the Ban as 'there are no British soldiers in Ireland now'; and in any event over half the members of the GAA were not adhering to the ban rules. There were a few opinions supporting the Central Council saying they should stick by their leader, McNamee. On a whole, though, Kildare GAA was firmly of the viewpoint that Hyde had been wronged and supported the motion to restore him as patron.[106] In contrast, a similar motion to have Hyde reinstated was defeated at the Wexford GAA Convention on the basis that the Central Council had no intention of besmirching the name of Hyde but had no choice but to treat him as they would anyone else who broke the rules.[107] The Longford GAA County Board also supported the Central Council. The chairman, Fr McLoughlin, claimed that the GAA was a democratic organisation and the Central Council, which was representative of all members, was just carrying out its duties. One dissident at the Longford meeting said an exception should be made for the Head of State or even the mayor of a city.[108] The Lord Mayor of Drogheda, Alderman L. J. Walsh TD, at the Louth GAA Convention, blamed 'the hard and fast hidebound rules' of the Ban for the removal of Hyde and was in favour of removing the Ban. This was ruled out of order by the chairman as it was not on the agenda and not in good taste to pass a vote of censure on the Central Council. Walsh withdrew his remarks.[109]

There was no formal discussion on the Hyde incident at the Leinster GAA Annual Convention held on 18 February 1939. Offaly man Sean Robbins, president of the Leinster GAA Council, in a hard-hitting address at the convention, came down heavily in favour of the Central Council, of which he was a member, saying:

> For in these days of easy travelling, of cheap and appealing indoor entertainment in Cinemas and elsewhere, it is imperative on all who recognise the importance of a sound mind in a sound body to direct the minds of the youth of Ireland to the GAA playing fields, where they will play their own native games, and be taught to work

and labour for an Irish Ireland. For remember the work of nation building is just as urgent, if not more so, now than when Cusack called together Ireland's manhood under the GAA banner and made possible what took place in Easter in 1916. When we read about Ministers of State attending games played under foreign codes, and when we read all the excuses and flapdoodle about Irish hospitality and Irish courtesy, we are inclined to think that the present ideal is far from the high standard of a score of years or so ago. If those in high places were anxious to receive these people as distinguished visitors, they need not have gone to the playing grounds and throw their mantles of hospitality over them as exponents of foreign games ... Our games as well as our language and customs are part of the National heritage and must at all costs be jealously nursed and guarded.[110]

The removal of Hyde as patron caused intense debate within the GAA. It had been the main topic within GAA circles for months, with many high ranking GAA members fiercely opposed to the removal of Hyde. However, the more senior administration people within the Association and the chairmen and secretaries of county boards and provincial councils, in general, were fully behind the Central Council. Many of them had been in attendance at the meeting removing Hyde on 17 December 1938. They were firm advocates of the traditionalist stance that espoused the Irish-Ireland ideal. There was, therefore, little chance of any u-turn occurring at the Annual Congress, due to be held in April 1939.

14

Hyde's Removal Ratified

By the time of the GAA Annual Congress, held in City Hall, Dublin, on 9 and 10 April 1939, the story of Hyde being removed as patron had dominated the news for months. GAA conventions up and down the country were divided on the issue but it was clear that the general consensus amongst most counties was not to reverse the decision removing Hyde as patron.

The majority of the general public was opposed to the GAA's stance. The newspapers, by and large, whether provincial or national, were scathing of the GAA's decision and opinion pieces appeared regularly from December 1938 to April 1939 deriding the GAA. The letter pages followed the same trend. The main arguments used against the GAA were: Hyde as President of Ireland represented all of the people of Ireland and was duty bound to fraternise other sports, regardless of his personal views; Hyde was showing courtesy to a foreign nation; patrons were different to members and should not be subject to the same rules; the ban rules were antiquated and no longer needed in a country that had achieved independence; the ban rules should not apply to spectators; Hyde was there in his official capacity and should be treated like other officials, including gardaí, who were exempt from the Ban whilst on duty; the ban rules were sporadically administered, with many GAA members openly flouting them – particularly pronounced on the 'foreign dance' rule – and were not punished for doing so. There were also attacks on the GAA's strong Irish-Ireland rhetoric not being backed up by the reality; the most glaring example used was the paying of mere lip service by the GAA to the Irish language. It was suggested that Hyde should have been afforded the same opportunity to defend himself as other GAA members who were accused of breaking the ban rule. The overriding feeling was one of disgust and astonishment at the decision to remove a man such as Hyde, who had done more than anyone else for the Irish-Ireland movement. Only for Hyde, according to many, the GAA would not have survived its early turmoil. The manner in which his removal came about and was handled by the GAA left a lot to be desired. McNamee had blamed the press for making the Hyde incident an issue. On occasions, he had a point. *The Irish Times*, it could be argued, was being mischievous when, on 24 February 1939, it published a picture, taken some thirty years earlier, of de Valera in his Blackrock rugby jersey and mentioning that he would probably deputise for Hyde at an international rugby match the following day between Ireland and Scotland.[1] This picture would not have been a welcome sight for those GAA members who were pro-Ban. Some papers sympathised with the GAA, saying the Central Council had no choice but to remove Hyde. Pato, *The Irish Times* GAA columnist, claimed the debate on Hyde had been calm and orderly within the GAA and that there was no chance of cleavage, saying, 'It is clear that the vast majority of members and associates of the Gaelic Athletic Association have the highest regards for Dr Douglas Hyde, who has devoted his life to Gaelic culture. The rules on the official book are clear, and the Central Council rely on those rules in their action'.[2] It was also mentioned in the *Irish Press* when the 'Aryan Dr Hyde became, in the brief time of one football match, a most non-Aryan Mr Jekyll', the GAA 'acted in strict accordance with their written rules, which is praise-worthy'.[3] But such comments were rare and the press generally did not agree with the reasons offered by the GAA for its decision.

The primary argument used by the GAA was that it had no option but to remove Hyde. The rules applied to everyone, regardless of their position in the country. The Ban was sacrosanct in many people's eyes: without it, the GAA would not have been successful. To dilute the Ban in any way would weaken the Association as a result. Although most of Ireland had achieved a degree of independence, six counties still had not. Their right to practise Gaelic games was being jeopardised on a daily basis. And the rest of Ireland was as far away from the Irish-Ireland ideal as ever. Hyde had removed himself as patron by going to the soccer match. He did not have to go to the match to show courtesy, he could have received the Polish as guests at Áras an Uachtaráin.

Regardless of the arguments put forward by those supporting the Central Council or not, the men at the helm were in no mood to compromise by the time the Annual Congress came about. Some reasonable suggestions on how the GAA could have saved face and restored Hyde as patron were ignored. Instead, the GAA 'dug its heels in' and ratified its initial decision to remove Hyde as patron.

Pádraig Ó Caoimh, in his Secretary's Report to Congress, made an unbending speech highlighting his belief in the Irish-Ireland cause, a cause still very far from being achieved. He asserted:

> We have no desire to retain those whose allegiance to the games is failing or divided. The Gaelic Athletic Association was established to serve the manhood of this country who held all things belonging to Ireland first in their affections ... We are, therefore, under no obligation to compromise principle to suit external exigencies, nor to submit our policy to outside approval any more than we

are obliged to surrender the facilities and resources we have created to alien exploitation. And, above all else, we cannot betray the spirit of the founders of our movement and of those who brought the Organisation through years of adversity and distraction to strength and confidence. Some may think that, under altered conditions, we might dispense with proven safeguards as a gesture of good will. As ever before, this would be interpreted as a signal of distress. That is the lesson history has taught here and a lot more history will have to be made in Ireland before the lessons become out-dated or inapplicable. Where they offend against laws that are an essential part of the Gaelic code they cannot be tolerated. The continued success of the organisation depends upon an honourable fulfilment of the conditions of membership and resorts which seek to hold a privilege denied to others are particularly reprehensible. They strike at the balance of fair play which it is the duty of the Association to maintain and they are unworthy of Gaels. Nor will the enactment of prohibitions and obligations alone promote the cause of Gaelicism unless the rank and file realise that divided allegiance is no allegiance and that the restoration of the Gaelic State can never be assured until it is complete in every function and feature.[4]

We can see from these comments the mind of Ó Caoimh, a man of deep passionate beliefs, who felt he had a duty to uphold the traditions passed down to him since he became general secretary in 1929, a position he held with brilliant distinction until the day he died in 1964. His speech also demonstrates an unbending mind, one which believes compromise in any form is a sign of weakness. His speech was, ultimately, a defensive one, treating opponents of his views with disdain.

Pádraig McNamee's address was of a similar vein, strongly demonstrating his belief in the Association's right to have a ban and his quest for a 'Gaelic Front'. Commenting on the events arising from the removal of Hyde as patron, he conceded that the year had been a difficult one and that the Association had had more than its share of troubles. He also said it was a momentous one for the GAA with the Cusack Stand being opened and a record attendance at the All-Ireland football final highlighting its continued strength and popularity. He went on to say:

> During the year, our critics have been more than usually busy informing us of the best way to mind our own business. The suitable retort is so obvious that I refrain from making it. At the outset let me make it clear that this Association does not object to intelligent, constructive criticism, on the contrary we welcome it. There is no member so foolish as to claim that our organisation is perfect. County and Provincial Conventions and Annual Congress afford opportunities for healthy, helpful criticism … But what do we have to say to those arm-chair critics, who know what we need better than we know ourselves? They wish to direct our policy from without; let me tell them the policy in this Association is and will be directed only by its members through the Annual Congress. Change in rules can be made; any rule, even the 'ban' rules can be changed when the Gaels of Ireland so decide.[5]

Although this may have been technically true, the higher echelons within the Association did wield significant power. At County and Provincial Conventions and at Annual Congress, the chairmen were able to exert almost total control over proceedings. There certainly were democratic mechanisms within the GAA, more so than in many other organisations, but on many occasions too much reverence for the Central Council and the leading officials was shown by the rank and file members.

McNamee continued, 'It is not my intention to-day to defend the "ban", but it is my intention to defend our right to have a ban if we think it advisable', saying that anyone was entitled to have their opinion on the Ban, for or against. If someone joins the GAA, they are bound by its rules and must stick to them. In a clear attack on the international nature of soccer, McNamee asserted:

> The critics tell of a wonderful thing called 'internationalism' ... The people who talk of internationalism really mean Anglicism. They describe English games as international; they pander deliberately or unwittingly to England's superiority complex. They talk of 'bans', even English critics admit the superiority of hurling as a field game, but I wonder how many English colleges have introduced it as part of their athletic curriculum ... The too recent history of this country should teach Irishmen that we cannot afford to toy with any so-called 'international' but really anglicising influences.[6]

He also claimed he hoped for a day when there would be no bans because there would be no need for bans. He concluded by promoting a theme very close to his own heart, the quest for a truly Gaelic Ireland:

> On one point I agree with our critics, and that is when they say that we are intolerant. My only complaint is that we are not half intolerant enough. We and all Irishmen who value the inheritance of the Gael must always be intolerant of everything foreign in this country. We can never rest until the last vestige of foreign dominion is gone beyond recall ... It is my firm conviction that unless the old national spirit be re-awakened the struggle for the revival of the national language and the spread of our native culture is in very serious danger of failure. Government and government departments can help, but

only the united will of the nation can save the language of the Gael … I dream of the day when a 'Gaelic Front' will come into existence – a 'Front' consisting of a union of organisations, each looking after its own particular part of the Gaelic revival, and all united in the ultimate aim – 'A Gaelic Ireland'.[7]

McNamee, like Ó Caoimh, was a man of deep convictions and a man known for his eloquence; Hyde would have appreciated McNamee's communication skills. Both McNamee and Ó Caoimh, in this instance, showed an uncompromising side to their characters, men who had done so much to make the Association what it was and what it would become, although, in their treatment of Hyde, their strength had become their weakness by their unwillingness to concede they should have handled the episode differently.

At the Annual Congress there was a motion on the Irish language, so in order not 'to anticipate the decision of congress', McNamee decided not to speak on the subject during his address but he was not so impartial when it came to the motions on Hyde's reinstatement: 'The President said that there were three motions – Numbers 39 [from Roscommon], 40 [from Kildare] and 41 [from Mayo] [all looking to have the name of Hyde reinstated as patron] – on the Agenda which, in his opinion, were out of order. As long as the "Ban" remained in force no exception could be made. However, he would leave it to Congress to pass judgement'.[8] McNamee was clearly exercising his authority here by trying to have the three motions to restore Hyde removed from the agenda or, at the very least, voted on without debate.

As a result of this intervention by McNamee, the Mayo and Roscommon motions were withdrawn. Kildare still wanted its motion to be put to a vote, without a need for debate. 'On a vote being taken, 11 voted for the motion, 120 against and 5 delegates did not vote. The motion was therefore defeated.'[9]

And so it came to pass that any chance of the decision being reversed was lost and Hyde's connections with the GAA on a national level were severed for good. He still maintained, on a whole, cordial relationships with the GAA board of his home county of Roscommon, whose members had stood by him over his removal as GAA patron. He donated £1 in 1939 and again in 1941 towards the county team's training expenses,[10] as well as offering them his 'goodwill for their Connacht football final match against Galway'[11] in 1941. Even though Hyde was not particularly interested in Gaelic football as a spectacle, it could be safely assumed that he would have had a deep pang of regret for not being in attendance at Croke Park, as Head of State, to celebrate with the Roscommon team its finest hours of 1943 and 1944 when they won back-to-back All-Ireland football finals, a title that had eluded them beforehand and has done so ever since. There was an unwelcome incident during the build up to the 1943 final, though, involving Hyde and the Roscommon Men's Association who hosted a reception on behalf of the Roscommon Gaelic football team before their final against Cavan on 26 September.[12] They asked Hyde to make a donation to the reception. McDunphy replied on behalf of Hyde saying that whilst Hyde 'is naturally interested in anything that appertains to his native County the President does not think it necessary for him to be associated with the reception in question'.[13] At a subsequent meeting of the Roscommon Men's Association, a motion was passed expressing disappointment 'that the President, as a Roscommon man, could not see his way to meet the committee's wishes'.[14] This could be construed as a backlash by Hyde at the treatment he received from the GAA previously or, perhaps, a more likely reason could be that he genuinely felt it was not a worthy venture to be involved with.

Looking back on those extraordinary events in the cold light of time gone by, it is hard to comprehend how the GAA allowed itself to come to the position of removing Hyde as patron. Logic would have suggested that some form of compromise was required. Most of the reasonable arguments came from people supporting Hyde's reinstatement. He was President of Ireland; he had to attend other sporting events in his role. The GAA allowed gardaí to attend 'foreign games' in their official capacity, why not the President of Ireland? And not just any President but the person most associated with the Irish-Ireland movement since its inception as a concept, Douglas Hyde. One of the main defences of the decision was that the ban rules applied to everyone, and yet within the GAA it was accepted that the 'foreign dance' rule was being flagrantly violated without sanction. To inconsistency could be added hypocrisy. Highlighting this hypocrisy were events that happened at the Gaelic League Annual Convention at the same time. The Gaelic League, at its 1939 Annual Convention, re-imposed its bans on 'foreign dances and games', primarily due to pressure exerted on it by the GAA. At the same meeting, a resolution was put forward 'criticising the GAA for its foreign dances'.[15] In defence of the GAA, McNamee was meek in the extreme, saying they would do better to hold *céilithe*.

At the Annual Congress of 1939, Ó Caoimh and McNamee both took defensive stances in respect of Hyde's removal. There was no chance of them changing their minds based on the suggestions of 'outsiders'. It would mean that the GAA's relationship with the government would be severely strained for most of 'The Emergency' years of the Second World War: a resolution was not reached until 1945 when the GAA had to climb down in how it treated future Presidents on the Ban rule; an outcome all the more galling as it should never have come to such an impasse.

15

The GAA Versus the Government

The removal of Hyde as patron was not only a snub to Hyde himself: it was also a snub to the Fianna Fáil government and its leader Éamon de Valera, the man most responsible for the new constitution and bringing the Office of President into being. Hyde was accompanied by de Valera and other government representatives at the soccer match in November 1938. The relationship between the GAA and the government was certainly strained after the Hyde incident and this manifested itself in a number of ways.

In 1942, the GAA published a 130-page booklet entitled *National Action*, written by Joseph Hanly under the pseudonym Josephus Anelius.[1] Pádraig McNamee provided the foreword. It was a plan for National Recovery in Ireland, a New Departure. It advocated a cause very close to the hearts of people like McNamee and Ó Caoimh, an Irish-Ireland, strongly supporting the Irish language and Irish industry. Unsurprisingly, it also advocated the practicing of native games and dances.[2] The author of the book received no profits from sales of the book; funds were donated to the Irish-Ireland movement.[3] In the book it states:

> The object of the work is to formulate, in outline, a plan for National Government for this country, together with

revised or reorganised public systems and services ... The factors which are introduced should be sufficient to show that our present major systems are unsound, that from them there is little hope of either good or great results, and that they must, therefore, be radically revised.[4]

It was also stated in the booklet:

Our duty now, and our only hope for a national future, lies in making Ireland once again, not only free but Gaelic, not only Gaelic but a missionary power and example of practical Christianity in the only way that twentieth century scepticism will heed it – a successful example of an exemplary Christian State ... Will it continue on its downward course, through national idleness, foreign imitation and social slavery, towards inevitable national defeat?[5]

The controversial work was clearly in opposition to the current government. It was looking to tear down the structures of the day. It advocated a single party regime as a form of government.[6] This was at a time when the world was engulfed in its most deadly of wars, a war dominated by countries with single party models on the lines of fascism or communism. Due to its belief that party politics proved a failure, the booklet recommended two alternative systems of government; a dictatorship or a national government. The author clearly favours the national government model with officials elected directly by the people of Ireland and parish guilds and councils providing the opposition such a system would need,[7] believing a dictator could easily become a tyrant.[8] The author looked to Portugal as an ideal model to follow – António de Oliveira Salazar, the country's leader at the time, had removed political parties and created his own authoritarian *Estado Novo* (New State) – 'With faith, courage, common sense, and the backing of his people, who understood him, because he was simple and sincere, his plan worked like magic. As a result, Portugal is to-day an example to Europe of nationalism based on Christian Social Teaching put to the test, and not found wanting.'[9] Admittedly without the benefit of historical perspective, the author was recommending a state that had more in common with fascism than with democracy, a state that was seen as one of the poorest in Europe and which, through its secret police, was repressive of all opposition. The booklet did offer some worthwhile solutions too, particularly in the areas of Irish industry and the revival of the Irish language, suggesting economic activity should be focussed in Gaeltacht areas and more emphasis should be placed on oral testing during examinations, as well as teaching the spoken word as opposed to learning by 'the book'.[10]

The GAA publicly declared itself as a non-political body. Based on past actions and with its belief in its important role in the national rejuvenation of the country, this was something people viewed with a high degree of scepticism. With the publication of this book by the GAA with its apparent promotion of a national government political system along the lines of totalitarian states, the facade of non-political involvement was blown away completely. This fact was raised by Dan O'Rourke, a Fianna Fáil TD from Roscommon and future president of the GAA, at the GAA Annual Congress of 1943. O'Rourke, quoted in *The Irish Times*, said that the preface to *National Action* was 'by the president of the GAA. The fact of the matter was that it was nothing if not political. It was published under the auspices of the Central Council. He found that it proposed to abolish the old party system and substitute a one party … It was a serious matter that it should emanate from the Gaelic Athletic Association as representing their views. They were on very dangerous ground.'[11] McNamee claimed there was nothing untoward with the GAA's engagement with the book; it had come before the Central Council in the usual way. He was unwilling to disclose the author's name, other than to say he was involved in national

Dan O'Rourke, GAA president from 1946–1949, was also a Fianna Fáil TD. O'Rourke found his loyalties were divided on more than one occasion during the Second World War when the relationship between the GAA and the Irish government was severely strained. *(Courtesy of the GAA Museum, Croke Park)*

and Irish-Ireland affairs, prompting *The Irish Times* to call it a 'mysterious publication'.[12] McNamee, incredibly, asserted that, 'there was nothing political in the book. It did not want to abolish all political parties: but he did not think that it was politics to abolish the whole lot. It seemed to him that it was a plan for a national reconstruction on national lines, and the new government was to be non-political.'[13] For McNamee to state that there was nothing political in the booklet is an astounding statement. *National Action* was a political manifesto condemning the current system of government as a failed entity. It advocated a new system along the lines of McNamee's and O'Caoimh's dream, an Irish-Ireland. The GAA's previous cordial relationship with politicians had been sorely tested over Hyde's removal as GAA patron; this was an outright attack by the GAA on everything those politicians stood for. O'Rourke was correct when he said the GAA was entering dangerous territory.

Pádraig Ó Caoimh also justified the GAA's publication of the book, stating, 'That, before the book was published' he 'consulted the heads of the Church and colleges, and he got their approval'. He claimed the book 'gives a survey of the plan of campaign necessary in the reconstruction of a Gaelic Ireland. The reception given to it by the Press, as well as the demand for it by the public, has justified our venture.'[14] The booklet was a success, selling over 100,000 copies in its first year of publication.[15] Ó Caoimh and McNamee deserve to be admired for their tenacious and passionate belief in everything Gaelic. There is no doubt that they genuinely believed this Gaelic Ireland they cared for so deeply was being compromised by all around them, including by the politicians of the day, driving them to take drastic actions to halt the move away from Ireland's Gaelic past and towards a nation inherently anglicised and internationalised. To say that they were not involving themselves or the body they represented, the GAA, in politics, was an absurd comment to make. They conceded this at a later date when they agreed the publication of *National Action* was in breach of the GAA Constitutional commitment to non-involvement in politics.[16]

The views expressed in *National Action* were very similar, in many ways, to a new right-wing fascist movement spawned from a branch of the Gaelic League. The branch, known as Craobh na hAiséirghe (Branch of the Resurrection), was founded in 1940 by a former civil servant, Gearóid Ó Cuinneagáin. Ó Cuinneagáin had been active in the pro-Nazi organisation, the Friends of Germany, before that body was disintegrated after some of its leading members were interned.[17] He planned for Craobh na hAiséirghe to become a 'Hitler Youth Movement' and eventually to take over the whole of the Gaelic League.[18] Between 1,200 and 1,500 people became members of the branch but Ó Cuinneagáin was unsuccessful in his bid to take over the entire Gaelic League. He left Craobh na hAiséirghe and then founded a political party, Ailtirí na hAiséirghe (Architects of the Resurrection) in 1942. Ailtirí na hAiséirghe was an extreme right-wing movement that called for the:

> Creation of a one party system, with all power in the hands of a Ceannaire, or 'Leader', for a period of seven years in the first instance. Aiséirghe promised full employment to all citizens; an end to emigration (by the straightforward if draconian means of making it a criminal offence to leave the country); a massive state-directed economic expansion scheme; discrimination against Jews and freemasons; and the reconquest [sic] of Northern Ireland by the massive conscript army Ó Cuinneagáin proposed to build. Lastly, Irish would be restored as the national vernacular. Five years after the accession to power of an Aiséirghe régime, the use of the English language in public was to become unlawful.[19]

Ailtirí na hAiséirghe aspired to create a Gaelic Christian Corporatist State along the lines of Salazar's regime in Portugal. The countrywide adoption of the Irish language was central to its plans, 'Irish would protect the people against insidious

J. J. Walsh, seated third from right, at the unveiling of a memorial to Sam Maguire in Dunmanway, County Cork, in 1941. Former cabinet minister and businessman, Walsh was an active member of the GAA. He opposed Hyde's attendance at a rugby match in 1940. He was also a supporter of the far right political party, Ailtiri na hAiséirghe. *(Courtesy of the Irish Examiner)*

modern ideas: "The importance of the national language as a shield against modern material and atheistic cultural influences is obvious. We shall be most Christian when most Gaelic.'"[20] Ó Cuinneagáin claimed that under his leadership Ireland would become the 'Mistress of the Atlantic' and the 'Masters in the Pacific'[21] and would 'settle the affairs of the universe for another 2,000 years'.[22] Ailtirí na hAiséirghe's solution to partition was best summed up with one of its more well known slogans, 'Six Counties, Six Divisions, Six Minutes'.[23]

The Irish electorate were not captivated by Ó Cuinneagáin's lofty ambitions and in the general elections of 1943 and 1944, all of the Ailtirí na hAiséirghe candidates lost their deposits, finishing last on the ballot paper in many cases.[24] Despite the extreme nature of its programme, Ailtirí na hAiséirghe did attract some prominent supporters. Ernest Blythe, the finance minister during the Cumann na nGaedhael governments from 1922 to 1932, gave his backing, as did future Ceann Comhairle of Dáil Éireann, Sean Treacy who started his political career with Ailtirí na hAiséirghe.[25] Its main mouthpiece in the Dáil was independent TD from Laois-Offaly, Oliver J. Flanagan who supplied the party with 'blank parliamentary question forms to enable Aiséirghe to quiz the government in Flanagan's name and intervened with ministers to secure permission for the launch of the party newspaper'.[26] Flanagan held deep anti-Semitic views and notoriously claimed in the Dáil in July 1943, 'There is one thing that Germany did, and that was to rout the Jews out of their country. Until we rout the Jews out of this country it does not matter a hair's breadth what orders you make. Where the bees are there is the honey, and where the Jews are there is the money.'[27]

Ailtirí na hAiséirghe also had links with some GAA figures. One of its candidates in the 1944 general election was Willie Walsh, a GAA official and referee, who stood in the constituency of Waterford.[28] Occasionally, events organised by the Ailtirí na hAiséirghe were held on GAA grounds, including an event, entitled 'An Aeridheacht Mhor', held in O'Growney GAA Park in Athboy, County Meath, in August 1943, that included a challenge hurling match.[29] J. J. Walsh, who played a significant role in building the GAA in his native Cork and had served as a Cumann na nGaedhael Minister for Posts and Telegraphs before forging out a successful career as a businessman,[30] was responsible for providing much needed funding for Ailtirí na hAiséirghe. He provided the money and the offices for the publication of *Aiséirghe 1942*, a manifesto for the party,[31] and he covered many of the election deposits for the party for the 1944 general election.[32] Other than a few examples of involvement from GAA members, the evidence would suggest that the GAA was as unconvinced as everyone else on the merits of Ailtirí na hAiséirghe and provided it with little support.

The Annual Congress of 1943 unquestionably had the GAA's relationship with the government at the heart of its programme. As well as the discussion on the GAA's sponsorship of *National Action*, there was a debate on the pastimes enjoyed by the national army that would cause a clearer divide between the government and the GAA. It would lead to open and public hostility between the two for some time. Former soccer player Oscar Traynor was at the centre of the dispute. It was believed by the GAA that Traynor, as Minister for Defence, instructed the army to open itself up to sports other than Gaelic games early in 1943, a move which naturally received the wrath of the GAA. Since the foundation of the State in 1922 Gaelic games were the only sports approved to be played by soldiers in the Irish army. If soldiers or officers did play other games, they did not receive compensation if they got injured whilst playing and they also had to pay personally for whatever equipment they required to participate in those 'foreign games'; Gaelic games equipment was fully provided for by the army and injured players received full payment whilst out of action.[33] There had been a motion put before the Irish Free State Army Athletic Association in 1923 to allow non-Gaelic games in the army but this was defeated.[34] Considering Traynor's history with soccer, it is no surprise that he would make such a move to open the army to other sports. Traynor, who was deeply passionate about soccer as well as the national cause he had played such a prominent role in, was incensed at the allegation that people playing 'foreign games' were, in any way, not 100 per cent Irishmen. He made a vigorous defence of his actions along with a scathing attack on the GAA at the Fianna Fáil Árd Fhéis of 1943, stating:

> The attitude of the GAA, in my view … is a partition of this section of our people – it is an attempt to divide one section of the people against the other. The man who plays these so-called foreign games is as much entitled to justice as anyone else. And, they are not foreign games,

inasmuch as the game to which I believe the GAA offers the strongest opposition is a game that came from the Highlands of Scotland – a Gaelic game. No one is going to tell me that Gaelic football is a purely national game; it is a composite of a number of types of football. I have done nothing that I have to apologise to any man in this nation for. I have righted what I have deemed to be an injustice, and wherever I meet injustice I will always try to right it … We want our people united, not alone in national matters, but in their ordinary lives and recreation as well.[35]

At the 1943 GAA Annual Congress, outgoing GAA president, McNamee, commented:

That [we], as an Association, did not and never had denied the right of any citizen, least of all of any soldier, to play the game of his choice. But [we] most emphatically [hold] that the policy of putting foreign games on the same status as Gaelic games in the Army was a nationally retrograde step. [Our] games, historically, [are] a part of [our] national heritage and, as such, [are] to be guarded as jealously as [our] national flag.[36]

McNamee had served for five years as president instead of the standard three. He had been unanimously re-elected in 1941 and 1942 due to the Second World War and the symbolism of having an Ulsterman at the helm of the GAA was believed to help towards national reintegration.[37] The consensus within the GAA was also that McNamee, the man who had to deal with the testing Hyde incident, had done an exceptional job as president, with the succeeding president, Seamus Gardiner, claiming 'McNamee was one of the greatest presidents the Association had known'.[38]

Ó Caoimh, at the same meeting, also condemned the new army policy saying, 'It was not merely a sabotage of the GAA but a national betrayal and a nullification of the recognised ideals of Irish-Ireland'.[39] Another delegate was vociferous in his attacks on those seen as responsible for the decision, saying, 'Two men were responsible – the Taoiseach and the Minister for Defence. The Central Council should decide on appropriate action. These people had been received with all honours at Croke Park. The question of refusing to associate or co-operate with them should be left to the Council.'[40] It was believed by many GAA members that members of the government were trying to kill off Gaelic games by this action. Vincent O'Donoghue from Waterford, and future president of the GAA, alleged, 'The question of foreign games in the army was part of the "general offensive" and [I believe] that it was not unconnected with the attack on the Irish-Ireland movement that caused scenes and a riot outside Earlsfort terrace'.[41] There were calls for the GAA to make the reimposition of solely Gaelic games in the army an issue for the upcoming general election.[42] Another delegate suggested a similar solution to the one the GAA used in dealing with Hyde in 1938, remarking, 'They had some years ago; with a much bigger figure than Mr Traynor, shown their disapproval by withdrawing his name as one of the patrons of the Association. They should show their disapproval of Mr Traynor entering Croke Park; if he had any sense of decency, he would not appear there at all.'[43] There were also calls for de Valera to remove Traynor from office for his betrayal of the ideals of the Irish-Ireland cause. At the same Annual Congress, there was mention of government grants being denied to GAA sports fields where 'foreign games' were not permitted on their grounds, a clear indication of a government putting pressure on the GAA for continuing with its Ban.[44] There were some dissenting voices to the GAA's stance on the army decision with one man in particular voicing his support for the government: Dan O'Rourke. O'Rourke must have found his loyalties to two bodies of which he was a member tested severely. O'Rourke who, as well as being a senior GAA figure, was a Fianna Fáil TD, was dismayed by the

Éamon de Valera at the 1941 All-Ireland hurling final between Cork and Dublin. De Valera believed that rugby and hurling were the two games best suited to the Irish temperament. An opponent of the Ban, he believed it was preventing the 'great national game of hurling' being adopted throughout many schools and colleges. *(Courtesy of the* Irish Examiner*)*

disintegration of the relationship between the GAA and Fianna Fáil, which in many ways had been instigated by the removal of Hyde as patron in 1938. During the debate on the games played by the army, he highlighted the unfairness of injured army personnel not being compensated if they played 'foreign games' instead of Gaelic games.[45] At the same Annual Congress, O'Rourke was defeated by Gardiner for the position of president. One of the reasons cited by O'Rourke for his loss was 'forces at work against the election as president of a member of the Dáil'.[46] This would be remedied when he succeeded Gardiner as president in 1946; his election was, no doubt, helped by the improvement of the relationship between Fianna Fáil and the GAA after de Valera's intervention in 1945.

Calls by the GAA for the action to be reversed were ignored by the army:'The Army authorities cannot accept interference by outside bodies in a matter of Army administration'.[47] A spokesman for the army asserted that the army was 'not prepared to give privilege to any game, and their policy is to afford facilities to all sports and games, provided they are of military value'. On O'Caoimh's allegation that it was a betrayal of the Irish-Ireland ideal to allow 'foreign games' in the army, it was stated, 'The fact that a considerable number of keen participants and supporters of these games were patriotic enough to offer their services to the nation at a time of grave national danger is an effective answer to this absurd allegation'.[48]

At the same Fianna Fáil Árd Fhéis where Traynor defended the army's decision to give equal status to 'foreign games', the Taoiseach Éamon de Valera defended his Defence minister, agreeing with him wholeheartedly. In an open attack on the Ban, he claimed the GAA did have pride of place in the army, as it did throughout the country and 'the national sports, if they are fit to survive, will survive and will get the support they deserve, and we do not need the narrow methods which had to be used in the past'.[49] He believed the Ban was preventing the 'great national game of hurling' from being adopted throughout many schools and colleges. De Valera made no mention of Gaelic football, a game he had no real interest in, believing rugby and hurling were the two games best suited to the Irish temperament. Continuing his attack on the Ban, he thought:

> [...] the GAA were making a mistake: that there was an attitude of mind continued on from a period in which the conditions were different. It was an awful mistake from a national point of view that this should be continued. It would be just as reasonable to have an organisation for the protection of Catholic interests, where 93 p.c. were Catholics. What the Minister had done in the Army should be supported by every right-thinking person.[50]

This was also an attack on secretive Catholic organisations such as the Knights of Saint Columbanus.[51] It was not the first time that de Valera had expressed views that appeared to be anti-Ban. In 1931, during a debate in the Dáil on an entertainments tax bill, de Valera remarked that all sports should be exempt from taxes, not just Gaelic games.[52] His attendance at the soccer match between Ireland and Poland in November 1938 was also an indication of his anti-Ban sentiments. He was further embroiled in controversy with the GAA in 1957 by declaring that he was against the Ban rule and had always been of that opinion.[53] At the same time he disclosed his preference for rugby over Gaelic football, stating, 'For Irishmen there is no football game to match rugby and if all our young men played rugby not only would we beat England and Wales, but France and the whole lot of them together'.[54] His biggest disagreement with the GAA was directly linked to the removal of Hyde as patron. In 1945, he intervened to make sure such an incident would never happen again. By this time, Sean T. O'Kelly had succeeded Hyde as President.

16

The GAA Completes a U-Turn

Douglas Hyde 'was not invited to, and was not present at the Senior Hurling Final between Cork and Kilkenny which took place at Croke Park on Sunday 3rd September, 1939',[1] a hurling final that went down in history as the 'Thunder and Lightning' final, played on the same day the Second World War broke out. Kilkenny won the match, an excellent spectacle, despite the conditions – it was played amid thunder, lightning and a severe downpour for the last twenty minutes of the match.[2] Hyde would not attend another GAA event as President.

President Hyde was invited by the IRFU to a rugby international held on 25 February 1939. He declined 'owing to his recent bereavement' but did add the caveat 'that he hopes to be present at a later date at an international fixture under the auspices of your Union'. After the death of his wife, Lucy, Hyde observed a period of three months of mourning. In that time, he held just one function, a reception for 300 children competing in a Gaelic Drama Festival in March 1939.[3] He did attend a charity rugby match between Ireland XV and The Rest of Ireland in Lansdowne Road on 10 February 1940[4] where he received a 'rousing reception' when he greeted both teams.[5] This met with the disapproval of ex-minster and businessman, J. J. Walsh who was perturbed by the

Programme cover for the 1939 All-Ireland hurling final between Cork and Kilkenny. Douglas Hyde was not invited to the final that went down in history as the 'Thunder and Lightning' final, played on Sunday 3 September 1939, the same day the Second World War broke out. *(Courtesy of the GAA Museum, Croke Park)*

President's attendance at what he viewed as a 'foreign game'.[6] On a point of principle he declined future invitations from the President as a result.[7] This stance changed, however, perhaps due to the President's Office setting up a meeting between Walsh and a French delegation interested in 'the development of Irish industries including the manufacture of electric light bulbs' in 1941.[8] Walsh was chairman of light bulb company Solus Teoranta. Walsh claimed that, 'with the passing of time he had changed his views and that in future he would be honoured to receive an invitation from the President'.[9]

Hyde's movements were seriously curtailed in April 1940 when he suffered a stroke. Initially his right hand, arm and leg were paralysed and, for a number of months, he was confined to his bed.[10] Gradually he improved, albeit confined to a wheelchair for the rest of his life. This was distressing for Hyde who, up to that point, had enjoyed an active life outdoors. As President, he was still a regular hunter, had ordered a boat to go fishing for pike in the lake near Áras an Uachtaráin and even had a golf course laid out at the presidential residence.[11]

Hyde decided to retire in 1945 after his term was up instead of seeking another seven years as was suggested to him at the time, declining to put his name forward again because he was eighty-five years of age and he believed it would be best if someone else was given the opportunity to shape the role of President.[12] He was succeeded by Sean T. O'Kelly. O'Kelly was a Fianna Fáil stalwart who had served as Tánaiste and Minister for Finance. In contrast, Hyde had been elected as President in 1938 precisely because he was above politics. O'Kelly had to fight an election where he defeated General Sean MacEoin, who was backed by the main opposition party, Fine Gael, and Dr Patrick McCartan, an independent candidate. O'Kelly won comfortably, receiving almost 50 per cent of the first preference vote.[13]

When O'Kelly took up his role as President in 1945, Seamus Gardiner, president of the GAA, 'thought it advisable that he would make a courtesy call on the President of Ireland'.[14] This was the first time there had been communication between the President's Office and the GAA since 1938. The GAA heard nothing until they were contacted by de Valera who 'asked that himself [Gardiner] and the General Secretary [Ó Caoimh] would call to see him'.[15] At the meeting the Taoiseach:

> Explained that the President could not ignore the slight which had been offered to Dr Hyde by the G.A.A. in December, 1938 when he was removed from his position as patron of that body and in view of what happened then it was essential that precautions should be taken now to avoid doing anything which might have embarrassing consequences as regards the future relations between the President and the G.A.A. In the case of Dr Hyde the Taoiseach said that when he entered upon his office and his name was being continued as a patron of the G.A.A. his permission should first have been sought and his attention drawn to the possible implications of 'foreign games' rule, if that rule was to apply to him. If this had been done in all probability Dr Hyde would have asked that he should be no longer continued as a patron of the G.A.A. and the unfortunate incident of December, 1938, would never have occurred.[16]

De Valera remarked that he believed patrons were different to members and should not be bound by the 'foreign games' ban rule. He also expressed the view that the President should be invited to important GAA events, regardless of whether he attended other sporting functions, saying: 'the GAA must understand, however, that the President is President of all sections of the community and cannot in any circumstances put himself in such a position as to seem, by implication or otherwise, to discriminate against any section of the community'.[17] He continued by stating that an acceptance by the President to attend any GAA event in the future was based on the understanding that in no way did the President condone the actions taken against Hyde in 1938 and would not restrict the President to accepting invitations to any athletic and sporting bodies in the future. He concluded by requesting that GAA members not publicly criticise the President in the future on related matters. The GAA representatives agreed that the Hyde incident was unfortunate but they claimed it was as much the President's advisers fault as it was theirs for not bringing to the attention of Hyde the possible implications as patron of the GAA. They agreed to convene a meeting of the Central Council to discuss de Valera's proposals and to revert back once the Central Council had reached a decision.[18]

At a Special Central Council Meeting of the GAA held on 17 August 1945 to discuss the meeting with the Taoiseach, it was agreed unanimously not to discuss the issue with the press, for silence to be maintained on the contents of that meeting. This was proposed by Pádraig McNamee. The following motion was passed:

> That the present Central Council accepts the principle embodied in the above memorandum that representatives of a national organisation such as the G.A.A. should be received by the President and that he should be invited to its principal functions such as the All-Ireland Finals. The President is President of all sections of the community and cannot in any circumstances put himself in such a position as to seem, by implication or otherwise, to discriminate against any section of the community.[19]

The Central Council added that they were speaking on behalf of the existing Central Council and future councils would have the authority to change their ruling, if they were to see fit. They could not agree with de Valera on his other point, related to GAA members criticising the President. As a democratic body, members had a right to air their views on the President or anyone else for that matter. This was relayed to the Taoiseach in a subsequent meeting. De Valera expressed

At his inauguration in 1938, Douglas Hyde (centre, in coat tails) is accompanied by two future Presidents of Ireland, Sean T. O'Kelly (third from left) and Éamon de Valera (fourth from left). O'Kelly and de Valera's intervention with the GAA in 1945 ensured that no future President would suffer the same fate as Hyde for attendance at a 'foreign game'. *(Courtesy of the National Library of Ireland)*

his hope that decisions would be made in a calm atmosphere and not based on an incident by incident basis. He told the GAA delegation that he would relay the message to O'Kelly who, if interested, would attend GAA events in 'state and should be received accordingly'. Ó Caoimh declared he would make sure the appropriate preparations were made befitting the Office of President.[20] The meetings between de Valera and the GAA in 1945 demonstrated the depth of feelings the government had regarding the whole affair involving Hyde. De Valera was determined that such an incident would never happen again. It was an embarrassing episode for both the GAA and the new Office of President. The willingness of the GAA to agree so readily to de Valera's primary request was the first clear indication from the GAA that it had acted imprudently. To say the President's Office was as much to blame as the GAA was a weak argument that attempted to take responsibility away from the GAA. De Valera was also entitled to be disappointed by the GAA in just making a decision for its current Central Council only and not future ones. Although no similar incident was to happen in the future, a non-binding commitment left the possibility that such an incident could occur again. The GAA was right, though, in not agreeing to de Valera's request that no GAA member be allowed to criticise the President's status regarding the Ban. Such an action would have undermined the democratic structures within the Association. Considering the trenchant outlook the GAA had taken when Hyde attended the soccer match in November 1938, and the absolute refusal of McNamee and Ó Caoimh to show flexibility in any way towards Hyde at that time puts this u-turn into perspective. It also makes it all the more frustrating that common sense did not prevail within the ranks of the GAA in 1938. Accepting that the President should be allowed to attend events organised under the auspices of 'foreign games' had been an acknow-ledgement by the GAA that it was wrong in the action it took against Hyde in 1938. The GAA had been offered a golden opportunity by the new President and the government to extract itself from similarly awkward episodes in the future; it was also allowed to do so discreetly, without any public humiliation. For this, de Valera and O'Kelly deserve to be commended and it did lead to a marked improvement in relations between the GAA and the government.

As a result of the meetings between the GAA and de Valera, President Sean T. O'Kelly decided to go to the All-Ireland hurling final between Tipperary and Kilkenny, held on 2 September 1945. He would also attend the All-Ireland football final that same year. This was considered by McDunphy as 'the renewal of friendly relations between the President of the country and the GAA'.[21]

Former President of Ireland Mary McAleese greets the Kilkenny team before the start of the 2009 All-Ireland hurling final. Today the President takes pride of place at every All-Ireland hurling and football final and is greeted with the 'Presidential Salute' before meeting the teams before the matches start.
(Courtesy of the GAA Museum, Croke Park)

The President, who had a motor cycle squadron as escort, was greeted with a fanfare of trumpets by buglers of the Artane Band and then was accorded the 'Presidential Salute.' He was escorted to his seat by Mr Seamus Gardiner, president of the GAA, Pádraig Mac Con Midhe (McNamee) and Fr MacGouran of the Colleges Council. The President was given a warm welcome on his arrival and, as he walked across the field at the head of the party, was cheered from every part of the densely crowded grounds. An Taoiseach was also given a hearty ovation.[22]

The President expressed to his secretary, Michael McDunphy, 'that he was quite satisfied with the manner in which he was received at the Match'.[23] McDunphy, however, was not. 'The accommodation for the President was not satisfactory. As far as visibility was concerned there was no objection, but there was no special enclosure and no privacy. I have suggested to the

President, and he agrees, that representations should be made to the G.A.A. to have proper accommodation in future, without, however, appearing to be pressing unduly on his behalf'.[24] When he put the issue to Pádraig Ó Caoimh, McDunphy 'gathered the impression that he [Ó Caoimh] was more anxious to stress the difficulties than to concern himself with finding a solution. I told him what was being done by the Rugby Union and by the Association Football Union in this regard, and suggested that the G.A.A. would not like to be regarded as less willing to show proper courtesies to the Head of the State than bodies which did not lay claim to such high national aims as the G.A.A. This seemed to put him more on his mettle and he promised to give the matter immediate attention.'[25] Ó Caoimh even promised to have a Presidential Stand erected in Croke Park, something that never came to fruition.[26] In fact, very little was done to improve the accommodation for the President for a number of years after, and it was still being raised as an issue by McDunphy in 1954.[27] Relations had improved, though, by 1959 between the GAA and the President's Office with O'Kelly, in one of his last duties as President (he served for two terms), providing a speech at the official opening of the new Hogan Stand in June 1959 where his praise for the GAA and Ó Caoimh in particular was fulsome, remarking 'a more rapid progress has been a noticeable feature of the history of the GAA since the first day that Pádraig Ó Caoimh became General Secretary of the organisation'.[28] Echoing sentiments his predecessor, Hyde, would have concurred with, O'Kelly claimed:

These founders of the GAA surely had in mind and desired to encourage and promote the growth – the rebirth, as it were of Gaelic Ireland. They were inspired by the same ideals as were those who later founded the Gaelic League. The spirit and the Irish Ireland principles which inspired these two organisations is the spirit which brought us a free Ireland. Without the work of these two organisations the Irish Republic, now existing thank God, would, I believe, scarcely have been a possibility in our time.[29]

Today the President takes pride of place at every All-Ireland hurling and football final, with the 'Presidential Salute' being played upon arrival, followed by the greeting of the teams before battle commences.

The new arrangement between the GAA Central Council and the President's Office was not well received by everyone within the GAA. Wexford GAA County Board decided to boycott the President on a trip he made to Wexford for attending 'foreign games' in May 1946.[30] Before the All-Ireland football final of 1946, a note was sent to the President's Office of a rumour that the Kerry team 'intended to stage a demonstration against the President at that Match at which he would be present. The demonstration would take the form of a refusal to go on the field, or if they were on the field when he arrived, to walk off. The object of the demonstration apparently was to protest against the President's attendance at Rugby and Association Football Matches.' It was also believed that there was a 'certain amount of resentment in Gaelic circles because of the fact that while members of the teams were presented to the President at Rugby and Association Football Matches at which he was present, this was not done at Hurling Matches under the auspices of the GAA'.[31] The President decided to go to the match in any event, and if a protest was to transpire he planned on quietly retiring from the match to be followed by members of the government. McDunphy requested that the government should intervene to ensure nothing unseemly be broadcast in the event of any protest.[32] The threat, however, never materialised. There was a protest at the match, though, with almost a hundred teachers invading the pitch at half time, bearing placards and inscribed bannerettes looking for support for their strike.[33] At the Dublin GAA County Board Convention of 1954, there was a motion put down: 'criticising the Central

Council for inviting to and officially receiving at Croke Park any person who officiates at functions organised by bodies promoting foreign games'.[34] At the meeting one person said: 'We suspended one President – I do not see why we should not suspend another if he has not abided by the rules of the association.'[35] The chairman of the meeting quashed the motion before it went to a vote. Such incidents were sporadic and there is no evidence there was much public backing or support within the GAA for them.

17

Modernism – A Mental Cancer

The Hyde incident had brought the issue of the Ban to the forefront of the GAA agenda again. According to Breandán Ó hEithir, due to the Hyde incident, 'most sensitive people wished the Ban would wither away of shame. That the absurd law was not merely an ass but a monstrous mule incapable of generating anything but dissension and acrimony was clear to most dispassionate observers.'[1] The Ban was never seriously threatened, though. It would be a long time before it would have to justify itself thoroughly to GAA members. The ruling that the Ban could only be debated every three years certainly helped. There were no motions at the Annual Congress in 1939 to remove the Ban; there would have been no point as they could not be discussed. Considering the depth of feelings towards the removal of Hyde, it is fair to assume that such motions would have reached the Congress floor if the three-year ruling was not in place.

There were certain rumblings of expressions of disapproval towards the Ban during the 1940s. They were infrequent and had little impact within the GAA overall. For example, in a survey conducted in 1943, 94 per cent of the students of UCD were in favour of removing the Ban. This did not come from just students who were members of the soccer and rugby clubs, but also from GAA members who commented, 'The

Éamon de Valera speaking at the fiftieth anniversary of the Central Branch of the Gaelic League in 1944 – he was president of the branch at that time. The Gaelic League was faced with a dilemma in 1945 when de Valera attended a Tattoo Ball (a ballroom dance) and was in breach of its rule prohibiting committee members from attending 'foreign dances'. Instead of reprimanding him, the Gaelic League removed its ban. *(Courtesy of the National Library of Ireland)*

position with regard to our national culture, language and games is precarious enough … without suffering interference and dictation from short-sighted cranks'.[2] Interestingly, in the same survey, 60 per cent of UCD students were not in favour of women students being allowed into the college. The row between the GAA and the government in 1943 over the army playing non-Gaelic games spilled over into county conventions the following year, with some conventions calling for not just the army to allow 'foreign games', but for the GAA to remove its Ban too. Motions in Mohill club in Leitrim,[3] Louth[4] and Derry[5] calling for the abolition of the Ban were defeated at those conventions and never made their way to the 1944 Annual Congress.

In 1945, the Gaelic League were faced with a dilemma similar to that experienced by the GAA by the Hyde incident in 1938. The Taoiseach Éamon de Valera attended a Tattoo Ball on 10 August 1945 where ballroom dancing was part of the programme for the evening; the event was organised by the military with over 5,000 dancers participating.[6] Ballroom dancing was considered a 'foreign dance' by the Gaelic League, and de Valera, an official in his capacity as president of the Central Branch of the Gaelic League since 1919, was in breach of the rule banning Gaelic League officials from attending or promoting 'foreign games or dances'. Commenting on the dilemma facing the Gaelic League, *The Irish Times* remarked, 'Mr De Valera's attendance is going to have undoubted repercussions in Gaelic League circles. It will be recalled that when Dr Douglas Hyde who was then Patron of the GAA, some years ago attended, with Mr De Valera, an Association football match between Poland and Ireland, the Central Council of the GAA removed his name from the list of patrons.'[7] News of de Valera's attendance at the Tattoo Ball travelled even as far afield as Australia.[8] Faced with the alternatives of removing de Valera or ignoring his attendance, the Gaelic League chose a third way and removed the bans on 'foreign games and dances',[9] a move heralded by *The Irish Times* as 'a gesture to common sense' allowing members to '"swing it" to the tune of "Meet Me in St. Louis, Louis", or to cheer in English at Soccer or Rugby games'.[10] This was the second attempt the Gaelic League had made to remove their bans and unlike the previous occasion in 1938, the GAA was not as vocal in its opposition and the bans were allowed to be removed without the acrimony of the past.

In Ulster, the province most vehemently opposed to the removal of the GAA's Ban, a number of counties changed tack in the 1940s. In Derry, the nationalist Member of Parliament, Edward 'Big Eddie' McAteer, as well as many other Derry

GAA members, supported the removal of the Ban as it was impacting negatively on the number of people Derry GAA was attracting.[11] At the Annual Congress of 1947, motions for removal of the Ban were on the agenda for the first time since 1929. The motions were from Counties Cavan, Monaghan and Down. Supporting Down's motion to remove the Ban was the one solitary voice that supported Hyde on that night in December 1938 when Hyde was removed as patron, Peter O'Farrell, from Roscommon, who stated 'the President [Sean T. O'Kelly] of their country was allowed attend a foreign game, a privilege that was denied to his predecessor, Dr Douglas Hyde, one of the greatest Gaels that the country had ever produced. Their Gaelic games had flourished, not because of the ban, but in spite of it.'[12] Opening old wounds did not help O'Farrell's or Down's case and the motion to remove the Ban was defeated by 188 to 5 votes. Interestingly, around the same time as county conventions were discussing the Ban in the lead up to the Annual Congress of 1947, Ó Caoimh received correspondence from a Mr J. H. Mulrooney, from the Australian Commission's office, who was anxious to organise international contests between teams representing Gaelic football and Australian rules football, a venture that would come into being decades later.[13]

Motions on the Ban were defeated again in 1950.[14] The world was changing rapidly but it took Ireland longer to modernise. Many in the GAA saw modernism, even in its primitive Irish guise, as 'a mental cancer' and it became as important as ever to face opponents of the Ban with absolute resistance.[15] Opposing any attempts to remove the Ban in 1953 the then GAA president, Vincent O'Donoghue, said the Ban 'was there to remind members of the dishonour of associating with British Imperialism, and would aid in opposing the subtle plan for the proselytising of Irish youths, who were being enticed, by various enducements, to become happy little English children, and heirs to the joy of a soccer paradise'.[16] Opposition to the Ban had always been quite strong from people outside of the GAA; the opposition became more vocal as it was covered more in the national media from the 1950s onward, and many of the people opposed to the Ban used the Hyde incident as a tool to hammer home their point. In a letter written to *The Irish Times* in 1950, the GAA was condemned for mixing up nationalism with tribalism by its enforcement of the Ban. The writer took particular issue with the removal of Hyde as patron, commenting:

> He was struck off the list of the GAA patrons, in punish-
> ment for this act of courtesy, due from the head of a State
> that includes citizens who like all sorts of games. The
> Tricolour, the National Anthem, are honoured at Croke
> Park, but the living symbol of the nation, its President,
> was disloyally ejected. At that time, a Protestant clergyman
> who was striving to interest his people in Irish patriotic
> works met the objection: 'We are not wanted; see what
> the GAA has done to a Protestant patriot.' The objection
> was difficult, almost impossible to answer; for the insult
> to Dr Hyde, the great Irishman who initiated the Gaelic
> revival and all that flowed from it, was pure, ignorant,
> savage tribalism.[17]

In 1953 the Lord Mayor of Waterford, Alderman Martin Cullen was removed from the GAA for attending a 'foreign game' even though he was acting in his official capacity.[18] This reminded many people of Hyde's removal, with one com-mentator observing on the absurdity of the GAA removing a man who had done more deeds than any GAA member for the Irish language and Irish culture, saying it 'Sounds like the Orangeman's query: "Is the King Loyal"'.[19] The oft-remarked accusation of GAA members wantonly flouting the Ban was still reported on in the 1950s.[20] The IRFU, who was not afraid to voice its opinion on the narrow-mindedness of the GAA, could still be relied upon to give ample proof to any wavering GAA members that 'foreign games' such as rugby were still heavily anglicised, by persisting in playing the British national anthem, 'God Save the Queen', at internationals in Ravenhill, Belfast.[21] The Minister for External Affairs at the time, Frank Aiken of Fianna Fáil, was inundated with complaints from many people and groups about how the Tricolour was not flown at rugby matches at Ravenhill as well as at international matches abroad, and about the playing of the British national anthem and not the Irish national anthem at Ravenhill whenever the Irish team played. Groups who protested included the Old IRA Association, Westmeath County Council and some Fianna Fáil cumainn.[22] Sean T. O'Kelly had previously withdrawn his acceptance of attendance at a rugby international between Scotland and Ireland in 1948, as a protest at the Irish national anthem not being played at Twickenham before a match between Ireland and England.[23]

Radio Éireann made a decision in 1954 to broadcast a soccer match on St Patrick's Day, in addition to its customary broadcasting of the hurling and Gaelic football matches from Croke Park on that day. The GAA protested and threatened to ban the broadcast of the GAA games on Radio Éireann if it was decided to go ahead with the soccer airing. However, Radio Éireann stood firm and covered the soccer match in Dalymount Park, much to the consternation of the GAA.[24] Commenting, in 1957, on the changing media landscape, the GAA president, Antrim man Seamus McFerran, the second Ulsterman to hold the title, referred 'to the "hotch-potch sports mixtures in which the national games and issues are featured in a very inferior manner with games that are foreign and insignificant". As a national association they had a right to demand and expect specialised GAA features commensurate with their public appeal and their status.'[25] In the same address, he declared the Ban was 'by no means a fundamental principle' but 'it would always be justified as long as a border existed in the country'. He also condemned the attitude of some Irish schools and colleges who were still promoting 'foreign games' at the expense of the native ones.[26] With the establishment of RTÉ in 1961 and the increased access for consumers to televisions, the GAA would face an even greater media threat with world sporting events, like the FIFA World Cup, accessible in people's living rooms.

18

Death and Burial of a President

When Hyde finished his term as President of Ireland in 1945, he did not move back to 'Ratra', his residence in Frenchpark, County Roscommon. Instead, a residence in the Phoenix Park, that had been home to the private secretaries of previous Lord Lieutenants, was made available to him.[1] This residence became known as 'Little Ratra' and it was here that Douglas Hyde died on 12 July 1949, aged eighty-nine years of age. Glowing tributes poured in from the world over to this 'kindly, gentle and tolerant'[2] man. *The Manchester Guardian*, in a comprehensive obituary, claimed it was Hyde 'who had brought back to the minds of men Ireland's past which the nineteenth century had sought as it were to bury alive. It was this feat of his which made it inevitable that Ireland should claim independent status as a nation.'[3] *The Irish Times* called Hyde 'cultured, strenuous and far-seeing, his ideals were constructive. Intensely sociable, companionable and magnetic, his name will remain an inspiration.'[4] Speaking in the Dáil, opposition leader at the time, Éamon de Valera said that people involved in the Gaelic League 'were well aware that Dr Hyde was the foundation and the inspiration of the movement. It was Dr Hyde who had attracted the people into the League,

An Taoiseach, John A. Costello, (with tall hat in hand, to the right of the photograph) with members of his cabinet outside St Patrick's Cathedral, Dublin, for Douglas Hyde's funeral in July 1949. For fear of excommunication from the Catholic Church, they were not able to enter the Protestant cathedral. *(Courtesy of British Pathé)*

who had set them to work on the revival of the language, and had taught them to learn and love it.'[5] The Taoiseach, John A. Costello, leading the tributes in the Dáil, said that Hyde, through the founding of the Gaelic League had 'aroused the dormant spirit of the people and stimulated their intellectual, social, political and artistic activities'.[6] Messages of sympathy were also received from the Gaelic League and the GAA who wished 'to record their great sorrow on the death of An Craoibhín Aoibhinn. Great was his prowess for country and language.'[7]

Both Costello and de Valera were at the funeral service for Hyde at St Patrick's Cathedral in Dublin, held on 14 July. For fear of excommunication from the Catholic Church, who had introduced their own ban prohibiting their members from attending Protestant services or institutions such as Trinity College Dublin, they were not able to enter the Protestant cathedral. They waited outside. After the service in St Patrick's Cathedral, the cortège moved to Frenchpark in Roscommon where Hyde was buried. Some people commented on the shame of the leading politicians of Ireland not attending the service, and saw it as treating Irish Protestants 'as pariahs and that their worship is considered contaminating and unclean'. Another said, 'What will the world at large think of a nationalism which makes so pathetic a failure to do full homage to one of its greatest men?'[8] One of the few people who was in attendance at the service in St Patrick's Cathedral was poet Austin Clarke. He wrote a poem sharing his thoughts on those who waited outside, named 'The Burial of an Irish President';

> At the last bench
> Two Catholics, the French
> Ambassador and I, knelt down.
> The vergers waited. Outside.
> The hush of Dublin town,
> Professors of cap and gown,
> Costello, his Cabinet
> In Government cars, hiding
> Around the corner, ready
> Tall hat in hand, dreading
> Our Father in English. Better
> Not hear that 'which' for 'who'
> And risk eternal doom.[9]

Hyde's house in Roscommon, Ratra, was donated to the Gaelic League after his death but the local branch was unable to keep paying its rates and they failed to interest the Department of Education or Roscommon VEC to take it over. 'It fell into disrepair and, in a most potent symbol of modern Ireland, was used in the early 1970s as in-fill for the foundations of a local milk powder factory'.[10] His grave was

Douglas Hyde's graveside in Portahard, Frenchpark, County Roscommon. In 1984, GAA president, Paddy Buggy, placed a GAA memorial plaque on Hyde's grave.

also neglected for years, covered with nettles and briars. The first efforts to clean it up were on the seventy-fifth anniversary of the founding of the Gaelic League in 1968. The grave was cleaned up completely in 1988 and a Dr Douglas Hyde Interpretative Centre was established in the neglected church beside his grave, the same church in which his father preached.[11] He has had Gaelscoileanna named after him in Tallaght, Dublin, and Roscommon, and in 1978, Trinity College Dublin opened the Douglas Hyde Gallery which is used for art exhibitions.[12] In addition to this, a Hyde Summer School, devoted to the Irish language, was set up in 1993 in Ballaghaderreen, County Roscommon, and was opened by a successor to Hyde as President, Mary Robinson.[13] In November 1995, the Central Bank of Ireland commissioned a new £50 banknote, designed by artist Robert Ballagh. The front featured a portrait of Hyde with a picture of Áras an Uachtaráin in the background and the crest of the Gaelic League appearing on the back of the note.[14] A poem of Hyde's, 'Mise Raifteri an File', also featured on the £5 banknote commissioned by the Central Bank in 1992.[15]

Years after Hyde died, the GAA would make amends for what had happened to him in 1938. The Roscommon GAA Council, which had always stood by their most famous countyman, opened a new GAA grounds in Hyde's honour, named the Dr Douglas Hyde Park, in the same year the Ban came to an end, 1971.[16] It is the main GAA ground in Roscommon today. The decision was not without its critics. One person claimed the GAA had one 'helluva neck' for naming the ground in Hyde's honour, saying the GAA 'should have made a public apology to the memory of a great Irishman first' for its action in removing him as patron.[17] An attempt at an apology was made by the GAA in 1984, the year of the GAA's centenary. On 16 August of that year, ceremonies for leading GAA members were held in Roscommon. There was an unveiling of a plaque at a ceremony for Pádraig Ó Caoimh.

Ó Caoimh is most associated with County Cork, although he was born in Roscommon in 1897. A plaque was placed on the grave of Dan O'Rourke, former GAA president, and, immediately after that, a similar ceremony was conducted at the graveside of Hyde in Portahard, Frenchpark. The memorial plaque was placed on Hyde's grave by the then GAA president Paddy Buggy. In attendance also was the President-Elect, Dr Mick Loftus; Liam Mulvihill, the general secretary; Seán Ó Siocháin Mulvhill's predecessor; and a number of other former GAA presidents as well as representatives from the Connacht Provincial Council.[18] This simple plaque can be still seen on Hyde's grave today, a small gesture acknowledging that the GAA had made a mistake and was, in some way, seeking atonement for the humiliating treatment of a true Irish-Irelander.

19

Woulfe Attack

Although the Ban appeared to be secure, in 1959 the Dublin Civil Service GAA Club, led by its chairman Kerryman Tom Woulfe, made a move that would lead to the Ban's eventual removal in 1971. Woulfe deserves the lion's share of the credit for the success of this campaign. His tenacity and perseverance were tested to the limits over the next decade with more lows than highs until the ultimate goal was achieved. His personal motivation stemmed from an incident in 1948 when he was involved in a Vigilance Committee for Dublin County Board where a person was suspended for playing a foreign game and that person subsequently took no further part in the GAA. Woulfe was disgusted by the experience and refused to act as vigilante again.[1] Woulfe started a nation-wide campaign, which was played out fully in the media throughout the 1960s. He was ably assisted by many journalists, including Eamon Mongey, former Mayo footballer and Gaelic games correspondent with the *Sunday Press* at the time.[2] The Dublin Civil Service Club passed a motion in 1959, not necessarily seeking the Ban's removal, but to have an investigation committee set up to determine the usefulness of the Ban.[3] It appeared a futile exercise, though, as motions on the Ban would have to wait until the Annual Congress of 1962. Woulfe

Tom Woulfe from the Dublin Civil Service GAA Club led a decade-long campaign that culminated in the removal of the Ban in 1971. *(Courtesy of the* Irish Press)

was not repelled that easily and he published a thesis on the Ban, which was published in *The Irish Times* on 28 November 1961, recounting the history of the Ban and the various arguments for and against. He attacked one of the primary defences of the Ban; the Ban was carrying out the ideals of the founders of the GAA. He proceeded to produce evidence suggesting that all three primary founders – Cusack, Croke and Davin – wrote documents clearly showing their opposition to the banning of 'foreign games'. He also attacked one of the staunchest defenders of the Ban, Monsignor Hamilton, remarking:

> Monsignor Hamilton went on to assert that only a member of the GAA can be a 100 per cent Irish man, and in defence of this assertion he said: 'We are also told that good Irishmen have played foreign games and the

ex-Taoiseach [de Valera] and Kevin Barry [in an iconic picture, Barry is wearing his Belvedere rugby jersey[4]] are sometime quoted as examples. It is true that some good Irishmen have played foreign games, but in so far as they did they were not 100 per cent good Irishmen.' So there you have it – 1st and 2nd class Irishmen based on an allegiance to sport – and apparently the crown of martyrdom does not suffice to erase the barrier.[5]

The Irish Times article, clearly an anti-Ban one by Woulfe, re-opened the Ban debate for the upcoming county conventions in preparation for the Annual Congress in 1962. The Dublin County Board decided to back the Civil Service motions to have ban motions voted on by ballot as opposed to a show of hands and for a Commission of Inquiry to be set up to review the Ban.[6] Other counties were still fully behind the Ban with Longford, Laois and Westmeath voting to retain it.[7] An acrimonious debate followed at the Annual Congress of 1962 with one delegate from Kerry comparing GAA players to schoolchildren who had no right to be consulted on anything.[8] Woulfe cited the banning of Hyde as well as the banning of such distinguished people as de Valera, Kevin Barry, Cathal Brugha and Archbishop John Charles McQuaid from the GAA as reasons for the Ban's removal.[9] Woulfe was incorrect in claiming the others were banned, however; it was just Hyde. The 'fantastic situation' of the nature of removing Hyde as patron was an argument used on more than one occasion by opponents of the Ban.[10] It was to no avail. By an overwhelming majority of 180 to 40, the motion to investigate the Ban was defeated.[11] Unperturbed, Woulfe's Civil Service Club passed a motion later that year to amend the rule limiting motions on the Ban to every three years.[12] Woulfe kept the Ban high up on the agenda through the years when the Ban could not be discussed before Congress. He reiterated his views on the founding fathers and their opinion towards the Ban to the Dublin County Board in early 1964. He found many willing

Delegates for the GAA Annual Congress of 1961 outside the Gresham Hotel, Dublin. The 1960s were dominated by debates on the Ban. *(Courtesy of the National Library of Ireland)*

advocates in the Irish media, some calling for the GAA 'who, ostrich-like, continue to bury their heads in the sands' to get behind the country. 'At a time when this country is making such a commendable effort to throw off the social shackles of the past 40 years, it would be nice to think that the Gaelic Athletic Association, which has such an important role to play in the growth of the nation, will not be found wanting.'[13] Another commentator mentioned the removal of Hyde as GAA patron as 'something the GAA will never live down'[14] considering other professionals, like gardaí, were allowed to attend 'foreign games' in their official capacity and Hyde, as President of the State, was not. Later that same year, with the prospect of a Minister for Sport portfolio being mooted as a potential position within the Irish government, it was pondered if that person would suffer the same fate as Hyde if they attended a 'foreign game'.[15]

In 1965, motions on the Ban were allowed to be debated on again and it was Woulfe and the Dublin County Board who led the way once more with their opposition. Again, Woulfe used the same arguments: there was strong evidence to suggest Croke and Davin in particular were not against 'foreign games' and due to the Ban the GAA had lost people like Hyde and de Valera.[16] Those supporting the Ban also claimed the founding fathers were pro-Ban and if the Ban was removed, the GAA would be reduced to just being a sporting organisation with nothing to stop the advent of professionalism.[17] One Mr M. Costigan, from the Laois County Board, wildly exaggerated the situation, by making the outlandish claim, 'The ban should be retained. Men like Davis, Pearse and Wolfe Tone died for its retention.'[18] Mr Costigan failed to follow up on how he had come to the conclusion that Davis and Wolfe Tone had died for the Ban considering they were dead long before the GAA was founded. He also did not explain the remark attributed to Pearse, 'Do not condemn English games, play Irish ones'.[19] The division between the two camps had become steadily more acrimonious over the years with both sides becoming entrenched in their views. There was talk of legal action being threatened,[20] and RTÉ came in for criticism for bowing to intimidation tactics adopted by the GAA. Woulfe alleged that the president of the GAA, Alf Murray, and Pat Fanning, outgoing chairman of the Munster Council (and the man who would be president when the Ban was removed), made a visit to the Director General of Telefís Éireann, Kevin McCourt. They pressurised McCourt to withhold any airings on television of debates on the Ban before it was debated at Congress that year.[21] The outcome of the 1965 Annual Congress would follow a similar pattern to 1962. Even with Counties Dublin, Waterford, Roscommon, Sligo, Wicklow and the East Midlands of Britain supporting a removal of the Ban,[22] the anti-Ban lobby received only 52 votes out of a possible 282.[23]

Fianna Fáil Minister for Education, Donogh O'Malley, in a picture taken shortly before his premature death in 1968. He believed students in schools should be consulted on their choice of sport. President of the FAI and a former inter-provincial rugby player with Munster, Connacht and Ulster, he stated, 'Rugby and soccer people, as well as others, are sick and tired of having the finger pointed at them as if we were any worse Irishmen for playing these games. We are proud of our games and do not see anything wrong in our sons playing them.' (Courtesy of the Irish Press)

Jack Lynch (third from left) and Éamon de Valera (second from left) instruct King Baudouin of Belgium (right) how to play hurling at Áras an Uachtaráin in 1968. Also pictured is GAA general secretary, Seán Ó Siocháin (left). Lynch, one of the most decorated GAA players of all time, was threatened with removal from the GAA for attending a rugby international at Lansdowne Road in 1967. *(Courtesy of the National Library of Ireland)*

The soccer World Cup was held in England in 1966, a competition the host nation subsequently won. RTÉ provided extensive coverage of the competition. This 'brought increased interest in soccer throughout the country, and also induced heightened GAA paranoia'.[24] One commentator, An Fear Ciuin, remarked that the World Cup was having 'disturbing effects here amongst those followers and imitators who contaminate their minds with world-disturbing, unnatural and degrading recreations. Every effort will be made to preserve our Gaelic people from falling into boisterous belligerency.'[25] It also brought into focus the impossibility of stopping people from watching 'foreign games'. Would members of GAA

Vigilance Committees have to visit every house up and down the country to see if GAA members were adhering to Rule 27? Or did 'spectating' mean attending a match as opposed to watching the match on the television?

Opposition to the Ban continued to grow with leading politicians expressing hostile views towards the Ban. Fianna Fáil TD and Minister for Health, Donogh O'Malley, who would go down in history as the person who brought in free secondary level education to Ireland, criticised Radio Éireann in 1966 for not broadcasting the FAI Cup final in Dalymount Park.[26] In late 1967, as Minister for Education, at a Shannon Rugby Club dinner, he stated that 'students at secondary schools should be consulted on their choice of sport'.[27] O'Malley, who was president of the FAI and a former inter-provincial rugby player with Munster, Connacht and Ulster, also stated, 'Rugby and soccer people, as well as others, are sick and tired of having the finger pointed at them as if we were any worse Irishmen for playing these games. We are proud of our games and do not see anything wrong in our sons playing them.'[28] The GAA angrily attacked O'Malley for ridiculing the GAA's methods for promoting its games. O'Malley's comments also raised tension within the Fianna Fáil party. Fianna Fáil TD, Paddy Lalor, who was president of Abbeyleix GAA Club in Laois, said the Ban was entirely a matter for the GAA. He 'strongly resented the GAA being told how it should run its business by these outsiders, no matter who they might be' and 'he did not agree at all that pupils of secondary schools should be consulted about their choice of games no more than about their choice of subjects'.[29] As the controversy unfolded, following on from O'Malley's comments, *The Irish Times* wrote an article on a showing of goodwill between a Roscommon GAA club and the Dublin soccer club Shamrock Rovers. The GAA club in question, Celtic, was participating in an indoor Gaelic football tournament organised by the Roscommon Gaels GAA club. Looking for distinctive green jerseys, they wrote to Shamrock Rovers who duly supplied them with six new green jerseys.[30] Such levels of co-operation were not uncommon amongst grass-roots GAA members who, it was felt, were overwhelmingly in favour of removal of the Ban by the late 1960s. This sentiment was still not shared by GAA officials who debated the Ban again at the 1968 Annual Congress, with an outcome that was all too familiar.

Another politician who entered the debate was a Gaelic games legend, Jack Lynch. Jack Lynch, to this date, holds the record for winning the most All-Irelands in a row – five in hurling and one in Gaelic football. After retiring from both Gaelic games codes, he embarked on a spectacularly successful political career with Fianna Fáil, culminating with his election as Taoiseach in 1966. It was recorded soon after Lynch became Taoiseach that he was against the Ban.[31] At the beginning of 1967 there were calls for Lynch to be removed from the GAA for attending a rugby international at Lansdowne Road in his official capacity as Taoiseach. One advocate from Galway wrote:

> Some years ago, a truly great Irishman and Gaelic scholar, Dr Douglas Hyde, who was then Ireland's first President, attended a Soccer match at Dalymount Park and as a result he was banned by the Gaelic League [the writer was mistaken, it was the GAA] and rightly so. On Saturday last, the Taoiseach, John Lynch, attended a Rugby match at Lansdowne Road, and he should also get the axe by supporting Shoneenism while head of our country's Government. If we are to be consistent he must be shown that any such fellow-travelling will not be tolerated. Gaels worthy of that proud title must be either 'fish or flesh' and there can be no in-betweens. This can be demonstrated by taking firm action in this regrettable case.[32]

Responding, the *Connacht Tribune* remarked that the axe would be very blunt as there were many other former All-Ireland winners who would have to be axed, along with Lynch, for

President Éamon de Valera with former French president General Charles de Gaulle at Áras an Uachtaráin in 1969. Some believed de Gaulle could oppose Ireland's entry to the European Economic Community (EEC) due to the inward and divisive nature of the Ban. *(Courtesy of the National Library of Ireland)*

attending the same rugby match.[33] The language may have been as colourful as it was in the 1930s but there was no stomach to take action against such a decorated star of the GAA as Jack Lynch. Lynch's attendance at a rugby match still had people uncertain of his opposition to the Ban but remarks he made in 1968 removed all doubt. Speaking at a Munster sports stars award evening in March 1968, he commented on the divisive nature of the Ban, stating that all sportspeople should be united as they all shared a common bond.[34] It was also observed that Lynch could have difficult discussions with General Charles de Gaulle in France due to the inward and divisive nature of the Ban.[35] Ireland, at that time, was looking to gain entry into the European Economic Community (EEC) – they achieved this in 1972, officially joining in January 1973. De Gaulle, the president of France, was seen as the power broker for Ireland to join. He had vetoed British entry twice in the 1960s, which also put an end to Irish hopes of joining at that time. As the European Project talked of unity with no barriers, this would surely mean unity in sport too and it was believed the Ban would not be tolerated by de Gaulle.[36] This was probably an exaggeration on the overall political impact of the Ban.

Senior figures within the clergy added their opposition to the Ban too. Tomás Ó Fiaich, in 1966, who was Professor of Modern History in Maynooth at the time and who later became Archbishop of Armagh and the Primate of All-Ireland, claimed the Ban did not help the GAA's aim to end partition, it did the opposite. It was causing disunity between Catholic and Protestant communities in the North.[37] The Archbishop of Cashel Thomas Morris who, like all his predecessors since Archbishop Croke, was a patron of the GAA, suggested that the GAA should gauge public opinion by employing professional sociologists to study the Ban. This contribution came in for criticism from certain quarters in the GAA who suggested that the Archbishop should instead use his connections to convince certain schools and colleges to employ the same professional sociologists to examine why those schools and colleges had an 'unofficial ban' on Gaelic games.[38]

From 1965, the fractious nature of the debates between the two opposing camps dissipated to some degree, with pro-Ban supporters recognising that their opponents within the GAA had the best interests of the Association at heart.[39] Realising the possibility of the Ban being removed was significant, the pro-Ban faction went on the offensive from 1965 to the next Annual Congress debate on the Ban in 1968.[40] Brendan MacLua's book supporting the Ban, *The Steadfast Rule*, was published in this period. MacLua was a journalist and editor of the *Gaelic Weekly* and an Executive Officer of the GAA; the foreword was from the GAA president.[41] Advance publicity of the book stated, 'This book contains the full history of the Ban

– based on extensive research, official documents and correspondence. This is the book to end all arguments.'[42] MacLua attacked the assertion made primarily by Woulfe that the three leading founders of the GAA were against bans on 'foreign games'. He claimed Croke's request in November 1885 to remove the ban on the IAAA did not necessarily mean he was against bans per se,[43] and he provided ample evidence of Cusack's comment supporting bans. He claimed that Cusack stated in 1903 that the mission of foreign games 'was to absorb into their system all that was manful in Ireland and have them chalked down as British'.[44] Cusack is also famously reported as saying that rugby was 'a denationalising plague to carry on through winter the work of ruin that cricket was doing during the summer'.[45] These revisionist arguments on where the founders stood regarding bans on 'foreign games' from both sides were, to all intents and purposes, futile. Ireland had changed radically since the days the GAA was founded and the GAA's position in Ireland could not have been more different from when the founders met in Hayes Hotel to revive the national pastimes. Yet, one of the staple arguments used throughout the 1960s for and against the Ban was the opinions of the founders.

MacLua also devoted a full chapter, entitled 'A Poignant Moment', to one of the incidents that had been used as a key argument throughout the 1960s to remove the Ban, the ejection of Hyde as patron. Calling the Hyde incident 'the most dolorific moment in the history of the Ban',[46] MacLua claims the GAA had no option but to remove Hyde. Any other decision 'would have been a breach of trust and of tradition; it might also have marked the beginning of the disintegration which weakness or indecision, in the face of such confrontation, invariably begets'.[47] Commenting on the criticism the decision received at the time, particularly from the press, MacLua said, 'All in all, though, the criticism was not particularly harsh. There appears to have been a realisation of how painful the decision was for the Association – and also, perhaps, something by way of mild admiration for a group of men who had, most definitely, shown the courage of their convictions.'[48] This is not entirely true – outrage and disgust were some of the more common expressions used by the press at the time. He also failed to mention the eventual outcome reached with de Valera in 1945 when the GAA agreed that the President of the State should be allowed to attend all events in the future, including those organised by 'foreign games'.

MacLua made a rallying call for the Ban with his closing remarks, saying:

> The GAA remains the only sizeable organisation still committed to an unchanged ideal. The Ban is its binding link with the past and its commitment to give that past a future. To snap that link would be to cut the Association adrift from the tradition that has made it, and from its appeal to the patriotic young men who have always shouldered its burdens. To remove the Ban would ... amount to the assassination of the GAA's intrepid vitality. Ireland can ill-afford to lose so valuable a prize.[49]

There is validity to those comments. Of all the organisations that encompassed the Irish-Ireland ideal, the GAA was, by the late 1960s, the only one left standing. Members of the GAA were genuine in their belief in this ideal and felt the removal of the Ban would damage the GAA as well as the whole Irish-Ireland movement irrevocably. Their problem was that most people did not agree with this concept of sticking to the ideals of the past; they were hungry to face the brave new world of modernism and, as years passed, more and more within the GAA ranks were of this viewpoint. Ó hEithir described reading MacLua's book, 'rather like entering the caves at Mitchelstown to find men dressed in bearskins painting little pictures on the walls'.[50]

MacLua's book was published at the end of 1967, just as county conventions were occurring in preparation for the Annual Congress of 1968. Many of the old arguments were rehashed for the now three-yearly event of the Ban debate at Annual Congress; there was, however, a notable increase in opposition to the Ban.[51] Woulfe, tenacious as ever, led the way. In a reasoned and forceful article he wrote for *The Kerryman* in March 1968, devoid of some of his previous revisionist comments on the three founding members, he said he too wanted what was best for the GAA and country. He asserted:

> That the promotion of the national games is the primary object of the GAA. I believe that the GAA has an important role to play in other areas of the national life. I believe that the GAA should support our culture and way of life. It should support the language revival. It should support the national dances. It should support Irish industry.[52]

He claimed that with the Ban being more popular in rural than urban areas and the ever increasing move away from the land, the GAA needed to attract townspeople and the Ban was a huge obstacle. He claimed that the removal would help re-unification and would, ultimately, attract more people to the GAA without losing anyone. He also returned to his familiar theme of Hyde's removal saying:

> I have heard that outrageous decision defended some time ago on the ground that there was a principle involved. All I want to say in like [sic] Dr Douglas Hyde who did so much for the revival of the Irish language and Irish culture had to be exposed to the public humiliation of expulsion from the GAA in the name of principle, the principle must be a foul one indeed.[53]

At the Annual Congress a month later, Galway and Dublin tabled motions to have the Ban removed outright, Louth wanted spectators permitted to attend 'foreign games', Clare wanted British Security forces to be allowed to join the GAA, Down sought a relaxation of the dance rules, and Limerick, Mayo and Louth called for a committee to investigate the Ban. Dublin's motion to delete the Ban was heavily defeated again, by 220 votes to 80.[54] This Annual Congress marked the beginning of the end for the Ban, even though it was not realised at the time. Mayo's motion for a committee to be set up to investigate the Ban passed. On the face of it, this seemed like a pyrrhic victory for anti-Ban supporters as the terms of reference of the new committee was to establish the validity of the retention of the Ban and the pro-Ban Central Council chose the committee. Maurice Hayes, former secretary of Down County Board, commented on the committee make-up, saying that it was 'rather like the Unionist Party appointing a committee of ex-Grand Masters to discuss the validity of the Orange order'.[55] The committee's findings led indirectly to the removal of the Ban just three years later.

20

The Ban Goes With a Whimper

Some people were determined not to give up the Ban without a fight. In 1968, the Lord Mayor of Waterford refused to attend a European Cup soccer match between the new European champions, Manchester United and Waterford City, as he was a member of the GAA. Unlike Hyde and his predecessor some years ago, Martin Cullen, he granted his famous visitors a civic reception but instructed a deputy to go in his place to the match.[1] The new GAA president, also from Waterford, Pat Fanning, admitted that he respected the viewpoints of those within the GAA who opposed the Ban, but that he supported the Ban because:

> I suggest that Rule 27 enables us to project an image of an association still dedicated to an ideal, still governed by principle, still declaring to the world at large that, come what may, in addition to its wish to serve the people of Ireland through its games, it also holds before its own membership the ideal of an Ireland that is Gaelic, that is proud of and willing to preserve its traditions. That is the way I feel about it, very sincerely.[2]

Public opposition to the Ban was as vocal as ever as the decade closed, in some cases more so. The South African rugby team, the Springboks, toured Ireland at the end of 1969 and on into

1970, amid huge protests from the Irish public for their government's policy of Apartheid. One game in Lansdowne Road was even played with the crowd behind barbed wire fences. During the tour the RTÉ programme, *The Late Late Show,* had a discussion on Apartheid where the GAA's Ban was compared, rather harshly, to the policy of the South African government.[3] The Ban was seen as discriminatory, as was the commonly held belief that Jews were barred from 'Dublin golf clubs because of the fear that they would dominate business deals in the clubhouse bars'.[4] The GAA's Ban was also compared to the Berlin Wall, with one commentator stating, 'the Gaelic Athletic Association's ban which remains, like the Berlin wall, cutting down the middle of sport in Ireland'.[5] Sean Flanagan, Fianna Fáil Minister for Lands and a former All-Ireland football winner with Mayo, believed the GAA would become 'an empire without citizens' if it did not remove the Ban.[6] Protests were even seen outside the grounds of Croke Park at the Leinster Gaelic football final of 1970, with people holding up placards reading, 'Ban the Ban' and 'Gaelic players, take your stand'.[7]

There were some notable exceptions to the barrage of antagonism towards the GAA, including Dr Conor Cruise O'Brien who, in later years, would be considered no friend of Irish nationalism. In his book, *Writers and Politics*, he wrote:

> It [the GAA] organised with faith and enthusiasm the replacement of what had been a servile spirit by a spirit of manliness and freedom … More than the Gaelic League, more than Arthur's Griffith Sinn Féin, more even than the Transport and General Workers' Union and of course far more than the movement which created the Abbey Theatre, more than any of these, the Gaelic Athletic movement aroused the interest of large numbers of ordinary people throughout Ireland. One of the most successful and original mass movements of its day, its importance has perhaps not even yet been fully realised.[8]

The committee charged with reviewing the Ban also felt this sense of history and the importance of the role the GAA played within the national movement. Unsurprisingly, the result of their deliberations, published in November 1970, was that the Ban should stay. In a thoroughly-researched report, the committee claimed, 'the Ban has come to be accepted as a means by which the purpose and principles of the GAA are proclaimed: that it is an outward sign of the association's exclusively and national motivation'.[9] The report went on to say the Ban should be retained for practical and idealistic reasons. Practical reasons included: GAA players were already overloaded with fixtures and the addition of other sporting codes would add to further congestions for players; hurling would be affected in many counties as Gaelic footballers could be more drawn toward soccer as their second sport; the removal of the Ban would reduce people's commitment to the GAA. From the idealistic and national point of view, it was felt the Ban should be retained for the following reasons:

> Rule 27 is one of a number of rules which mark out the GAA as more than a mere sporting organisation – as a National organisation interested in the Irish language, Irish goods, Irish dancers, etc. Experience establishes that the fostering of the language, Irish industry and Irish goods, no less than the propagation of Gaelic games, requires guide-lines and firm directives. If Rule 27 were removed this would weaken the idealistic motive which inspires so many people to give voluntary service to the GAA ... By its demand for exclusive allegiance to a National course, the GAA claims an attribute that no mere sporting organisation can claim. This puts its games above other sports – games with a mission – and it would be foolish to allow this 'patriotic motive' to be reduced.[10]

For people playing other sports in the six counties of Northern Ireland, this could entail playing under the Union Jack, thus recognising two states in Ireland.[11]

Just as unsurprising as the decision of the committee was the reaction they received from almost everyone else. *The Irish Times* called the report astonishing and saddening, and questioned the wisdom of the men who conceived the report.[12] Tom Woulfe claimed, by the report's total dismissal of the genuine views of the anti-Ban side, the report had become, in effect, 'the best anti-ban material produced in the past ten years'.[13]

The pro-Ban side had made a fatal political flaw at the Annual Congress preceding the publication of the report in 1970: they allowed a motion, put forward by Meath, to be passed – it demanded that all clubs and county boards put their views forward on the Ban before the Annual Congress of 1971.[14] Alf Murray, former president of the GAA, in predicting the report on the Ban would put an end to all debates on the Ban, could not have been more wrong.[15] There were ninety-six motions relating to the Ban up for discussion at the following Annual Congress held in Belfast in April 1971.[16] A substantial majority of clubs and counties came out in favour of removing the Ban. Thirty counties in all called for the deletion of Rule 27. Antrim and Sligo were the only two that did not.[17] One of the most famous symbols of the Ban's impending demise was the picture that appeared in the *Irish Independent* of legendary Kerry footballer, Mick O'Connell, standing tall in the crowd at an FAI soccer match months before the Ban rule was removed in April 1971.[18] The death of the Ban was as swift as it was comprehensive; it was almost an anti-climax in the way it disappeared. Leading up to the Annual Congress, it was widely accepted the Ban would be removed but that there would be a severe schism within the GAA. The Ban rule, Rule 27, was removed on Easter Sunday 11 April 1971, along with the ban on 'foreign dances'. Twelve counties called for the deletion of the RUC ban; this rule remained, though, due to the escalating conflict in Northern Ireland.[19]

GAA players were quick to embrace their new freedom to play other sports. A high profile rugby seven-a-side charity match was organised just weeks later with Irish rugby internationals pitting

Pat Fanning was GAA president in 1971 when the Ban was removed. His handling of the Ban's removal was seen by many as vital in helping to heal the wounds caused by the Ban debates. *(Courtesy of the GAA Museum, Croke Park)*

themselves against such GAA luminaries as Des Foley, Kevin Heffernan, John Donnellan and Sean Flanagan.[20] There were reports of GAA figures making names for themselves in other sports,[21] and sportspeople from other codes taking up Gaelic games again.[22] There was even hope that GAA grounds would be made available for other sports. Limerick Football Club, winners of the FAI Cup in soccer, sought permission from the GAA to use the Gaelic Grounds in Limerick for their European Cup Winners Cup match against Torino of Italy in 1971.[23] Unfortunately for Limerick F.C., their request was not granted and it was not until 2007 that Rule 42 was rescinded, temporarily, to allow the playing of non-Gaelic games on GAA grounds, when France played Ireland at a rugby international in Croke Park.

The predicted split in the GAA did not materialise and one person who can justifiably take great credit for this was the GAA president, Pat Fanning. In a speech at the Annual Congress of 1971, widely recognised as magnanimous and stirring, Fanning said:

> Let us then delete this rule, but in a 'banless' GAA let us maintain the spirit that made this association great. Let us remain a national organisation pledge to work, as always towards an Irish Ireland, proud not only of our games, but of our language, our songs, our dances, our nationhood. Today let there be no sounding of trumpets as a rule disappears. Nor should there be talk of defeat. If victory there be, let it be a victory for the association. If defeat there be, let it be for those who had hoped that change would give them a less nationally motivated GAA.[24]

Accepting the events as traumatic, he asked delegates to set about the mammoth task of reorganising the GAA through a new charter, to make sure it remained relevant to Irish culture and firmly committed to the Irish-Ireland ideal. This certainly helped appease those who were pro-Ban.[25]

The GAA can be admired for its commitment to the Irish-Ireland ideal. The men who led the Association sincerely believed in this cause. They looked to the past as a vision for what they wanted their future to be, even if views of that Gaelic past were from a myopic outlook, only seeing elements they wanted to see. Their views could be considered strong and consistent despite huge opposition. This differed starkly from others who espoused the same principles, but failed to back those lofty principles with action. A case in point was the desire, expressed by most people, to speak Irish, backed up by the disheartening 80 per cent decrease in native Irish speakers in the fifty years after 1922.[26]

The GAA's persistence in sticking with the Ban was also their weakness. Ireland had transformed fundamentally from the time the GAA was founded. Irish people were no longer as insular; through tourism and emigration, people were now embracing the modern world directly and culturally through television and other forms of media. The GAA's doggedness in relation to the Ban as well as its false belief that the best future for Ireland was only through its Gaelic past, bore some similarities to Fianna Fáil's self-sufficiency tariff-driven economic policy of the 1930s, borne of the same ideals as the GAA's, until it was abandoned as a failed economic strategy in the 1950s. The Irish-Ireland movement was at its strongest during the first fifty years of the twentieth century when its principles pervaded all aspects of Irish life, from the political and religious classes to the imprint it implanted on the Irish cultural landscape. 'The second half of the twentieth century was characterised by a gradual waning of the Irish Ireland outlook and a progressive entry into the European economic and political mainstream'.[27] This more outward-looking ethos prevailed within body politic first before it dawned on the GAA that, as an Association, it too had to embrace the modern world and that part of that was accepting that an Irish identity should be 'a possession rather than an obsession'.[28]

Conclusion

The GAA celebrated 125 illustrious years in 2009. From humble beginnings the GAA's success over that period has been remarkable. There are few, if any, peer organisations worldwide that are comparable to this amateur body. As an organisation it has had to contend with seismic historical events of a worldwide and Irish nature throughout its history. It has overcome huge obstacles internally and externally and has still managed to organise games that have captivated people for decades. It built grounds the length and breadth of the country that evolved into impressive stadia, in particular the centrepiece stadium, Croke Park. The Association has enjoyed exceptional success in terms of the number of people participating in its sports and the spectators who watch them. Of the bodies that encompass the Irish-Ireland ideal, the GAA is the one body that stands out as its only true success story.

It is true that the GAA followed a similar trend to other sporting bodies that started in Victorian Britain in the late nineteenth century and enjoyed success over the course of the twentieth century and beyond. It could be argued that it is an easier task to promote the playing and support of native pastimes than it is to revive the Irish language or contribute towards a national literary revival, particularly when they are seen as entertaining spectacles in their own right. Regardless, the GAA has faced significant threats, some of its own making, and has overcome them to remain the premier sporting body in Ireland. The GAA has achieved this success in no small part due to its organisers, people like James Nowlan, Luke O'Toole, Pádraig McNamee and Pádraig Ó Caoimh. These men made great sacrifices to make the GAA what it is today. Look back at the lives and careers of McNamee and Ó Caoimh within the GAA – the countless months and years they spent promoting its cause, even through poor health, are a testament to their selfless dedication. This passion, commendable in most ways, led to some negative outcomes. The most striking example of this was their blind adherence to the ban on 'foreign games', Rule 27, regardless of the situation, particularly when it involved an Irish-Ireland treasure, Dr Douglas Hyde.

It is easy for commentators today to dismiss the Ban as a backward, inward-looking, divisive and ultimately outrageous rule. The Ban, in its different guises, served a useful purpose, particularly in its earlier years. Trying to gain a foothold, the new sporting body successfully used boycotting techniques to bring people away from more elitist sporting bodies to its folds. The Irish-Ireland movement with its ethos of de-anglicisation, in many ways instigated by Hyde, changed the way Irish people thought about themselves. The GAA, through its reintroduction of the Ban at the start of the twentieth century, embraced this new atmosphere. The Ban was their most potent tool in their bid to depart from all that was foreign and welcome all that was Irish. During the struggle for independence the Ban became a strong symbol of the GAA's nationalism. The British authorities saw it as such and they helped, in no small measure, in increasing its aura, by trying to force the GAA to remove it. The GAA's place at the centre of the struggle was copperfastened by the events of 21 November 1920, now known as Bloody Sunday, when fourteen innocent civilians, who were watching a Gaelic football match between Dublin and Tipperary, were gunned down in Croke Park by the British Auxiliaries, an act of reprisal for the assassination of twelve British agents, carried out on the instructions of Michael Collins, that same morning.[1] This image of the GAA as an integral part of the fight for independence, illusory in many respects, was something its members clung to deeply and more dearly as the years progressed. The Ban was seen as sacrosanct by many members and overcame stiff internal opposition to become a rigid rule by the late 1930s.

As time went by, retaining the Ban was akin to the sting of a dying wasp and its credibility was severely tested by a number of incidents that brought it sharply into focus, on many occasions garnering the incredulity of people both inside and outside the Association. The incident that did the most damage to the Ban's credibility was unquestionably the removal of Hyde as patron.

It is hard to quantify the full impact Hyde has made on the Ireland of today, as in many ways he changed Ireland intangibly and indirectly. He helped changed the spirit of the Irish. He gave Irish people, whose confidence was bruised sharply, the self-belief and confidence to accept themselves for who they were and to believe anything Irish – be it the language, native games, arts or industrial outputs – was as good as, if not better, than something foreign or British. This pacifist who never looked for conflict and who was a genuine consensus builder was, ironically, in many ways the architect of the ideology behind the campaigns that led to the violent struggles of the Easter Rising, the War of Independence and the subsequent Anglo-Irish Treaty of 1921, something he conceded himself years later.[2] He could, justifiably, be called one of the main architects of the Irish state.

The impact Hyde made on Irish culture through his role in the Irish-Ireland movement is substantial. Hyde played a major part in the three main facets of this movement; the Gaelic League, the GAA and the Irish Literary Revival. The inspiration behind the founding of the Gaelic League and its president throughout its golden era, Hyde's name is synonymous with the language revival movement. He also made his mark on the Irish Literary Revival, writing and performing some of the first plays produced in the Abbey

Theatre. His role in the GAA, although not documented extensively before now, was also significant. He was the one voice regularly calling for co-operation, even union, between the GAA and Gaelic League. He was never slow in his praise for the GAA. The Gaelic League played a decisive role in helping to turn around the fortunes of the GAA at the beginning of the twentieth century, thanks in no small part to its president.

Very few men have been made GAA patron; no woman has yet received this tribute. Hyde, in 1902, was the last non-Catholic and last layperson to be awarded this honour; he was the sixth person to become so up to that date. He was an active patron too, contributing to and supporting the GAA at every opportunity. The GAA could not have selected a more committed devotee to the Irish-Ireland cause than Hyde. Yet, a decision was made to remove him as patron. Questioning Hyde's devotion to the Irish-Ireland cause was the same as asking, as one commentator remarked, is the King loyal?[3]

In defence of the GAA's decision, it could be argued that Hyde, in attending a soccer match, had broken Rule 27 and, like all members, was subject to the same rules. The Central Council was just doing its job, interpreting the rules. The GAA had faced a number of trying episodes that same year, 1938, relating to the Ban and any sign of swaying or dithering would, it was feared, have caused a domino effect, bringing the whole Ban tumbling down. Many members of the GAA, particularly people in administrative roles, genuinely believed the Ban was essential to the GAA's success, even its survival. There was good cause for them to question many others within Irish society on their commitment to the Irish-Ireland ideal. Even people such as Éamon de Valera were softening their approach towards the British – he ended the Economic War and his utterances on ending partition were more like smokescreens than a genuine call to action. The strength of Ulster opposition to Hyde and particularly to the removal of the Ban was understandable, considering the trying times they were experiencing in expressing themselves culturally within the Northern Ireland state.

The removal of Hyde could have been more palatable if the GAA were consistent in its enforcement of the ban rules. Referees are acceptable if they are tough on the basis they are tough with everyone. The GAA was not consistent. It was tough with some people, like Hyde and Jim Cooney, and turned a blind eye to all of its members wantonly breaking the 'foreign dances' rule up and down the country. The accounts of people breaking the 'foreign games' rule were too numerous and persistent to be considered figments of naysayers' imaginations, yet the GAA's implementation of Rule 27 was sporadic in nature.

The removal of Hyde could also have been more acceptable if the GAA had been as committed to the Irish-Ireland cause as it liked to portray. As we have seen, its commitment to Irish dances was a mere illusion; the finances earned from hosting 'foreign dances' throughout GAA halls in the country were too much of an incentive for members to abide by the rule on 'foreign dances'. The Central Council, instead of stamping out this blatant breaking of the rules, chose to do nothing. The GAA has unquestionably contributed to the Irish language. Through provision of funding to the Gaelic League and some efforts to use the language at GAA events, it has put the revival of the Irish language high on its agenda, at least superficially. Looking beyond this facade, the GAA's endeavours to help revive the language were, like the government's, a sham. With a few exceptions, all GAA meetings were conducted in English. Its support of the Gaelic League was at a cost, in some respects bullying its sister organisation to acquiesce to the GAA's agenda with threats of withdrawal of support if the Gaelic League did not. Hyde had previously commented on the paltry efforts made by the GAA to promote the language.[4] It is true that the GAA's primary aim has always been to promote its sporting endeavours. It has, through its officers, also seen itself in a different light, at the vanguard of the Irish-Ireland movement fighting for a Gaelic Ireland. In reality, these lofty statements were mere talk and were not backed up by tangible actions to make their dream a reality.

Hyde, as President of Ireland, had no choice but to break Rule 27. For Hyde not to attend any event organised by the sporting bodies in Ireland of soccer, rugby, cricket or hockey for his term as President would have caused a greater scandal than the one that transpired by his attendance at the soccer match in November 1938. He would not have been a President for all of the people of Ireland; he would not have been above politics and would have alienated more people than he would have pleased. The fact that he was at the soccer match in an official capacity should have been ample reason for the GAA to take no action against Hyde. It is incredible that the GAA never even considered this in view of the incident involving Garda George Ormsby the previous spring, which caused such consternation in Connacht.

The GAA was also extremely discourteous to Hyde. On no occasion did it communicate with him before or after its decision to remove him. It is difficult to avoid the conclusion that the GAA knew it had made a mistake and was too embarrassed to admit it, unwilling to accept this 'astounding moment of aberration'[5] should never have happened. The GAA's admittance of erring finally came about in 1945 when, under pressure from de Valera, it conceded the whole incident involving Hyde was an unfortunate one and the President of the country was entitled to attend events organised by the sports banned under Rule 27.

Although the Ban survived for over thirty more years after the Hyde incident, its credibility was dented considerably by the affair. Time and time again opponents of the Ban used this as a glaring reason to remove the Ban, particularly the opponent-in-chief, Tom Woulfe, who cited the Hyde incident regularly in his decade-long campaign, which ultimately led to the removal of the Ban in 1971.

The GAA doggedly tried to retain its Ban, its crown jewel in opposing the 'mental cancer'[6] that was modernity. The Ireland of the 1970s had changed considerably from the Ireland at the start of the twentieth century and even more from the Ireland of 'The Emergency' of the Second World War. The world had been opened up to what had been an essentially insular country in the interim period, with advances in technology leading to easier and more frequent communication. With people emigrating in their thousands during the dark decade of the 1950s, the Fianna Fáil government accepted its self-sufficiency policy was a failure and opened its doors to foreign investment and strengthened its ties with other countries, culminating in its bid to gain entry to the European Economic Community. It was inevitable the vast changes that Ireland underwent as it modernised would affect the GAA. A gradual realisation dawned on the body that its quest for an Ireland based on its Gaelic past only, without engaging with the modern internationalised world, did not have the support of the rank and file membership, with the result that the Ban finally had to go.

Endnotes

Introduction

1   *Irish Press*, 4 June 1945, p. 2.
2   Gaelic Athletic Association (hereafter referred to as GAA) Central Council Executive Meeting Minutes, GAA/CC/01/06, 17 December 1938.
3   *Ibid.*

Chapter 1. 'I Dream in Irish'

1   Doiminic Ó Dálaigh, *The Young Douglas Hyde*, excerpts appeared in *Studia Hibernica*, No. 10 (1970), p. 108.
2   Gerard Murphy, 'Douglas Hyde 1860–1949', *An Irish Quarterly Review*, Vol. 38, No. 151 (Sep., 1949), p. 275.
3   Risteárd Ó Glaisne, 'This Is No Political Matter', *An Irish Quarterly Review*, Vol. 82, No. 328 (Winter, 1993), p.471.
4   Seán Ó Lúing, 'Douglas Hyde and the Gaelic League', *An Irish Quarterly Review*, Vol. 62, No. 246 (Summer, 1973), p. 124.
5   J. E. Dunleavy and G. Dunleavy, *Douglas Hyde: A Maker of Modern Ireland* (Berkeley, 1991), p. 26.
6   Ó Lúing, 'Douglas Hyde and the Gaelic League', *An Irish Quarterly Review*, p. 124.
7   Murphy, 'Douglas Hyde 1860–1949', *An Irish Quarterly Review*, p. 276.
8   Dunleavy and Dunleavy, *Douglas Hyde: A Maker of Modern Ireland*, p. 30.
9   Murphy, 'Douglas Hyde 1860–1949', *An Irish Quarterly Review*, p. 276.
10 Ó Dálaigh, 'The Young Douglas Hyde', *Studia Hibernica*, p. 111.
11 *Ibid.*, p. 113.
12 *Ibid.*, p. 110.
13 Ó Lúing, 'Douglas Hyde and the Gaelic League', *An Irish Quarterly Review*, p. 124.
14 Ó Dálaigh, 'The Young Douglas Hyde', *Studia Hibernica*, No. 10, pp. 108–25.
15 Ó Lúing, 'Douglas Hyde and the Gaelic League', *An Irish Quarterly Review*, p. 124.
16 Ó Dálaigh, 'The Young Douglas Hyde', *Studia Hibernica*, No. 10, p. 116.

17 *Ibid.*, p. 120.
18 *Ibid.*, p. 134.
19 *Ibid.*, pp. 129–30.
20 Ó Lúing, 'Douglas Hyde and the Gaelic League', *An Irish Quarterly Review*, p. 125.
21 *Ibid.*, p. 126.
22 *Ibid.*, p. 126.
23 *Ibid.*, p. 126.
24 J. B. Hughes, 'The Pan-Celtic Society (1888–1891)', *The Irish Monthly*, Vol. 81, No. 953 (Jan. 1953), p. 17.
25 *Freeman's Journal*, 3 October 1877.
26 *The Nation*, 16 February 1884, p. 8.

Chapter 2. 'Sweeping the Country Like a Prairie Fire'

1 Marcus de Búrca, *Michael Cusack and the GAA* (Dublin, 1989), p. 20.
2 *Freeman's Journal*, 14 November 1882.
3 Marcus de Búrca, *The G.A.A.: A History* (Dublin, 1999), p. 10.
4 De Búrca, *Michael Cusack and the GAA*, p. 62.
5 *Freeman's Journal*, 27 January 1894.
6 De Búrca, *The G.A.A.: A History*, p. 6.
7 *Freeman's Journal*, 3 August 1896.
8 Owen McGee, *Dictionary of Irish Biography*, available from http://dib.cambridge.org/; accessed on 1 June 2011.
9 De Búrca, *The G.A.A.: A History*, pp. 12–3.
10 Brendan MacLua, *The Steadfast Rule* (Dublin, 1967), p. 13.
11 *Freeman's Journal*, 12 November 1882.
12 *Freeman's Journal*, 8 January 1883.
13 Paul Rouse, 'Sport and The Politics of Culture: A History Of The G.A.A. Ban 1884–1971', (UCD Master's Thesis, 1991), p. 6.
14 W. F. Mandle, 'The IRB and the Beginnings of the Gaelic Athletic Association', *Irish Historical Studies*, Vol. 20, No. 80 (Sept., 1977), p. 421.
15 W. F. Mandle, 'Parnell and Sport', *Studia Hibernica*, No. 28 (1994), p. 103.
16 *Freeman's Journal*, 24 December 1884.
17 *Freeman's Journal*, 18 December 1882.
18 *Glasgow Herald*, 21 March 1892.
19 Cormac Bourke, 'Northern Flames: Remembering Columba & Adomnán', *History Ireland*, Vol. 7, No. 3, *Scotland and Ireland through the Ages* (Autumn, 1999), p. 16.
20 *Freeman's Journal*, 6 August 1894.
21 De Búrca, *The G.A.A.: A History*, p. 15.
22 Neal Garnham, 'Accounting for the Early Success of the Gaelic Athletic Association', *Irish Historical Studies*, Vol. 34, No. 133 (May, 2004), p. 65.
23 *Ibid.*, p. 65.
24 *Ibid.*, p. 72.

25 *Ibid.*, p. 72.
26 *Ibid.*, p. 74.
27 *Ibid.*, p. 77.
28 R. F. Foster, *Modern Ireland 1600–1972*, (London, 1988), p. 406.
29 MacLua, *The Steadfast Rule*, p. 15.
30 Mandle, 'The IRB and the Beginnings of the Gaelic Athletic Association',
    Irish Historical Studies, pp. 422–3.
31 *Freeman's Journal*, 30 October 1885.
32 MacLua, *The Steadfast Rule*, p. 17.
33 Rouse, 'Sport and The Politics of Culture: A History Of The G.A.A. Ban
    1884–1971', p. 11.
34 *Ibid.*, p. 12.
35 MacLua, *The Steadfast Rule*, p. 27.
36 De Búrca, *The G.A.A.: A History*, p. 49.
37 Breandán Ó hEithir, *Over the Bar*, (Dublin, 1984), p. 203.
38 Mandle, 'The IRB and the Beginnings of the Gaelic Athletic Association',
    Irish Historical Studies, p. 426.
39 *Freeman's Journal*, 23 March 1886.
40 *Freeman's Journal*, 24 March 1886.
41 MacLua, *The Steadfast Rule*, pp. 27–8.
42 Rouse, 'Sport and the Politics of Culture: A History of the G.A.A. Ban
    1884–1971', p. 17.
43 *Ibid.*, p. 17.
44 Mandle, 'The IRB and the Beginnings of the Gaelic Athletic Association',
    Irish Historical Studies, p. 425.
45 W. F. Mandle, *The Gaelic Athletic Association and Irish Nationalist Politics 1884–
    1924* (London and Dublin, 1987), p. 31.
46 Mandle, 'The IRB and the Beginnings of the Gaelic Athletic Association',
    Irish Historical Studies, p. 432.
47 Mandle, *The Gaelic Athletic Association and Irish Nationalist Politics 1884–1924*,
    p. 50.
48 *Ibid.*, p. 66.
49 Robert Kee, *The Laurel and the Ivy: The Story of Charles Stewart Parnell and
    Irish Nationalism* (London, 1993), p. 597.
50 *Ibid.*, p. 6.
51 MacLua, *The Steadfast Rule*, p. 31.
52 Rouse, 'Sport and the Politics of Culture: A History of the G.A.A. Ban
    1884–1971', p. 18.
53 *Ibid.*, p. 18.

Chapter 3. The De-Anglicising of Ireland

1 *Freeman's Journal*, 30 August 1893.
2 Declan Kiberd, *Inventing Ireland: The Literature of the Modern Nation* (London,
   1995), p. 141.

3   Gerard Murphy, 'Douglas Hyde 1860–1949', *An Irish Quarterly Review*, Vol. 38, No. 151 (Sep., 1949), p. 276.
4   Seán Ó Lúing, 'Douglas Hyde and the Gaelic League', *An Irish Quarterly Review*, Vol. 62, No. 246 (Summer, 1973), p. 127.
5   Murphy, 'Douglas Hyde 1860–1949', *An Irish Quarterly Review*, p. 277.
6   Ó Lúing, 'Douglas Hyde and the Gaelic League', *An Irish Quarterly Review*, p. 127.
7   *Freeman's Journal*, 30 August 1893.
8   Maureen O'Rourke Murphy and James MacKillop, *An Irish Literature Reader: Poetry, Prose, Drama* (New York, 2006), p. 140.
9   *Ibid.*, p. 146.
10   *Ibid.*, p. 146.
11   Kiberd, *Inventing Ireland: The Literature of the Modern Nation*, p. 142.
12   *Freeman's Journal*, 24 January 1893.
13   *Freeman's Journal*, 21 September 1893.
14   *Freeman's Journal*, 29 August 1893.
15   Arthur E. Clery, 'The Gaelic League, 1893–1919', *An Irish Quarterly Review*, Vol. 8, No. 31, (Sep., 1919), p. 401.
16   *Freeman's Journal*, 15 February 1899.
17   Clery, 'The Gaelic League, 1893–1919', *An Irish Quarterly Review*, p. 398.
18   Murphy, 'Douglas Hyde 1860–1949', *An Irish Quarterly Review*, p. 278.
19   Kiberd, *Inventing Ireland: The Literature of the Modern Nation*, p. 145.
20   Ó Lúing, 'Douglas Hyde and the Gaelic League', *An Irish Quarterly Review*, p. 130.
21   *Ibid.*, p. 130.
22   Clery, 'The Gaelic League, 1893–1919', *An Irish Quarterly Review*, p. 402.
23   Ó Lúing, 'Douglas Hyde and the Gaelic League', *An Irish Quarterly Review*, pp. 130–1.
24   Clery, 'The Gaelic League, 1893–1919', *An Irish Quarterly Review*, p. 403.
25   Kiberd, *Inventing Ireland: The Literature of the Modern Nation*, p. 145.
26   *Freeman's Journal*, 15 February 1899.
27   Kiberd, *Inventing Ireland: The Literature of the Modern Nation*, p. 149.
28   R. F. Foster, *Modern Ireland 1600–1972*, (London, 1988), p. 451.
29   Kiberd, *Inventing Ireland: The Literature of the Modern Nation*, p. 149.

Chapter 4. The GAA Reborn

1   *Irish Press*, 4 September 1937.
2   Brendan MacLua, *The Steadfast Rule* (Dublin, 1967), p. 33.
3   *Freeman's Journal*, 3 August 1896.
4   William Murphy, *Dictionary of Irish Biography*, available from http://dib.cambridge.org/; accessed on 1 June 2011.
5   MacLua, *The Steadfast Rule*, p. 36.
6   *Ibid.*, p. 37.
7   *Ibid.*, p. 40.

8   Marcus de Búrca, *The G.A.A.: A History* (Dublin, 1999), p. 70.

9   *Meath Chronicle*, 3 January 1903 and *The Anglo-Celt*, 24 January 1903.

10 Regina Fitzpatrick, Paul Rouse and Dónal McAnallen, 'The Freedom of the Field: Camogie before 1950', *The Evolution of the GAA: Ulaidh, Éire agus Eile* (Stair Uladh, 2009), ed. Dónal McAnallen, David Hassan and Roddy Hegarty, pp. 124–5.

11 Marcus de Búrca, *Dictionary of Irish Biography*, available from http://dib.cambridge.org/; accessed on 25 May 2011.

12 Paul Rouse, 'Sport and the Politics of Culture: A History of the G.A.A. Ban 1884–1971', (UCD Master's Thesis, 1991), p. 23.

13 MacLua, *The Steadfast Rule*, pp. 40–1.

14 *Ibid.*, p. 43.

15 *Ibid.*, p. 45.

16 David Hassan, 'The GAA in Ulster', *The Gaelic Athletic Association 1884–2009*, ed. Mike Cronin, William Murphy and Paul Rouse (Dublin, 2009), p. 81.

17 Conor Curran, *Sport in Donegal: A History* (Dublin, 2010), pp. 80–1.

18 Tom Hunt, 'The GAA: Social Structure and Associated Clubs', *The Gaelic Athletic Association 1884–2009*, ed. Cronin, Murphy, Rouse, pp. 200–1.

Chapter 5. Hyde Becomes Patron of the GAA

1   *The Irish Times*, 14 June 1982, p. 9.

2   W. F. Mandle, *The Gaelic Athletic Association and Irish Nationalist Politics 1884–1924* (London and Dublin, 1987), p. 20.

3   *Nenagh Guardian,* 20 December 1924, article by Douglas Hyde where he claims he was one of the GAA's earliest members.

4   *Freeman's Journal*, 29 November 1893.

5   *Freeman's Journal*, 17 January 1894.

6   *The Anglo-Celt*, 8 August 1896.

7   *Ibid.*

8   *New Zealand Tablet*, 30 July 1897.

9   National Archives of Ireland (hereafter referred to as NAI), Office of the Secretary of the President (hereafter referred to as PRES 1) P1131, 30 December 1938.

10 *Meath Chronicle*, 29 November 1902, p. 7.

11 *Evening Herald,* 19 December 1938, and Pádraig Puirséal, *The GAA in its Time* (Dublin, 1982), p. 129.

12 *Westmeath Examiner*, 13 December 1902, p. 7.

13 J. E. Dunleavy and G. Dunleavy, *Douglas Hyde: A Maker of Modern Ireland* (Berkeley, 1991), pp. 200–1.

14 Gerard Murphy, 'Douglas Hyde 1860–1949', *An Irish Quarterly Review*, Vol. 38, No. 151 (Sep., 1949), p. 278.

15 *Irish Independent*, 6 November 1905.

16 Brendan MacLua, *The Steadfast Rule* (Dublin, 1967), p. 82.

17 *Sunday Independent,* 17 July 1949, p. 6.

18 *Irish Independent,* 8 November 1905.

19 *Southern Star,* 11 November 1905.

20 *The New York Times,* 26 November 1905.

21 Dunleavy and Dunleavy, *Douglas Hyde: A Maker of Modern Ireland,* p. 12.

22 *Ibid.,* p. 269.

23 *The New York Times,* 5 December 1905.

24 Diarmaid Ferriter, *The Transformation of Ireland: 1900–2000* (London, 2005), p. 98.

25 *The Register,* 16 March 1906, p. 3.

26 *The New York Times,* 16 June 1906.

27 *Irish Independent,* 14 June 1906.

28 Dunleavy and Dunleavy, *Douglas Hyde: A Maker of Modern Ireland,* p. 314.

29 Seán Ó Lúing, 'Douglas Hyde and the Gaelic League', *An Irish Quarterly Review,* Vol. 62, No. 246 (Summer, 1973), p. 132.

30 Declan Kiberd, *Inventing Ireland: The Literature of the Modern Nation* (London, 1995), p. 149.

31 Ó Lúing, 'Douglas Hyde and the Gaelic League', *An Irish Quarterly Review,* p. 136.

32 Kiberd, *Inventing Ireland: The Literature of the Modern Nation,* p. 154.

33 Murphy, 'Douglas Hyde 1860–1949', *An Irish Quarterly Review,* p. 275.

34 Ó Lúing, 'Douglas Hyde and the Gaelic League', *An Irish Quarterly Review,* p. 137.

35 León Ó Broin, 'The President and the Irish Revival', *The Irish Monthly,* Vol. 66, No. 783 (Sep., 1938), p. 588.

Chapter 6. The Ban – A Fundamental Principle of the GAA

1 Paul Rouse, 'Sport and the Politics of Culture: A History of the G.A.A. Ban 1884–1971', (UCD Master's Thesis, 1991), p. 27.

2 Brendan MacLua, *The Steadfast Rule* (Dublin, 1967), p. 47.

3 *Ibid.,* p. 47.

4 Rouse, 'Sport and the Politics of Culture: A History of the G.A.A. Ban 1884–1971', p. 27.

5 MacLua, *The Steadfast Rule,* p. 48.

6 Rouse, 'Sport and the Politics of Culture: A History of the G.A.A. Ban 1884–1971', p. 28.

7 *Southern Star,* 6 December 1913, p. 6.

8 W. F. Mandle, *The Gaelic Athletic Association and Irish Nationalist Politics 1884–1924* (London and Dublin, 1987), p. 167.

9 *Ibid.,* pp. 166–7.

10 William Murphy, 'The GAA During the Irish Revolution, 1913–1923', *The Gaelic Athletic Association 1884–2009,* ed. Mike Cronin, William Murphy and Paul Rouse, (Dublin, 2009), p. 67.

11 Mandle, *The Gaelic Athletic Association and Irish Nationalist Politics 1884–1924,* p. 178.

12 Murphy, 'The GAA During the Irish Revolution, 1913–1923', *The Gaelic Athletic Association 1884–2009*, ed. Cronin, Murphy, Rouse, p. 67.

13 Mandle, *The Gaelic Athletic Association and Irish Nationalist Politics 1884–1924*, p. 178.

14 *Ibid.*, p. 178.

15 Rouse, 'Sport and the Politics of Culture: A History of the G.A.A. Ban 1884–1971', p. 35.

16 Mandle, *The Gaelic Athletic Association and Irish Nationalist Politics 1884–1924*, p. 178.

17 *Ibid.*, p. 179.

18 Rouse, 'Sport and the Politics of Culture: A History of the G.A.A. Ban 1884–1971', p. 36.

19 *Ibid.*, p. 36.

20 MacLua, *The Steadfast Rule*, p. 53.

21 Rouse, 'Sport and the Politics of Culture: A History of the G.A.A. Ban 1884–1971', p. 37.

22 *Ibid.*, p. 37.

23 MacLua, *The Steadfast Rule*, p. 52.

24 *Daily News*, 5 August 1918, p. 6.

25 Rouse, 'Sport and the Politics of Culture: A History of the G.A.A. Ban 1884–1971', p. 38.

26 *Daily News*, 5 August 1918, p. 6.

27 *The Irish Times*, 13 January 1919, p. 3.

28 Rouse, 'Sport and the Politics of Culture: A History of the G.A.A. Ban 1884–1971', p. 39.

29 MacLua, *The Steadfast Rule*, p. 56.

30 Marcus de Búrca, *The G.A.A.: A History* (Dublin, 1999), p. 133.

31 Rouse, 'Sport and the Politics of Culture: A History of the G.A.A. Ban 1884–1971', p. 41.

32 MacLua, *The Steadfast Rule*, p. 57.

33 Rouse, 'Sport and the Politics of Culture: A History of the G.A.A. Ban 1884–1971', pp. 41–3.

34 MacLua, *The Steadfast Rule*, p. 58.

35 De Búrca, *The G.A.A.: A History*, p. 133.

36 Rouse, 'Sport and the Politics of Culture: A History of the G.A.A. Ban 1884–1971', p. 43.

37 *Ibid.*, p. 42.

38 *Ibid.*, p. 42.

39 MacLua, *The Steadfast Rule*, p. 58.

40 *Ibid.*, p. 58.

41 *Ibid.*, p. 59.

42 *Ibid.*, p. 59.

43 Rouse, 'Sport and the Politics of Culture: A History of the G.A.A. Ban 1884–1971', p. 43.

44 *Ibid.*, p. 44.

45 De Búrca, *The G.A.A.: A History*, p. 134.

46 Rouse, 'Sport and the Politics of Culture: A History of the G.A.A. Ban 1884–1971', p. 47.

47 Marcus de Búrca, *Dictionary of Irish Biography,* available from http://dib. cambridge.org/; accessed on 25 May 2011.

48 *The Irish Times,* 23 December 2009, p. A7.

49 Marie Coleman, *Dictionary of Irish Biography,* available from http://dib. cambridge.org/; accessed on 26 May 2010.

50 Pádraig Puirséal, *The GAA in its Time* (Dublin, 1982), p. 347.

51 Coleman, Dictionary of Irish Biography, available from http://dib.cambridge. org/; accessed on 26 May 2010.

52 De Búrca, *The G.A.A.: A History,* p. 144.

53 Mike Cronin, Mark Duncan and Paul Rouse, *The GAA: A People's History* (Cork, 2009), p. 278.

54 Puirséal, *The GAA in its Time,* p. 223.

55 De Búrca, *The G.A.A.: A History,* p. 173.

56 *Irish Independent,* 16 May 1964, p. 15.

57 *Ibid.,* p. 15

58 *The Kerryman,* 23 May 1964, p. 23.

59 *Irish Independent,* 16 May 1964, p. 15.

60 *The Irish Times,* 23 December 2009, p. A7.

61 *The Irish Times,* 18 May 1964, p. 12.

62 *Irish Independent,* 16 May 1964, p. 15.

63 *The Irish Times,* 23 December 2009, p. A7.

64 *Irish Independent,* 16 May 1964, p. 15.

65 *The Irish Times,* 23 December 2009, p. A7.

66 *The Anglo-Celt,* 23 May 1964, p. 8.

67 *The Irish Times,* 18 May 1964, p. 12.

Chapter 7. Hyde Becomes Ireland's First President

1 Gerard Murphy, 'Douglas Hyde 1860–1949', *An Irish Quarterly Review,* Vol. 38, No. 151 (Sep., 1949), p. 279.

2 *Irish Independent,* 17 July 1993, p. 29.

3 Murphy, 'Douglas Hyde 1860–1949', *An Irish Quarterly Review,* p. 279.

4 J. J. Lee, *Ireland: 1912–1985: Politics and Society* (Cambridge, 1989), p. 132.

5 *Ibid.,* p. 133.

6 *Ibid.,* p. 133.

7 *Ibid.,* p. 135.

8 *The Irish Times,* 5 February 1925.

9 *The Irish Times,* 30 September 1925.

10 J. E. Dunleavy, and G. Dunleavy, *Douglas Hyde: A Maker of Modern Ireland* (Berkeley, 1991), pp. 355–6.

11 *Ibid.,* p. 356.

12 *The Irish Times,* 1 October 1925.

13 *NZ Truth,* 28 November 1925.

14 *The Irish Times,* 9 January 1925, p. 4.

15 *The Irish Times,* 9 January 1926, p. 5.

16 *The Irish Times,* 13 July 1949, p. 4.

17 Marie Coleman, *Dictionary of Irish Biography*, available from http://dib.
cambridge.org/; accessed on 5 August 2010.

18 *Bunreacht na hÉireann*, Article 12 (1.)

19 Michael McDunphy, *The President of Ireland: His Powers, Functions and Duties*
(Dublin, 1945), p. 5.

20 *Bunreacht na hÉireann*, Article 12 (9.)

21 *Bunreacht na hÉireann*, Article 12 (6.)

22 *The Manchester Guardian*, 13 June 1945, p. 4.

23 McDunphy, *The President of Ireland: His Powers, Functions and Duties*, p. 41.

24 *The Irish Times*, 13 May 1937.

25 Dermot Keogh and Andrew J. McCarthy, *The Making of the Irish Constitution
1937: Bunreacht na hÉireann* (Cork, 2007), p. 180.

26 *Ibid.,* p. 181.

27 *Ibid.,* p. 207.

28 Alan J. Ward, *The Irish Constitutional Tradition: Responsible Government and
Modern Ireland, 1782–1992* (Dublin, 1994), p. 294.

29 *Ibid.,* p. 294.

30 *The Irish Times*, 8 May 1937, p. 3.

31 *Ibid.,* p.3.

32 *The Irish Times*, 22 April 1938, p. 6.

33 *Time Magazine,* 16 May 1938.

34 *Sunday Independent,* 24 April 1938, p. 12.

35 *Ibid.,* p. 12.

36 *Irish Press*, 9 July 1938, p. 1.

37 *Irish Press*, 2 May 1938, p. 9.

38 Keogh and McCarthy, *The Making of the Irish Constitution 1937: Bunreacht na
hÉireann,* p. 206.

39 *Irish Press,* 27 June 1938.

40 *The Irish Times,* 28 June 1938, p. 7A.

Chapter 8. Jazzing Every Night of the Week

1 Paul Rouse, 'Sport and the Politics of Culture: A History of the G.A.A. Ban
1884–1971', (UCD Master's Thesis, 1991), p. 48.

2 Marcus de Búrca, *The G.A.A.: A History* (Dublin, 1999), p. 134.

3 Brendan MacLua, *The Steadfast Rule* (Dublin, 1967), p. 61.

4 Ernest Blythe, TD, 'Public Business – Finance Bill, 1931', Dáil Éireann
Debates, Vol. 39, 2 July 1931; available from www.oireachtas-debates.gov.ie;
accessed 12 June 2010.

5 Éamon de Valera TD, 'Public Business – Finance Bill, 1931', Dáil Éireann
Debates, Vol. 39, 2 July 1931; available from www.oireachtas-debates.gov.ie;
accessed 12 June 2010.

6   Sean MacEntee TD, 'Public Business – Finance Bill, 1931', Dáil Éireann Debates, Vol. 39, 2 July 1931; available from www.oireachtas-debates.gov.ie; accessed 12 June 2010.

7   Richard Walsh TD, 'Public Business – Finance Bill, 1931', Dáil Éireann Debates, Vol. 39, 2 July 1931; available from www.oireachtas-debates.gov.ie; accessed 12 June 2010.

8   Mark O'Brien, *De Valera, Fianna Fáil and the Irish Press – The Truth in the News?* (Dublin, 2001), p. xii.

9   De Búrca, *The G.A.A.: A History*, p. 148.

10   Diarmaid Ferriter, *The Transformation of Ireland: 1900–2000* (London, 2005), p. 98.

11   Richard Walsh TD, 'Public Business – Finance Bill, 1931', Dáil Éireann Debates, Vol. 39, 2 July 1931; available from www.oireachtas-debates.gov.ie; accessed 12 June 2010.

12   *Irish Independent*, 5 January 1932, p. 1.

13   *The Irish Times*, 1 February 1932, p. 11.

14   *The Irish Times*, 6 February 1932, p. 9.

15   NAI, Department of Foreign Affairs and Trade, DFA2/1/38, 5 February 1932.

16   *Irish Press*, 2 July 1934, p. 7.

17   *The Irish Times*, 8 July 1932, p. 13.

18   *The Irish Times*, 28 July 1932, p. 8.

19   *The Irish Times*, 8 July 1932, p. 13.

20   *Irish Press,* 2 January 1934, p. 7.

21   Pádraig Ó Fearail, *The Story of Conradh na Gaeilge* (Dublin, 1975), pp. 49 and 51.

22   *The Irish Times*, 19 December 1931, p. 5.

23   *The Irish Times*, 22 December 1987, p. 10.

24   Jim Smyth, 'Dancing, Depravity and All That Jazz: The Public Dance Halls Act of 1935', *History Ireland,* Vol. 1, No. 2 (Summer, 1993), p. 53.

25   *The Pittsburgh Press*, 19 February 1928, p. 1.

26   *Schenectady Gazette*, 20 July 1928, p. 2.

27   *The New York Times*, 28 February 1921.

28   *The Irish Times*, 30 March 1932, p. 8.

29   Ó Fearail, *The Story of Conradh na Gaeilge,* p. 47.

30   *The Irish Times*, 2 January 1934, p. 8.

31   *Ibid.*, p. 8.

32   *Ibid.*, p. 8.

33   Smyth, 'Dancing, Depravity and All That Jazz: The Public Dance Halls Act of 1935', *History Ireland*, p. 54.

Chapter 9. Hyde the Committed Patron

1   Marcus de Búrca, *The G.A.A.: A History* (Dublin, 1999), p. 166.

2   *Nenagh Guardian*, 20 December 1924, p. 5.

3   *Ibid.*, p. 5.

4   *Ibid.*, p. 5.

5   *Ibid.*, p. 5.
6   *Ibid.*, p. 5.
7   *The Irish Times*, 7 November 1930, p. 8.
8   *Nenagh Guardian*, 7 April 1934, p. 2.
9   *The Irish Times*, 2 April 1934, p. 4.
10 *The Irish Times*, 14 May 1935, p. 6.
11 *The Irish Times*, 5 February 1949, p. 1.
12 *The Irish Times*, 9 March 1940, p. 4.
13 *The Irish Press*, 22 August 1938, p. 7.
14 NAI, PRES 1/P600, 21 December 1938.
15 NAI, PRES 1/P2901, 31 October 1938.
16 *Connacht Tribune*, 1 October 1938, p. 28.
17 NAI, PRES 1/P2901, 31 October 1938.
18 Marie Coleman, *Dictionary of Irish Biography*, available from http://dib.cambridge.org/; accessed on 26 May 2010.
19 *Ibid.*
20 NAI, PRES 1/P735, 11 October 1938.
21 *Ibid.*

Chapter 10. 1938 – The Year of Ban Controversies

1   Pádraig Puirséal, *The GAA in its Time* (Dublin, 1982), p. 232.
2   Brendan MacLua, *The Steadfast Rule* (Dublin, 1967), p. 60.
3   *Irish Independent*, 23 March 1938, p. 17.
4   *Irish Press*, 7 March 1938, p. 10.
5   *Irish Independent*, 14 March 1938, p. 15.
6   *Irish Press*, 23 March 1938, p. 15.
7   *The Irish Times*, 19 April 1938, p. 8.
8   *The Irish Times*, 28 April 1938, p. 13.
9   *The Irish Times*, 7 November 1960, p. 7.
10 *Irish Press*, 21 April 1938, p. 1.
11 *Irish Independent*, 12 May 1938, p. 2.
12 *Irish Press*, 20 May 1938, p. 2.
13 *Irish Press*, 16 May 1938, p. 4.
14 *Nenagh Guardian*, 30 April 1938, p. 12.
15 *Irish Independent*, 25 April 1938, p. 13.
16 *Nenagh Guardian*, 30 April 1938, p. 2.
17 *Irish Press*, 22 April 1938, p. 3.
18 *Irish Press*, 23 May 1938, p. 7.
19 *Sunday Independent*, 26 June 1938, p. 3.
20 *The Irish Times*, 12 April 1939, p. 3.
21 *Irish Press*, 29 April 1938, p. 7.
22 *Nenagh Guardian*, 2 July 1938, p. 2.
23 Marcus de Búrca, *The G.A.A.: A History* (Dublin, 1999), p. 165.
24 *The Irish Times*, 9 June 2000, p. 19.
25 De Búrca, *The G.A.A.: A History*, p. 166.

Chapter 11. The Soccer Match

1 *Irish Press*, 14 November 1938, p. 1.
2 *The Irish Times*, 12 November 1938, p. 13.
3 Brian Glanville, *The Story of the World Cup* (London, 2001), p. 36.
4 Peter Byrne, *Football Association of Ireland: 75 Years* (Dublin, 1996), p. 36.
5 *Irish Independent*, 9 November 1938, p. 16.
6 *Irish Independent*, 14 November 1938, p. 13.
7 NAI, PRES 1/P2901, 11 December 1938.
8 *The Irish Times*, 28 June 1938, p. 7A.
9 NAI, PRES 1/P1131, 5 December 1938.
10 NAI, PRES 1/P1170, 25 February 1939.
11 NAI, PRES 1/P607, 11 August 1938.
12 NAI, PRES 1 /P1131, 5 December 1938.
13 *The Irish Times*, 16 December 1963, p. 9.
14 *Irish Independent*, 17 December 1963, p. 19.
15 *Irish Independent*, 15 November 1938, p. 16.
16 *Irish Independent*, 16 December 1963, p. 14.
17 Marie Coleman, *Dictionary of Irish Biography*, available from http://dib.cambridge.org/; accessed on 31 May 2010.
18 *Irish Independent*, 16 December 1963, p. 14.
19 *The Irish Times*, 26 April 1943, p. 1.
20 Brian Hanley, 'Irish Republican Attitudes to Sport since 1921', *The Evolution of the GAA: Ulaidh, Éire agus Eile* (Stair Uladh, 2009), ed. Dónal McAnallen, David Hassan and Roddy Hegarty, p. 175.
21 NAI, PRES 1 /P1131, 5 December 1938.
22 Glanville, *The Story of the World Cup*, p. 15.
23 *Irish Press*, 14 November 1938, p. 9.
24 NAI, PRES 1 /P1131, 5 December 1938.
25 *Daily Mail*, 12 November 1938.
26 *The Sunday Times,* 13 November 1938.
27 *Irish News*, 14 November 1938, p. 5.
28 *The Irish Times*, 14 November 1938, p. 8.
29 *Irish News*, 14 November 1938, p. 5.
30 *Irish Independent*, 14 November 1938, p. 13.
31 *Sunday Independent*, 13 November 1938, p. 13.
32 *The Irish Times*, 30 January 1939, p. 8.
33 *Irish Independent*, 14 November 1938, p. 13.
34 *Irish Press*, 14 November 1938, p. 9.
35 *Daily Express*, 14 November 1938.
36 *Daily Express*, 16 November 1938, p. 18.
37 *Evening Herald*, 17 November 1938, p. 5.
38 *Evening Mail*, 21 November 1938, p. 7.
39 *Evening Herald*, 18 November 1938, p. 10, and *Evening Herald*, 21 November 1938, p. 7.
40 *The Leader*, 26 November 1938, pp. 299–300.

41 *Ibid.*

42 Cardinal Tomás Ó Fiaich Memorial Library and Archive, Armagh, Armagh GAA County Board Meeting Minutes, 18 November 1938.

43 *Irish Press,* 5 December 1938.

44 Marcus de Búrca, *Dictionary of Irish Biography,* available from http://dib. cambridge.org/; accessed on 26 May 2010.

45 *The Irish Times,* 13 October 1969, p. 11.

46 *Irish Independent,* 7 January 1939, p. 11.

47 *Evening Mail,* 5 December 1938, p. 4.

48 *Irish Independent,* 10 December 1938, p. 8.

49 *Ibid.,* p. 8.

50 *Irish News,* 7 December 1938, p. 5.

51 *Irish Press,* 5 December 1938, p. 1.

52 *Irish Press,* 12 December 1938, p. 11.

53 *Irish Independent,* 10 December 1938, p. 8.

54 *The Irish Times,* 7 December 1938, p. 8.

55 *Irish Press,* 21 February 1939, p. 7.

56 *The Irish Times,* 10 December 1938, p. 8.

57 *Irish Independent,* 12 December 1938, p. 12.

58 *Irish Press,* 16 December 1938, p. 9.

59 *Derry Journal,* 14 December 1938.

60 *The Irish Times,* 16 December 1938, p. 5.

61 *Irish News,* 13 December 1938.

62 *Evening Mail,* 13 December 1938, p. 7.

63 GAA Central Council Meeting Minutes, GAA/CC/01/06, 17 December 1938.

64 *News Review,* 15 December 1938.

Chapter 12. The Banned Patron

1 Tom Cullen, *A History of the G.A.A. in Ulster, 'Those With Whom I Walked the Way'* (Armagh, 2003), p. 10.

2 Marcus de Búrca, *Dictionary of Irish Biography,* available from http://dib. cambridge.org/; accessed on 26 May 2010.

3 Ruairi O Bleine, St Paul's GAA Club, Holywood, County Down, www.stpaulsgaa.com.

4 Ó Fearail, *The Story of Conradh na Gaeilge,* (Dublin, 1975), p. 47.

5 *The Anglo-Celt,* 17 June 1944, p. 6.

6 *Ibid.,* p. 6.

7 *The Irish Times,* 17 October 1957, p. 7.

8 *The Irish Times,* 2 December 1971, p. 3.

9 *The Irish Times,* 15 July 1969, p. 3.

10 *Irish Independent,* 3 April 1972, p. 10.

11 *Ibid.,* p. 10.

12 *The Irish Times,* 6 February 1976, p. 3.

13 GAA Annual Congress Meeting Minutes, GAA/CC/01/07, 9 and 10 April 1939.
14 *The Irish Times*, 31 December 1938, p. 6.
15 *Ibid.*, p. 6.
16 *Irish Press*, 20 December 1938, p. 10.
17 *Sunday Dispatch*, 18 December 1938, p. 1.
18 *Sunday Independent*, 18 December 1938, p. 1.
19 *Irish Press*, 19 December 1938, p. 1.
20 *The Irish Times*, 19 December 1938, p. 8.
21 *Irish Independent*, 19 December 1938, p. 13.
22 *Irish Daily Telegraph*, 19 December 1938.
23 *Daily Express*, 19 December 1938.
24 *Daily Sketch*, 19 December 1938.
25 *The Times*, 20 December 1938, p. 9.
26 *The Manchester Guardian*, 19 December 1938, p. 8.
27 *Glasgow Herald*, 24 December 1938, p. 5.
28 *Calgary Daily Herald*, 4 February 1939, p. 24.
29 *The New York Times*, 18 December 1938.
30 *Christian Science Monitor*, 19 December 1938, p. 12.
31 *Chicago Daily Tribune*, 20 January 1939, p. 10.
32 *Glasgow Herald*, 24 December 1938, p. 5.
33 *The Irish Times*, 19 December 1938, p. 8.
34 *Limerick Leader*, 19 December 1938, p. 2.
35 *Roscommon Herald*, 24 December 1938, p. 4.
36 *Roscommon Herald*, 24 December 1938, p. 4.
37 *The Manchester Guardian*, 20 December 1938, p. 20.
38 *Roscommon Herald*, 24 December 1938, p. 4.
39 *Evening Mail*, 13 December 1938, p. 7.
40 *Tuam Herald*, 31 December 1938, p. 2.
41 *Nenagh Guardian*, 4 February 1939, p. 3.
42 *The Irish Times*, 12 April 1939, p. 3.
43 NAI, PRES 1/P1131, 30 December 1938.
44 *Ibid.*
45 William Davin, TD, 'Questions – Offences Against the State Bill, Dáil Éireann Debates, Vol. 74, 7 March 1939; available from www.oireachtas-debates.gov.ie; accessed 9 April 2010.
46 NAI, PRES 1/P1131, 10 May 1941.
47 NAI, PRES 1/P1131, 30 December 1938.
48 *Ibid.*
49 *Ibid.*
50 *The Manchester Guardian*, 23 December 1938, p. 11.
51 *Irish Press*, 23 December 1938, p. 7.
52 *Irish Press*, 2 January 1939, p. 2.
53 *The Irish Times*, 2 January 1939, p. 8.
54 *Irish Press*, 2 January 1939, p. 2.
55 NAI, PRES 1/P1134, 1 January 1939.

56 NAI, PRES 1/P1134, 3 January 1939.
57 NAI, PRES 1/P1134, 4 January 1939.
58 *The Irish Times*, 7 January 1939, p. 11.
59 *Irish Press*, 2 January 1939, p. 2.
60 *The Irish Times*, 2 January 1939, p. 8.
61 The Connacht GAA Archive, Ballyhaunis, County Mayo, Connacht GAA Council Meeting Minutes, 6 January 1939.
62 NAI, PRES 1/P1135, 11 January 1939.

Chapter 13. GAA Conventions Debate Hyde's Removal

1   David Hassan, 'The GAA in Ulster', *The Gaelic Athletic Association 1884–2009* (Dublin, 2009), ed. Mike Cronin, William Murphy and Paul Rouse, p. 80.
2   *Ibid.*, p. 81.
3   *The Irish Times*, 26 August 1989, p. A3.
4   Eamon Phoenix, 'GAA's Era of Turmoil in Northern Ireland', *Fortnight*, No. 211 (17 Dec. 1984– 20 Jan. 1985), p. 8.
5   Hassan, 'The GAA in Ulster', *The Gaelic Athletic Association 1884–2009*, ed. Cronin, Murphy and Rouse, p. 82.
6   *Ibid.*, p. 84.
7   *Belfast Telegraph*, 20 December 1938, p. 9.
8   *Irish Independent*, 5 January 1939, p. 6.
9   Anon., *Na Fianna 1904–1984: A History of Coalisland Fianna G.F.C.*, (1985), p. 59.
10 *Sunday Independent*, 15 January 1939, p. 3.
11 *Ibid.*, p. 3.
12 *The Irish Times*, 11 January 1939, p. 8.
13 *Sunday Independent*, 26 February 1939, p. 9.
14 *Irish Independent*, 23 January 1939, p. 8.
15 NAI, PRES 1/P1131, 30 December 1938.
16 *Irish Press*, 30 January 1939, p. 9.
17 *Connacht Tribune*, 1 October 1938, p. 28.
18 *Irish Independent*, 23 January 1939, p. 8.
19 *The Irish Times*, 13 November 1944, p. 1.
20 Armagh GAA County Board A.G.M. Minutes, 29 January 1939.
21 Armagh GAA County Board Meeting Minutes, 21 February 1939.
22 Cardinal Tomás Ó Fiaich Memorial Library and Archive, Armagh, Ulster GAA Annual Convention Minutes, 25 February 1939.
23 *The Anglo-Celt*, 4 March 1939, p. 5.
24 Con Short, *The Ulster GAA Story 1884–1984*, (Monaghan, 1984), p. 140.
25 Ulster GAA Annual Convention Minutes, 25 February 1939.
26 *Ibid.*
27 *Ibid.*
28 *Roscommon Herald*, 28 January 1939, p. 3.

29 *Ibid.*, p. 3.
30 *Nenagh Guardian*, 20 December, 1924, p. 5.
31 *The Irish Times*, 23 November 1938, p. 11.
32 GAA Central Council Meeting Minutes, GAA/CC/01/06, 17 December 1938.
33 Marcus de Búrca, *The G.A.A.: A History* (Dublin, 1999), p. 185.
34 Pádraig Puirséal, *The GAA in its Time* (Dublin, 1982), pp. 225 and 245.
35 *Nenagh Guardian*, 30 April 1938, p. 12.
36 *Irish Independent*, 31 December 1938, p. 7.
37 *Meath Chronicle*, 14 October 1939, p. 1.
38 Breandán Ó hEithir, *Over the Bar*, (Dublin, 1984), p. 110.
39 Brian Ó Conchubhair, 'The GAA and the Irish Language', *The Gaelic Athletic Association 1884–2009,* ed. Cronin, Murphy, Rouse, p. 146.
40 *Roscommon Herald*, 28 January 1939, p. 3.
41 *Ibid.*, p. 3.
42 *Ibid.*, p. 3.
43 *Irish Independent*, 21 January 1939, p. 8.
44 *Irish Independent*, 31 December 1938, p. 13.
45 *Irish Press*, 14 January 1939, p. 8.
46 *Irish Independent*, 10 January 1939, p. 14.
47 *Irish Independent*, 17 January 1939, p. 12.
48 *Irish Independent*, 23 January 1939, p. 8.
49 *Irish Press*, 14 January 1939, p. 8.
50 *Irish Independent*, 23 January 1939, p. 8.
51 *Ibid.*, p. 8.
52 *Irish Independent*, 30 January 1939, p. 10.
53 *Irish Press*, 25 January 1939, p. 12.
54 *Connacht Tribune*, 28 January 1939, p. 17.
55 *Irish Press*, 23 January 1939, p. 8.
56 Connacht GAA Annual Convention Minutes, 26 February 1939.
57 *Roscommon Herald*, 4 March 1939, p. 4.
58 *Irish Press*, 20 January 1939, p. 11, and Ulster GAA Annual Convention Minutes, 25 February 1939.
59 *Irish Independent*, 4 April 1938, p. 14.
60 *Irish Independent*, 24 January 1939, p. 4 and 2 February 1939, p. 10.
61 *Irish Independent*, 10 February 1939, p. 12.
62 *The Irish Times*, 28 November 1961, p. 2.
63 *The Irish Times*, 1 September 1984, p. A21.
64 GAA Annual Congress Meeting Minutes, April 1939, GAA/CC/01/07.
65 *Irish Independent*, 17 January 1939, p. 10.
66 *The Irish Times*, 25 January 1939, p. 5.
67 *Nenagh Guardian*, 17 April 1948, p. 5.
68 Tim Carey, *Croke Park: A History*, (Cork, 2004), p. 115.
69 *Limerick Leader*, 25 January 1939, p. 4.
70 *Irish Independent*, 2 February 1939, p. 10.
71 *Leitrim Observer*, 21 January 1939, p. 7.
72 *Munster Express*, 3 February 1939, p. 6.

73 *Irish Independent*, 9 January 1939, p. 11.

74 *Limerick Leader*, 23 January 1939, p. 4.

75 *Irish Independent*, 17 January 1939, p. 12.

76 *Irish Press*, 17 January 1939, p. 2.

77 *The Irish Times*, 30 January 1939, p. 8.

78 *Irish Independent*, 9 January 1939, p. 10.

79 *Ibid.*, p. 10.

80 *Irish Independent*, 17 January 1939, p. 12.

81 *The Irish Times*, 1 September 1984, p. A8.

82 De Búrca, *The G.A.A.: A History,* p. 147.

83 *The Irish Times*, 1 September 1984, p. A8.

84 Mike Cronin, Mark Duncan and Paul Rouse, *The GAA: A People's History* (Cork, 2009), p. 245.

85 De Búrca, *The G.A.A.: A History*, p. 146.

86 *Sunday Independent*, 10 July 1938, p. 1.

87 *Nenagh Guardian*, 14 January 1939, p. 3.

88 *Nenagh Guardian*, 21 January 1939, p. 4.

89 *Ibid.*, p. 2.

90 *Limerick Leader*, 21 January 1939, p. 8.

91 *Nenagh Guardian*, 28 January 1939, p. 6.

92 *Nenagh Guardian*, 4 February 1939, p. 3.

93 Ó hEithir, *Over the Bar*, p. 103.

94 *Ibid.*, p. 107.

95 *Irish Farmers Journal*, 28 April 1990, p. 74.

96 *Limerick Leader*, 19 December 1938, p. 2.

97 *Limerick Leader*, 21 January 1939, p. 8.

98 *Limerick Leader*, 28 January 1939, p. 8.

99 *Limerick Leader*, 19 December 1938, p. 2.

100 *Limerick Leader*, 21 January 1939, p. 8.

101 *Limerick Leader*, 28 January 1939, p. 15.

102 *Ibid.*, p. 8.

103 *Limerick Leader*, 25 January 1939, p. 4.

104 *Limerick Leader*, 21 January 1939, p. 15.

105 *Limerick Leader*, 28 January 1939, p. 7.

106 *The Irish Times* 30 January 1939, p. 8.

107 *Irish Independent*, 30 January 1939, p. 10.

108 *Roscommon Herald*, 4 February 1939, p. 3.

109 *Irish Independent*, 23 January 1939, p. 8.

110 Leinster GAA Annual Convention Minutes, 18 February 1939.

Chapter 14. Hyde's Removal Ratified

1 *The Irish Times*, 24 February 1939, p. 7.

2 *The Irish Times*, 4 February 1939, p. 16.

3 *Irish Press*, 25 January 1939, p. 8.

4   GAA Annual Congress Meeting Minutes, April 1939, GAA/CC/01/07.

5   *Ibid.*

6   *Ibid.*

7   *Ibid.*

8   *Ibid.*

9   *Ibid.*

10 NAI, PRES 1/P2019, 8 September 1939 and 19 July 1941.

11 *Irish Press*, 19 July 1941, p. 2.

12 NAI, PRES 1/P3141, 26 August 1943.

13 NAI, PRES 1/P3141, 2 September 1943.

14 *Irish Press*, 18 September 1943, p. 3.

15 *Nenagh Guardian*, 15 April 1939, p. 2.

Chapter 15. The GAA Versus the Government

1   Marcus de Búrca, *The G.A.A.: A History* (Dublin, 1999), pp. 173–5.

2   Josephus Anelius, *National Action – A Plan For the National Recovery of Ireland*, (Dublin, 1942), p. 109.

3   *The Irish Times*, 26 April 1943, p. 1.

4   Anelius, *National Action*, p. ix.

5   *Ibid.*, p. x.

6   De Búrca, *The G.A.A.: A History*, p. 175.

7   Anelius, *National Action*, p. 37.

8   *Ibid.*, p. 36.

9   *Ibid.*, p. 41.

10 *Ibid.*, pp. 66–7.

11 *The Irish Times*, 26 April 1943, p. 1.

12 *Ibid.*, p. 1.

13 *Ibid.*, p. 1.

14 *Ibid.*, p. 1.

15 R. M. Douglas, *Architects of the Resurrection: Ailtirí na hAiséirghe and the fascist 'new order' in Ireland*, (Manchester, 2009), pp. 148–9.

16 De Búrca, *The G.A.A.: A History*, p. 175.

17 Patrick Maume, *Dictionary of Irish Biography*, available from http://dib.cambridge.org/; accessed on 18 November 2011.

18 R. M. Douglas, 'Ailtirí na hAiséirghe: Ireland's fascist New Order', *History Ireland*, Vol. 17, No. 5 (Sep./Oct., 2009), p. 42.

19 *Ibid.*, p. 43.

20 Michael Gallagher, *Politicial Parties in the Republic of Ireland* (Manchester, 1985), p. 107.

21 Douglas, 'Ailtirí na hAiséirghe: Ireland's fascist New Order', *History Ireland*, p. 43.

22 Gallagher, *Politicial Parties in the Republic of Ireland*, p. 108.

23 Douglas, *Architects of the Resurrection: Ailtirí na hAiséirghe and the fascist 'new order' in Ireland*, p. 260.

24 *Ibid.*, pp. 191 and 200.

25   Douglas, 'Ailtirí na hAiséirghe: Ireland's fascist New Order', *History Ireland*, p. 44.

26   *Ibid.*, p. 44.

27   Oliver J. Flanagan, TD, 'Emergency Powers (Continuance) Bill, 1943', Dáil Éireann Debates,Vol. 91, 9 July 1943; available from www.oireachtas-debates. gov.ie; accessed 19 January 2012.

28   *Munster Express*, 26 May 1944, p. 1.

29   *Meath Chronicle*, 28 August 1943, p. 2.

30   Patrick Maume, *Dictionary of Irish Biography*, available from http://dib.cambridge. org/; accessed on 5 October 2011.

31   Douglas, *Architects of the Resurrection: Ailtirí na hAiséirghe and the fascist 'new order' in Ireland*, p. 87.

32   *Ibid.*, p. 153.

33   *The Irish Times*, 26 April 1943, p. 1.

34   *The Irish Times*, 30 April 1923, p. 7.

35   *The Irish Times*, 30 September 1943, p. 1.

36   *The Anglo-Celt*, 1 May 1943, p. 13.

37   GAA Annual Congress Meeting Minutes, GAA/CC/01/08, 5 April 1942.

38   *Irish Independent*, 26 April 1943, p. 3.

39   *The Irish Times*, 26 April 1943, p. 1.

40   *Irish Independent*, 26 April 1943, p. 3.

41   *The Irish Times*, 26 April 1943, p. 1.

42   *Irish Independent*, 26 April 1943, p. 3.

43   *Ibid.*, p. 3.

44   *Ibid.*, p. 3.

45   *The Anglo-Celt*, 1 May 1943, p. 13.

46   *Irish Independent*, 26 April 1943, p. 3.

47   *The Irish Times*, 26 April 1943, p. 1.

48   *Ibid.*, p. 1.

49   *The Irish Times*, 30 September 1943, p. 1.

50   *Irish Independent*, 30 September 1943, p. 3.

51   Diarmaid Ferriter, *Judging Dev: A Reassessment of the Life and Legacy of Éamon De Valera,* (Dublin, 2007), p. 222.

52   Éamon de Valera, TD, 'Public Business – Finance Bill, 1931', Dáil Éireann Debates, Vol. 39, 2 July 1931; available from www.oireachtas-debates.gov.ie; accessed 12 June 2010.

53   UCD Archives, The Éamon de Valera Papers, P150/3110, 12 May 1957.

54   Ferriter, *Judging Dev*, p. 311.

Chapter 16. The GAA Completes a U-Turn

1   NAI, PRES 1/P1131, September 1939.

2   Séamus J. King, *A History of Hurling* (Dublin, 1996), p. 100.

3   NAI, PRES 1/P1134, 31 March 1939.

4   NAI, PRES 1/P1170, 11 February 1940.

5   *The Irish Times*, 12 February 1940, p. 8.
6   NAI, PRES 1/P1562, 9 February 1940: J. J. Walsh sent his comments to the President's Office when he heard Hyde planned to attend the match.
7   NAI, PRES 1/P1562, 7 March 1940.
8   NAI, PRES 1/P1562, 10 October 1941.
9   NAI, PRES 1/P1562, 8 October 1943.
10 J. E. Dunleavy and G. Dunleavy, *Douglas Hyde: A Maker of Modern Ireland* (Berkeley, 1991), pp. 422–3.
11 *The Irish Times*, 12 November 1938, p. 6.
12 Dunleavy and Dunleavy, *Douglas Hyde: A Maker of Modern Ireland*, p. 429.
13 ElectionsIreland.org, available from http://www.electionsireland.org/result. cfm?election=1945P&cons=194, accessed on 6 July 2011.
14 GAA Central Council Executive Meeting Minutes, GAA/CC/01/09, 17 August 1945.
15 *Ibid.*
16 *Ibid.*
17 *Ibid.*
18 *Ibid.*
19 *Ibid.*
20 NAI, PRES 1/P2577, 29 August 1945.
21 *Ibid.*
22 *Irish Press*, 3 September 1945, p. 1.
23 NAI, PRES 1/P2577, 29 August 1945.
24 *Ibid.*
25 NAI, PRES 1/P2901, 6 September 1945.
26 NAI, PRES 1/P2901, 8 October 1945.
27 NAI, PRES 1/P2901, 26 April 1954.
28 NAI, PRES 1/P2875, June 1959.
29 NAI, PRES 1/P2875, June 1959.
30 *Irish Press*, 17 May 1946, p. 5.
31 NAI, PRES 1/P2577, 5 October 1946.
32 *Ibid.*
33 *Irish Independent*, 7 October 1946, p. 5.
34 *Sunday Chronicle*, 19 December 1954, p. 9.
35 *Ibid.*, p. 9.

Chapter 17. Modernism – A Mental Cancer

1   Breandán Ó hEithir, *Over the Bar* (Dublin, 1984), p. 213.
2   *The Irish Times*, 19 May 1943, p. 1.
3   *The Irish Times*, 12 January 1944, p. 2.
4   *The Irish Times*, 19 January 1944, p. 2.
5   *The Irish Times*, 26 January 1944, p. 2.
6   *Irish Independent*, 11 August 1945, p. 3.
7   *The Irish Times*, 13 August 1945, p. 1.

8   *The Mercury* (Hobart, Tasmania), 30 August 1945, p. 3.

9   *The Irish Times*, 27 October 1945, p. 10.

10 *The Irish Times*, 3 November 1945, p. 2.

11 *Irish Press*, 30 December 1946, p. 7.

12 *Nenagh Guardian*, 12 April 1947, p. 2.

13 *The Irish Times*, 16 January 1947, p. 2.

14 Brendan MacLua, *The Steadfast Rule* (Dublin, 1967), p. 87.

15 Paul Rouse, 'Sport and the Politics of Culture: A History of the G.A.A. Ban 1884–1971', (UCD Master's Thesis, 1991), p. 56.

16 *Ibid.*, p. 55.

17 *The Irish Times*, 18 April 1950, p. 5.

18 *Irish Press*, 19 March 1953, p. 4.

19 *The Irish Times*, 28 March 1953, p. 18.

20 *The Irish Times*, 10 November 1951, p. 18.

21 *The Irish Times*, 29 January 1953, p. 5.

22 NAI, Department of Foreign Affairs and Trade, DFA/301/65(1), 5 March 1953.

23 NAI, PRES 1 /P2943, 23 February 1948.

24 *The Irish Times*, 9 March 1954, p. 7.

25 *The Irish Times*, 22 April 1957, p. 7.

26 *Ibid.*, p. 7.

Chapter 18. Death and Burial of a President

1   J. E. Dunleavy and G. Dunleavy, *Douglas Hyde: A Maker of Modern Ireland* (Berkeley, 1991), p. 430.

2   *Connacht Tribune*, 23 July 1949, p. 14.

3   *The Manchester Guardian*, 14 July 1949, p. 3.

4   *The Irish Times*, 13 July 1949, p. 4.

5   *The Irish Times*, 14 July 1949, p. 5.

6   *Ibid.*, p. 5.

7   *Irish Press*, 14 July 1949, p. 1.

8   *The Irish Times*, 18 July 1949, p. 5.

9   Austin Clarke, *Flight to Africa: and other poems* (Dublin, 1963), p. 18.

10 *Irish Independent*, 17 July 1993, p. 29.

11 *Ibid.*, p. 29.

12 Patrick Maume, *Dictionary of Irish Biography*, available from http://dib.cambridge.org/; accessed on 26 May 2010.

13 *Irish Independent*, 17 July 1993, p. 29.

14 *Sunday Independent*, 5 November 1995, p. 19.

15 Central Bank of Ireland website, www.centralbank.ie/paycurr/notescoin/history; accessed on 8 November 2011.

16 *Sunday Independent*, 25 April 1971, p. 24.

17 *Connacht Tribune*, 16 April 1976, p. 11.

18 *Connacht Tribune*, 10 August 1984, p. 24.

Chapter 19. Woulfe Attack

1 Paul Rouse, 'Sport and the Politics of Culture: A History of the G.A.A. Ban 1884–1971' (UCD Master's Thesis, 1991), p. 57.

2 Marcus de Búrca, *The G.A.A.: A History* (Dublin, 1999), p. 202.

3 *The Irish Times*, 4 December 1959, p. 2.

4 Gerard Siggins and Malachy Clerkin, *Lansdowne Road: The Stadium, The Matches, The Greatest Days* (Dublin, 2010), p. 106.

5 *The Irish Times*, 28 November 1961, p. 2.

6 *The Irish Times*, 12 December 1961, p. 3.

7 *The Irish Times*, 19 December 1961, p. 2.

8 *The Irish Times*, 23 April 1962, p. 7.

9 *Irish Independent*, 23 April 1962, p. 17.

10 *The Kerryman*, 21 April 1962, p. 8.

11 *The Irish Times*, 23 April 1962, p. 6.

12 *The Irish Times*, 30 October 1962, p. 1.

13 *The Irish Times*, 30 January 1964, p. 2.

14 *The Anglo-Celt,* 9 May 1964, p. 10.

15 *Connacht Tribune*, 14 November 1964, p. 13.

16 *The Irish Times*, 19 April 1965, p. 1.

17 *Ibid.*, p. 1.

18 *The Irish Times*, 16 January 1965, p. 11.

19 *The Irish Times*, 23 April 1962, p. 6.

20 Rouse, 'Sport and the Politics of Culture: A History of the G.A.A. Ban 1884–1971', p. 64.

21 *The Irish Times*, 24 March 1965, p. 3.

22 *The Irish Times*, 16 April 1965, p. 3.

23 *The Irish Times*, 19 April 1965, p. 1.

24 Rouse, 'Sport and the Politics of Culture: A History of the G.A.A. Ban 1884–1971', p. 65.

25 *Ibid.,* p. 65.

26 *Connacht Tribune*, 30 April 1966, p. 18.

27 *The Irish Times*, 4 January 1968, p. 1.

28 *Ibid.*, p. 1.

29 *The Irish Times*, 1 January 1968, p. 4.

30 *The Irish Times*, 4 January 1968, p. 2.

31 *Irish Independent*, 14 December 1966, p. 2.

32 *Connacht Tribune*, 27 January 1967, p. 17.

33 *Ibid.*, p. 17.

34 *The Irish Times*, 2 March 1968, p. 6.

35 *The Irish Times*, 25 January 1968, p. 3.

36 *Ibid.*, p. 3.

37 *The Irish Times*, 5 December 1966, p. 1.

38 *The Irish Times*, 14 March 1969, p. 3.

39 Rouse, 'Sport and the Politics of Culture: A History of the G.A.A. Ban 1884–1971', p. 65.

40 De Búrca, *The G.A.A.:A History*, p. 202.

41 *Ibid.*, p. 202.

42 *The Irish Times*, 9 November 1967, p. 3.

43 Brendan MacLua, *The Steadfast Rule* (Dublin, 1967), p. 20.

44 *Ibid.*, p. 96.

45 *Ibid.*, p. 96.

46 *Ibid.*, p. 83.

47 *Ibid.*, p. 82.

48 *Ibid.*, p. 83.

49 *Ibid.*, p. 107.

50 Breandán Ó hEithir, *Over the Bar* (Dublin, 1984), p. 213.

51 Rouse, 'Sport and the Politics of Culture: A History of the G.A.A. Ban 1884–1971', p. 66.

52 *The Kerryman*, 16 March 1968, p. 16.

53 *Ibid.*, p. 16.

54 Rouse, 'Sport and the Politics of Culture: A History of the G.A.A. Ban 1884–1971', p. 66.

55 *The Irish Times*, 4 November 1970, p. 3.

Chapter 20. The Ban Goes With a Whimper

1 *Munster Express*, 19 July 1968, p. 19.

2 *The Irish Times*, 15 April 1970, p. 3.

3 *The Irish Times*, 9 December 1969, p. 3.

4 *The Irish Times*, 18 February 1970, p. 9.

5 *The Irish Times*, 21 July 1969, p. 6.

6 *The Irish Times*, 18 February 1970, p. 9.

7 *The Irish Times*, 20 July 1970, p. 1.

8 An extract appeared in *The Irish Times*, 18 February 1970, p. 9.

9 *The Irish Times*, 3 November 1970, p. 3.

10 *Ibid.*, p. 3.

11 *Ibid.*, p. 3.

12 *The Irish Times*, 4 November 1970, p. 3.

13 Rouse, 'Sport and the Politics of Culture: A History of the G.A.A. Ban 1884–1971' (UCD Master's Thesis, 1991), p. 69.

14 Marcus de Búrca, *The G.A.A.:A History* (Dublin, 1999), p. 203.

15 Rouse, 'Sport and the Politics of Culture: A History of the G.A.A. Ban 1884–1971', p. 69.

16 *The Irish Times*, 7 April 1971, p. 3.

17 De Búrca, *The G.A.A.:A History*, p. 203.

18 *Irish Independent*, 25 February 1971, p. 1.

19 Rouse, 'Sport and the Politics of Culture: A History of the G.A.A. Ban 1884–1971', p. 71.

20 *The Irish Times*, 27 April 1971, p. 3.

21 *The Irish Times*, 28 April 1971, p. 3.

22 *The Irish Times*, 1 May 1971, p. 3.
23 *The Irish Times*, 16 July 1971, p. 3.
24 *The Irish Times*, 12 April 1971, p. 8.
25 De Búrca, *The G.A.A.: A History*, p. 204.
26 Rouse, 'Sport and the Politics of Culture: A History of the G.A.A. Ban 1884–1971', p. 73.
27 Dan Mulhall, 'Sean O'Faolain and the Evolution of Modern Ireland', *The Irish Review*, No. 26 (Autumn, 2000), p. 28.
28 *Ibid.,* p. 29.

Conclusion

1 Tim Carey, *Croke Park: A History* (Cork, 2004), pp. 48–52.
2 Seán Ó Lúing, 'Douglas Hyde and the Gaelic League', *An Irish Quarterly Review*, Vol. 62, No. 246 (Summer, 1973), p. 137.
3 *The Irish Times*, 28 March 1953, p. 18.
4 *Nenagh Guardian*, 20 December 1924, p. 5.
5 *The Irish Times*, 19 February 1970, p. 11.
6 Paul Rouse, 'Sport and the Politics of Culture: A History of the G.A.A. Ban 1884–1971' (UCD Master's Thesis, 1991), p. 56.

Sources and Bibliography

Primary Sources

**The Gaelic Athletic Association Archive,
Cusack Stand, St Joseph's Avenue, Croke Park, Dublin 3**
GAA Central Council Executive Meeting Minutes
GAA Annual Congress Meeting Minutes

**The Connacht GAA Archive,
Clare Road, Ballyhaunis, County Mayo**
Connacht GAA Council Meeting Minutes

**Cardinal Tomás Ó Fiaich Memorial Library and Archive,
15 Moy Road, Armagh, BT61 7LY, Northern Ireland**
Ulster GAA Council Meeting Minutes
Armagh GAA County Board Meeting Minutes

The Leinster GAA Archive, Portlaoise, County Laois
Leinster GAA Council Meeting Minutes

The National Archives of Ireland, Bishop Street, Dublin 8
Office of the Secretary to the President Papers (PRES)
Department of Foreign Affairs and Trade (DFA)

**University College Dublin Archives, School of History and
Archives, University College Dublin, Belfield, Dublin 4**
Papers of Éamon de Valera (UCDA P150)

Newspapers and Magazines

Belfast Telegraph	*Irish News*	*The Anglo-Celt*
Calgary Daily Herald	*Irish Press*	*The Irish Times*
Chicago Daily Tribune	*Leitrim Observer*	*The Kerryman*
Christian Science Monitor	*Limerick Leader*	*The Leader*
Connacht Tribune	*Meath Chronicle*	*The Manchester Guardian*
Daily Express	*Munster Express*	*The Mercury* (Hobart,
Daily Mail	*Nenagh Guardian*	Tasmania)
Daily News	*News Review*	*The Nation*
Daily Sketch	*New Zealand Tablet*	*The New York Times*
Derry Journal	*NZ Truth*	*The Register* (Adelaide,
Evening Herald	*Pittsburgh Press*	South Australia)
Evening Mail	*Roscommon Herald*	*The Sunday Times*
Freeman's Journal	*Schenectady Gazette*	*The Times*
Glasgow Herald	*Southern Star*	*Tuam Herald*
Irish Daily Telegraph	*Sunday Chronicle*	*Time Magazine*
Irish Farmers Journal	*Sunday Dispatch*	*Westmeath Examiner*
Irish Independent	*Sunday Independent*	

Secondary Sources

Books

Anelius, Josephus, *National Action – A Plan for the National Recovery of Ireland* (Dublin, 1942)

Anon., *Na Fianna 1904–1984: A History of Coalisland Fianna G.F.C.* (1985)

Byrne, Peter, *Football Association of Ireland: 75 Years* (Dublin, 1996)

Carey, Tim, *Croke Park: A History* (Cork, 2004)

Clarke, Austin, *Flight to Africa: and other poems* (Dublin, 1963)

Cronin, Mike; Duncan, Mark; and Rouse, Paul, *The G.A.A.: A People's History* (Cork, 2009)

Cronin, Mike; Murphy, William; and Rouse, Paul, *The Gaelic Athletic Association 1884–2009* (Dublin, 2009)

Cullen, Tom, *A History of the G.A.A. in Ulster 2003, 'Those With Whom I Walked the Way'* (Armagh, 2003)

Curran, Conor, *Sport in Donegal: A History* (Dublin, 2010)

De Búrca, Marcus, *Michael Cusack and the GAA* (Dublin, 1989)

— *The G.A.A.: A History* (Dublin, 1999)

Dunleavy, J. E., and Dunleavy, G., *Douglas Hyde: A Maker of Modern Ireland* (Berkeley, 1991)

Douglas, R. M., *Architects of the Resurrection: Ailtirí na hAiséirghe and the fascist 'new order' in Ireland* (Manchester, 2009)

Ferriter, Diarmaid, *Judging Dev: A Reassessment of the Life and Legacy of Éamon De Valera* (Dublin, 2007)

— *The Transformation of Ireland: 1900–2000* (London, 2005)

Foster, R. F., *Modern Ireland: 1600–1972* (London, 1988)

Gallagher, Michael, *Political Parties in the Republic of Ireland* (Manchester, 1985)

Glanville, Brian, *The Story of the World Cup* (London, 2001)

Kee, Robert, *The Laurel and the Ivy: The Story of Charles Stewart Parnell and Irish Nationalism* (London, 1993)

Keogh, Dermot, and McCarthy, Andrew J., *The Making of the Irish Constitution 1937: Bunreacht na hÉireann* (Cork, 2007)

Kiberd, Declan, *Inventing Ireland: The Literature of the Modern Nation* (London, 1995)

King, Séamus J., *A History of Hurling* (Dublin, 1996)

Lee, J. J., *Ireland: 1912–1985: Politics and Society* (Cambridge, 1989)

MacLua, Brendan, *The Steadfast Rule* (Dublin, 1967)

Mandle, W. F., *The Gaelic Athletic Association and Irish Nationalist Politics 1884–1924* (London and Dublin, 1987)

McAnallen, Dónal; Hassan, David; and Hegarty, Roddy, *The Evolution of the GAA: Ulaidh, Éire agus Eile* (Stair Uladh, 2009)

McDunphy, Michael, *The President of Ireland: His Powers, Functions and Duties* (Dublin, 1945)

O'Brien, Mark, *De Valera, Fianna Fáil and the Irish Press – The Truth in the News?* (Dublin, 2001)

Ó Fearail, Pádraig, *The Story of Conradh na Gaeilge* (Dublin, 1975)

Ó hEithir, Breandán, *Over the Bar* (Dublin, 1984)

Murphy, Maureen O'Rourke, and MacKillop, James, *An Irish Literature Reader: Poetry, Prose, Drama* (New York, 2006)

Puirséal, Pádraig, *The GAA in its Time* (Dublin, 1982)

Short, Con, *The Ulster GAA Story 1884–1984* (Monaghan, 1984)

Siggins, Gerard, and Clerkin, Malachy, *Lansdowne Road: The Stadium, The Matches, The Greatest Days* (Dublin, 2010)

Ward, Alan J., *The Irish Constitutional Tradition: Responsible Government and Modern Ireland, 1782–1992* (Dublin, 1994)

Journals and Periodicals

Bourke, Cormac, 'Northern Flames: Remembering Columba & Adomnán', *History Ireland*, Vol. 7, No. 3 (1999)

Clery, Arthur E., 'The Gaelic League, 1893–1919', *An Irish Quarterly Review*, Vol. 8, No. 31 (1919)

Douglas, R. M., 'Ailtirí na hAiséirghe: Ireland's fascist New Order', *History Ireland*, Vol. 17, No. 5 (2009)

Garnham, Neal, 'Accounting for the Early Success of the Gaelic Athletic Association', *Irish Historical Studies*, Vol. 34, No. 133 (2004)

Hughes, J. B., 'The Pan-Celtic Society (1888–1891)', *The Irish Monthly*, Vol. 81, No. 953 (1953)

Mandle, W. F., 'Parnell and Sport', *Studia Hibernica*, No. 28 (1994)

— 'The IRB and the Beginnings of the Gaelic Athletic Association', *Irish Historical Studies*, Vol. 20, No. 80 (1977)

Mulhall, Dan, 'Sean O'Faolain and the Evolution of Modern Ireland', *The Irish Review*, No. 26 (2000)

Murphy, Gerard, 'Douglas Hyde 1860–1949', *An Irish Quarterly Review*, Vol. 38, No. 151 (1949)

Ó Broin, León, 'The President and the Irish Revival', *The Irish Monthly*, Vol. 66, No. 783 (1938)

Ó Dálaigh, Doiminic, 'The Young Douglas Hyde', *Studia Hibernica*, No. 10 (1970)

Ó Glaisne, Risteárd, 'This Is No Political Matter', *An Irish Quarterly Review*, Vol. 82, No. 328 (1993)

Ó Lúing, Seán, 'Douglas Hyde and the Gaelic League', *An Irish Quarterly Review*, Vol. 62, No. 246 (1973)

Phoenix, Eamon, 'GAA's Era of Turmoil in Northern Ireland', *Fortnight*, No. 211 (1984–1985)

Smyth, Jim, 'Dancing, Depravity and All That Jazz: The Public Dance Halls Act of 1935', *History Ireland*, Vol. 1, No. 2 (1993)

Electronic Sources

Dáil Éireann Debates, www.oireachtas-debates.gov.ie
Dictionary of Irish Biography, http://dib.cambridge.org/
ElectionsIreland.org, www.electionsireland.org
St Paul's GAA Club, Holywood, County Down, www.stpaulsgaa.com

Other

Bunreacht na hÉireann (Constitution of Ireland), (Dublin, 1980)
Paul Rouse, 'Sport and the Politics of Culture: A History of the G.A.A. Ban 1884–1971', (UCD Master's Thesis, 1991)

Index

Pictures are indicated by page numbers in italics.

Index

Index